Death and Afterlife

Stephen T. Davis

Professor of Philosophy and Religion
Claremont McKenna College
Claremont, California

St. Martin's Press   New York

First published in the United States of America in 1989

Printed in Great Britain

ISBN 0–312–03537–3

Library of Congress Cataloging-in-Publication Data
Death and afterlife/[edited by] Stephen T. Davis.
p.   cm.
ISBN 0–312–03537–3
1. Death.   2. Death—Religious aspects.   3. Future life.
I. Davis, Stephen T., 1940–.
BD444.D34   1990
129—dc20   89–39431
                                            CIP

Contents

v

Notes on the Contributors

Paul Badham is Senior Lecturer in Theology and Religious Studies at Saint David's University College, Lampeter, in the University of Wales.

Francis H. Cook is Professor of Religious Studies at the University of California at Riverside.

Stephen T. Davis is Professor of Philosophy and Religion at Claremont McKenna College.

Ariel Glucklich is Assistant Professor of Modern Languages and Literature at Pomona College.

David Ray Griffin is Professor of the Philosophy of Religion at the School of Theology at Claremont.

John Hick is Danforth Professor of the Philosophy of Religion at Claremont Graduate School.

Edward J. Hughes is Assistant Professor of Philosophy at the University of LaVerne.

Jerry A. Irish is Vice-President and Dean of the College and Professor of Religion at Pomona College.

Kai Nielsen is Professor of Philosophy at the University of Calgary.

Joseph Prabhu is Professor of Philosophy at California State University at Los Angeles.

Introduction

Do we live after bodily death? This is surely one of the most pressing questions we human beings ask. Virtually everyone has an opinion. Virtually everyone is vitally interested in the answer. Does death end all, so to speak? Or do we (in some sense) continue as conscious, acting individuals after death?

It is sometimes said that death is the most fearful reality that we face. Perhaps this is true. Death is a universal human problem. We can find thinkers in all generations and cultures who are concerned about death, fear of death, and the possibility of survival of death. It might prove helpful to ask *why* death is such a frightening thing. Why do most people look upon their own death with dread? Perhaps there are (at least) the following six reasons that we fear death:

1. We all know that death is inevitable; but most of us do not know when we will die. Accordingly, we live constantly under death's threat.
2. Death is unknown. Death is not something that we experience but is rather (as Wittgenstein put it) the end of experience. So there are many opinions but few or no accepted truths about death and what happens to us (if anything) after we die.
3. Every person must face death alone. Perhaps if we could experience death together – if we could, so to speak, hold hands and leap together into the void – death would not be so alarming to us. Unfortunately we cannot.
4. In death we will be separated from our friends and loved ones.
5. In death our personal hopes and aims about the future will not be realized.
6. There is a real and fearful possibility that death does indeed 'end all', that my death means my annihilation as a person. After my death, I simply no longer exist.

These fears (and other factors like religious tradition) naturally lead people to wonder whether there is life after death. There seems to be four main answers to the question: What happens to me, if anything, after I die? These are the major options we find suggested by reflective people, both religious and irreligious, throughout history:

1. Nothing happens to me after I die because death is the end of me. I may live on in other people's memories, or perhaps my influence will continue for a time, but as a conscious, acting individual I do *not* survive my death. We can call this the 'death ends all' option.

2. After my death my body disintegrates permanently, but my immaterial essence (my mind, or soul, or *jiva*) is reborn in another body (animal or human) here on earth, perhaps to be reborn again many (or even an infinite number of) times. We can call this the 'reincarnation' option.

3. After death my body disintegrates, but my immaterial essence lives on forever in an immaterial world. We can call this the 'immortality of the soul' option.

4. After death my body disintegrates, but at some point in the future God will miraculously raise it from the ground and reconstitute me as a person. We can call this the 'resurrection' option. It might also be noted that these options are not necessarily mutually exclusive. Many Christian and Islamic scholars, for example, affirm both (3) and (4).

This is a book about death and the possibility of life after death. All four of the options mentioned above are defended and discussed here. The book began as a series of papers at a scholarly conference called 'Death and Afterlife' held in Claremont, California in January 1987 under the auspices of the Department of Religion of the Claremont Graduate School. All the papers included in the book were written especially for the conference (although two have appeared subsequently elsewhere). The responses to each paper that were read at the conference are also included here, as are several comments submitted later. The high level of the papers themselves, the many positions they reflect, and the informed nature of the debate led the participants to believe that the papers and comments on the papers would constitute a unique and helpful book. We trust that this has proved to be so.

Let me introduce the scholars who contributed the main chapters of the book (in the order in which their papers appear in it). Kai Nielsen is Professor of Philosophy at the University of Calgary. Well known in the philosophy of religion as well as in other areas of philosophy, Nielsen is an atheist who in this book defends his own version of the 'death ends all' option. Paul Badham is Senior Lecturer in Theology and Religious Studies at St David's University College, Lampeter, in the University of Wales, where he co-ordinates a unique master's degree programme in Death and Immortality. In his paper Badham defends the viability and necessity of the concept of the soul in Christian theology. Joseph Prabhu is Professor of Philosophy at California State University at Los Angeles. A native of India, in this book Prabhu steps outside his normal area of expertise (he is a Hegel scholar) and contributes an excellent contemporary defence of reincarnation. David Ray Griffin is Professor of the Philosophy of Religion at the School of Theology at Claremont. Griffin's orientation is Whiteheadean; his paper is interesting in that it goes beyond his own avowal earlier in his career of 'objective immortality' toward a notion of personal survival of death. Stephen T. Davis, the book's editor, is Professor of Philosophy at Claremont McKenna College. In his paper he defends a traditional Christian view of bodily resurrection. Francis H. Cook is Professor of Religious Studies at the University of California at Riverside. A Buddhist scholar and a practising Zen Buddhist, Cook presents a Buddhist version of the 'death ends all' option. (I should add that because of the lively nature of the debate stirred up by Cook's provocative paper, I have allowed him to contribute a reply to his two main critics.) John Hick is Danforth Professor of the Philosophy of Religion at Claremont Graduate School, and was the organiser of the conference. In his paper Hick summarises and defends his own survival of death thesis (developed originally in his *Death and Eternal Life*), a unique synthesis of insights from reincarnation, immortality, and resurrection.

Three other scholars contributed responses. Ariel Glucklich, an expert in Hinduism, is Visiting Assistant Professor of Modern Languages and Literatures at Pomona College. Edward J. Hughes is Assistant of Philosophy at the University of LaVerne. And Jerry A. Irish is Vice-President and Dean of the College and Professor of Religion at Pomona College.

Do we live after bodily death? Bishop Butler (in his *Of Personal Identity*) called that question 'the most important question which can possibly be asked'. Those of us who have contributed to this book may or may not agree with Butler's statement; we surely do agree, however, that the question of life after death is a very important question indeed. We are all of us professionally as well as personally interested in it. Our hope is that the book will help readers understand the various available answers to it, see the strengths and weaknesses of each position, and decide on a plausible answer.

It should be noted that John Hick's paper first appeared in *Consciousness and Survival*, edited by John Spong (Sausalito, California: Institute of Noetic Science, 1987), and an earlier version of Stephen Davis's paper appeared in *The New Scholasticism*, 62 (Winter, 1988). Both are reprinted here with permission of the respective editors.

STEPHEN T. DAVIS

1 The Faces of Immortality
Kai Nielsen

I

Is there an afterlife or any reasonable possibility of an afterlife, or is belief in an afterlife – of a post-mortem existence – somehow incoherent, or is it instead merely a false belief? Given the new philosophical dispensation in the aftermath of the undermining of foundationalism, it is better for secularists such as myself to 'split the difference' and contend that conceptions of the afterlife are so problematical that it is unreasonable for a philosophical and scientifically sophisticated person living in the west in the twentieth century to believe in life eternal, to believe that we shall survive the rotting or the burning or the mummification of our 'present bodies'. There are questions of fact here, questions of interpretation of fact, and questions of what it makes sense to say which come as part of a package, and it may well be that in some instances it is not so easy to divide these questions so neatly. In a good Quinean manner I will let philosophy range over all these considerations.

If immortality is taken, as I shall take it, in a reasonably robust way and not simply as the sentimentalism that we shall live in the thoughts of others, belief in the afterlife – or so I shall argue – is so problematical that it should not be something to be believed. It is a belief, depending on how exactly the afterlife is construed, that is either fantastically unlikely to be true, or is instead an incoherent belief which could not possibly be true. Bodily resurrection, one of the reigning conceptions of the afterlife, may well, on some of its formulations, be a coherent belief (at least on some readings of 'coherent'), but it is a belief which is very unlikely indeed to be true. Its unlikelihood rests, as I shall show, on a number of grounds. One of them is, of course, the non-existence of God. If there were a God and He was what, say, Orthodox Christianity takes Him to be, we might take bodily resurrection to be a straight matter of faith.[1] Even so, I will argue, there will still be extraordinary difficulties, difficulties so great that not a few believers in God have turned away from any such conception. They have, that is, opted for belief in God without belief in immortality. In this context we should keep firmly in

1

mind that if the grounds for believing in God are scant the grounds for believing in bodily resurrection are doubly scant. Belief in it is a considerable scandal to the intellect.

I shall, after some preliminaries, start with a discussion of bodily resurrection, go on to a discussion of disembodied existence, and finally turn to a last cluster of considerations of broadly moral and human rationales for having a concern for immortality and having a hope that it may, after all, be a reality. This last consideration will be linked to the claim made by some that belief in immortality is necessary to make life in an otherwise intolerable world have some sense in the face of what, some argue, would otherwise be human despair, a despair that is inescapable where human beings come to escape double-mindedness and face non-evasively the bleakness of their lives without God and the possibility of eternal life.[2]

II

In speaking of immortality we are speaking of the endless existence of a person after what we call her 'death' or at least the death of her body. What is agreed on all sides, and what is an inconvertible fact, is that after a time for all of us our bodies cease to be energised and left alone they will simply rot, and no matter how they are manipulated, when they are thoroughly in that state there is no evidence of their ever being re-energised. (In that respect we are not like batteries.) Believers in immortality believe that, all this to the contrary notwithstanding, we, as human beings, persons, selves, somehow do not really die but have instead an endless existence after such a de-energisation and disintegration of our bodies or (if you will) our 'earthly bodies'.

Jewish, Christian and Islamic defenders of immortality take two fundamentally different positions in their characterisation of the afterlife. The first position I shall characterise is probably the more religiously orthodox position and the second position, until rather recently, would more likely appeal to philosophers and perhaps even to common sense since the time of Descartes, and in certain strata of society extending down to our own time. Since I believe both views are fundamentally defective, I shall not be concerned to take sides with respect to them, but to be, after a characterisation of them, concerned to critique them both. The two views are, respectively, bodily resurrection by God to eternal life, and Cartesian dualism with its belief in an indestructible, immaterial individual self distinct from the body in which this self is said to be housed. This self is also thought to be capable of, without any body in which it must be housed, to exist as a disembodied individual who is also a person.

Belief in bodily resurrection is clearly something deeply embedded in the orthodox Judaeo-Christian-Islamic traditions. Unless we take seriously the idea that there could be, and indeed there actually is, a God and that He, being omnipotent, could do whatever is logically possible, bodily resurrection is a very difficult thing in which to believe on empirical grounds. On those grounds it just seems utterly fantastic and no doubt is something whose reality is very unlikely indeed. However, it appears at least not to be an incoherent notion, at least if we take an incoherent notion to be a notion which is logically impossible, for example, 'a round square', or not understandable (comprehensible), for example, 'Reagan sleeps faster than Thatcher'. People on such an account, when resurrected, do not have to be radically different from those men and women we meet on the street, including ourselves, where as Antony Flew once put it, 'People are what you meet. We do not meet only the sinewy containers in which other people are kept, and they do not encounter only the fleshy houses that we ourselves inhabit'.[3] Rather the people we meet are flesh and blood individuals: energised, purposively acting bodies through and through a part of the physical world (if that isn't a pleonasm).

What bodily resurrection teaches us is that we embodied beings will survive the death of our present bodies and that our post-mortem existence, though in certain respects it will be very different, will be, ontologically speaking, in a manner essentially similar to our pre-mortem existence. We will come to have, when resurrected, an energised physical body essentially like that of our present body except that it will be a better one, though better along familiar lines, and differing from our present bodies in that it cannot ever wear out or become de-energised. It must, and will, last forever. (It is like the suit in *The Man in the White Suit*.) We have an energised body, and, as we go along the history of our life trajectory, that body at some time ceases to be energised and then, perhaps after considerable decay or even disintegration, gets, according to the bodily resurrection story, a refurbished or a reconstituted body and, most importantly of all, it gets a re-energised body as a dead battery gets recharged. We are rather like a lake, to switch the analogy, that dries up and then, on the same lakebed, refills again. Peter Geach, a

stalwart defender of bodily resurrection, forcefully puts the matter in
this way:

> The traditional faith of Christianity, inherited from Judaism, is that
> at the end of this age the Messiah will come and men will rise from
> their graves to die no more. That faith is not going to be shaken by
> inquiries about bodies burned to ashes or eaten by beasts; those
> who might well suffer just such death in martyrdom were those
> who were most confident of a glorious reward in the resurrection.
> One who shares that hope will hardly wish to take out an occultistic
> or philosophical insurance policy, to guarantee some sort of
> survival as an annuity, in case God's promise of resurrection should
> fail.[4]

Leaving God out of it, the notions of inert bodies being re-
energised or even particles of dust being brought together and
formed again into a single body and then re-energised are logical
possibilities (in the philosopher's sense of that phrase) and in that
sense (a sense familiar to philosophers) these notions are coherent.
Of course, to say that something is logically possible is not to say
much. It is logically possible that Geach might sprint from Leeds to
London in three seconds or eat a thousand ears of corn in two
seconds, though we better not ask for a story about how he will do
these things. Similarly, it is logically possible that I might grow an
aluminium exo-skeleton just as the metamorphosis in the Kafka story
is, as the logical positivists used to say, consistently describable.
However, that is a kind of low-order coherence if coherence at all. It
is in reality no more than a necessary condition for coherence. What
it does mean is that we know what it would be like to see a metallic
substance spreading all over Nielsen's body and for his bones and the
like to turn into something like iron rods. And we can follow the
Kafka story. But we do not at all understand how such things are
causally possible. They make no sense at all in terms of what we know
about the world. (All we have are mental pictures here but still it
does not appear that any syntactical rules have been violated.) And it
is not even clear that we know what it would be like to see Geach run
from Leeds to London in three seconds or even in three minutes.
Suppose I were in an aeroplane at a very high altitude with very
powerful binoculars. I could possibly spy out Geach at Leeds in his
running shorts starting with the starter's gun and then track him as he
ran – now in three seconds – to London, though, if we get specific,

what it would be like to carry out such a tracking so rapidly is hard to say. However, I do know or think I know, what it would be like three seconds later – though I would have to move my binoculars awfully fast – to spy out Geach or a Geach-like replica at the outskirts of London. Given, as I remarked, the speed of his alleged running, the tracking (the very idea here) gets more obscure. What, for example, would it be like to see him running at such a speed? (But perhaps I could have a movie camera and replay the whole thing in very slow motion. Still he must have moved his arms and legs with incredible speed. And how did he do that? How is that possible? For God, all things are possible but not for Geach.)

Such stories depend for their intelligibility on their being under-described. The more we, remaining stubbornly literal, try to fill them in, the more problematical they become, namely, their intelligibility, and the less coherent they seem. (Philosophers talk of 'the limits of intelligibility' but we have no clear idea of what we are talking about here.)[5] Still, perhaps no contradictions are involved in their char-acterisations: problematicity and doubtful coherence yes, incon-sistency no, or perhaps no. (Still, what is or isn't consistent is not always easy to ascertain.) Where no disembodiment assumptions sneak in by the back door to carry the self from one body to the next, bodily resurrection seems at least to be some kind of obscure logical possibility. Still that is not saying very much at all.

Many logical possibilities are not genuine possibilities. It is totally irrational for me to believe I can levitate, survive in the winter outside in my swimming trunks at the North Pole, or that this body of mine will go on functioning in good order indefinitely. Is it not just as irrational to believe in bodily resurrection? Well certainly it is *without* a belief in the God of Judaism, Christianity or Islam. But with it, it is not so clear. Recall that for those religions God has promised such a resurrection and for God everything is possible. God, that is, is conceived of as omnipotent which entails that He can do anything that it is logically possible to do. (But He cannot create a round square – a clear logical impossibility.) So if you can come to believe in the God of these three sister religions – and continue to conceive of Him in a fairly orthodox way – you can come, readily enough, to believe in immortality in the sense of bodily resurrection though it also may cut the other way too, for some may feel that if to believe in God one must believe in bodily resurrection then one can hardly believe in God. (Perhaps we need something like reflective equili-brium here.) If our faith commits us to things like that, it is not unnatural to believe, then it is hard to be a person of faith.

However, again an extreme Fideist, remembering his James Joyce, may believe that if it is logically possible, and indeed humanly speaking necessary, to believe in one absurdity, that is, God, it is easy enough to believe in another, that is, bodily resurrection. Still, I think that it is reasonable enough to say that, if there is a God, and if He is as He is portrayed in the orthodox Judaic, Christian and Islamic traditions, then it is not unreasonable (scandal to the intellect that it is) to believe in survival through bodily resurrection. Theologians may debate over exactly what is the least imperspicuous representation of this, but that it will occur is itself reasonable to expect *given such background beliefs*. (But we should not forget how arcane and implausible these background beliefs are, beliefs which include the idea of there being an infinite disembodied individual who is both an *individual* and omnipresent, and is an individual, and a person as well, that is transcendent to the world.)

It is, I believe, for reasons such as this that Godfrey Vesey, after arguing that bodily resurrection is a coherent notion, remarks that 'bodily resurrection is a matter of faith, not of philosophy'.[6] If one has the faith of a Jew, Christian or Moslem, one can reasonably believe in bodily resurrection, if not, not. However, philosophy, or at least reflective deliberation, need not stop just where Vesey thinks it must, for we can, and should, ask whether this faith is reasonable or indeed, for us (that is we intelligentsia), standing where we are now, knowing what we know, not irrational (viewed from a purely cognitive perspective). We should also ask, irrational or not, whether we should, everything considered, crucify our intellects and believe in God and bodily resurrection even if such beliefs are irrational. (There may be a case – a reasonable case – as we shall see later, for sometimes, if we can bring it off, having, in certain very constrained circumstances, irrational beliefs.)[7]

It is because of such considerations that I, in several books, have laboured hard and long over questions about the necessity of faith and over whether belief in God is reasonable, if we have a good understanding of what our situation is.[8] I have argued, as has Antony Flew in a rather parallel way, that belief in an anthropomorphic god is little better than a superstition, and that belief in God, when conceptualised in the non-anthropomorphic way, is incoherent.[9] The non-anthropomorphic conceptualisation is where God has come to be conceptualised, in developed Judaic, Christian and Islamic traditions, as an infinite immaterial individual, omnipresent, but still a person transcendent to the world (to the whole universe). It is this conceptualisation that we are maintaining is incoherent. It is a conception, incoherent as it is, that is beyond reasonable belief for a person in the twentieth century with a good philosophical and scientific training. (For those who are not in a good position to be cognisant of its incoherency it is another matter.)

I hasten to add, lest I seem both unreasonable and arrogant in making the above claim, that reasonable people can have, and perhaps are likely to have, *some* unreasonable beliefs. I am not saying, let me repeat, that educated religious believers are unreasonable, while I am plainly reasonable. That would be gross hubris and silliness to boot. But I am saying that their belief in God, and with that, their belief in bodily resurrection, is unreasonable. However, I am also saying that *if* it were reasonable to believe in the God of our orthodox traditions, it would not be unreasonable to believe in bodily resurrection. So I have, in my work, concentrated on belief in God, and not on immortality, taking the former belief to be the central thing on which to concentrate.

It is hardly in place for me to repeat my arguments here or to try to develop new ones. However, if, on the one hand, they, or some more sophisticated rational reconstruction of them, are sound, or, if, on the other hand, arguments against the existence of God like those of Wallace Matson or J. L. Mackie are sound, or by some rational reconstruction could be made so, then belief in bodily resurrection is unjustified. (For the same conceptualisation of God, they cannot, of course, both be sound.) I should add here that both Matson and Mackie profess (strangely it seems to me as it does to Flew as well) to have no difficulties with the intelligibility or coherence of God-talk.[10] (They are the atheist counterparts or *alter egos* of Swinburne and Penelhum.) We say that belief in the God of developed forms of these traditions is incoherent; they say, by contrast, that the belief is merely false or at least on careful scrutiny clearly appears to be false. The Matson-Mackie arguments, that is, are arguments claiming to establish that belief in God, though coherent, is unjustified, and that it is more reasonable to believe that God exists is false than to believe in God or to remain agnostic. But in either eventuality, it is unreasonable to believe in bodily resurrection. If either the Flew-Nielsen coherence arguments, or the Matson-Mackie arguments about justifying belief in God, or an appeal to faith are sound, then, given the radical diversity of putative revelations, belief in God for philosophically informed people is unreasonable. And if belief in God is unreasonable, it is surely not reasonable to believe in bodily resurrection. But if one or another of these skeptical arguments are not sound or cannot be made so with a little fiddling, and if we are justified in believing in God or perhaps justified in accepting such a belief as an article of faith, then belief in bodily resurrection seems to be reasonable *if* God is what the orthodox say He is. (I say 'seems' for, as it does to Reinhold Niebuhr and Paul Tillich, such talk might still seem to be such an intellectual affront that it would be more reasonable and, morally more desirable, to somehow construe the whole matter symbolically as do Niebuhr and Tillich.)

Before I leave the topic of bodily resurrection I should note that there is a felt difficulty concerning it that some, in a way that baffles me, find naggingly worrisome.[11] Suppose Sven dies and rots and eventually turns to dust and indeed further suppose his grave gets upturned and the dust, which is all that he is now, is spread randomly by the wind. God, being omnipotent, at the Last Judgement gathers these specks of dust together and reconstitutes them into an energised body that looks exactly like Sven and has all the memories Sven had, but, the objection goes, what appears is not Sven,

> the very same person that died previously but merely a replica or simulacrum of him: for, since there is a time-gap between death and resurrection, during which the original body may very well have been destroyed altogether, the connecting link that would make it unambiguously the same person and not a replica will have disappeared.[12]

There are a number of things that should be said here. First, there is no reason, unless we gratuitously assume some very strange physics, to believe that the connecting link is broken: that there is not a bodily continuity. Those specks of dust scattered about and mixed with a lot of other dust are still the specks of dust of Sven, and God, being omnipotent, can readily gather up all the specks of dust and only those specks of dust that are Sven and reconstitute Sven and re-energise Sven's reconstituted corpse. For a while we have bits of Sven and then we have Sven all together again. That should not be difficult at all for God, given His intelligence and omnipotence. There is nothing there that should be *conceptually* puzzling. First we had Friday's *Globe and Mail* and then we had bits of paper scattered all over and then we had them all gathered up and pasted together into *The Globe and Mail*.

We no more need to speak of a gap-inclusive entity here than we need to speak of a gap-inclusive entity between my old battery which had gone dead and the same battery re-energised. There is no more a gap in identity between the human being first energised and then in turn de-energised and then re-energised again, than there is between the live battery, the dead battery and the battery charged up again. In both cases we maintain bodily continuity. The ashes of my pet canary, in a container on my desk, are still the ashes of my pet canary. The same physical entity transformed. God has a little more work cut out for Him in putting Sven back together again than the garage mechanic who charges my battery. (God, unlike the king's men, would have no trouble with Humpty-Dumpty.) But then again, God would not be God if He could not do it. There surely are no logical impossibilities here that omnipotence could not overcome unless perhaps omnipotence is itself an incoherent notion. (I shall assume here it is not.)

Secondly, certainly it could – and perhaps just as well – be a replica and perhaps there would be no verifiable difference between a situation describing the real Sven and a situation describing his replica. But this by now should not be in the least surprising. It is just the old story of theory being *undetermined* by data. Both descriptions make verifiable claims but perhaps there is no *further* verifiable claim that will enable us to decide between them, but post-Quinean philosophy of science has taught us to be neither surprised nor disturbed by that. There will often be a proliferation of theories all equally, or at least apparently equally, compatible with the same observed and perhaps even the same observable data. We must choose between theories on other grounds, and if Jews, Christians or Moslems have independent reason for accepting the God-centred narrative, then they can safely and reasonably ignore replica possibilities. They are not going to get certainty but then, as fallibilism has taught us, we never do in any interesting cases and, after all, why must they have certainty? They can instead be sturdy knights of faith confident that they have deflected philosophical arguments designed to show that talk of bodily resurrection is incoherent. Defeating such rationalism, they can live as persons of faith in their trust in God's promised resurrection: a promise that human beings will rise from their graves and die no more.

III

Let us now turn to an examination of a defence of immortality rooted in Cartesian dualism. That is, we will turn to claims to disembodied existence. There are Christians (Geach, for example) who vehemently reject such a conception of immortality as a philosophical myth which they take to be intellectually unsupportable and religiously unnecessary. There are other Christian philosphers who fervently wish that it would be true but are not even convinced that the very idea of disembodied personal survival is not nonsense.[13] Believers often see the claim to disembodied personal existence as a conception of Greek origin, refurbished and streamlined by Descartes. Many of them claim that it is in reality foreign to a genuinely biblical world view. Whatever may be the larger truth here, we should note that in contrast with the biblical world view, which is more communitarian in spirit, the Cartesian view nicely meshes with the intense individualism of the modern period.[14]

However, as has been pointed out, Jesus's own sayings about the afterlife are ambiguous as between the resurrection of a material body and a 'spiritual body' (whatever that means).[15] Later Christian thought has also waffled here. It has tended to teach the ultimate resurrection of our earthly bodies, no matter how long dead or in what state of decomposition, while permitting the average believer to expect an immediate transition of her soul at the moment of death.[16] Yet, a not inconsiderable number of believers, particularly *some* Protestant Christians, and, among them some philosophers, have opted (even in the age of Ryle, Wittgenstein and Dennett) for a disembodied self and the form of immortality that goes with it. Moreover, it should not be forgotten that even some atheists have believed in this form of immortality (for example, McTaggart). However, it is only against the background of a biblical world view that such a purely speculative conception, at least *prima facie* implausible, is of much interest. Christians, understandably, long for life eternal in the fellowship of God and it has come to seem to a not inconsiderable number of them that the best face that can be put on this is to see ourselves, if this can be justifiably done, as disembodied selves: spiritual continuants whose very spirituality (thinking, willing, feeling non-materially) is what makes us what we are. It is this that is our essence. This Cartesianism seems too much untutored common sense in many modern Christian environments (more likely so in Orange County than in Scarsdale) to be a clear enough notion, but many philosophers and theologians have found it very baffling indeed. Can we actually attach sense to the thesis that persons can exist disembodied? Can we be disembodied continuants who are also individuals who are, as well, persons? (Even if somehow we can attach some sense to the notion we have a long way to go to the making of it a belief that can plausibly be thought to be true.)

Hywel Lewis is just such a Christian philosopher. Lewis does not think 'that any case for immortality can begin to get off the ground if we fail to make a case for dualism'.[17] He is fully aware that many able philosophers think a belief in disembodied personal existence or in disembodied persons is an incoherent belief, devoid of any intelligible sense, and he is concerned to make a case for rejecting that (among philosophers) widely-held belief. He attempts, that is, to defend a belief in disembodied personal survival. In its classical Cartesian form it maintains that persons are real selves or souls, namely particular immaterial conscious things (continuants) which have feelings and thoughts, are capable of willing and acting and which are only contingently connected with the bodies ('physical bodies', if you will) in which they are sometimes housed.

It is this self – a self by which each person is what he is – which each of us, in our own direct, immediate experience, realises is distinct from the body and is capable of being what it is even if there is no body at all. We, the story goes, just experience ourselves as distinct from our bodies. Lewis thinks that this is just a *datum of experience*. Our sense of self-identity, which is prior to any conception we have of personal identity, just tells us that this is so. We are each directly aware of ourselves as we are directly aware of being in pain or of having a sudden thought.

A standard problem for any belief in an immaterial self is over how it is possible to individuate this self (distinguish it from other selves) since it does not have a body. Lewis in defending his view that a knowledge of an immaterial self is just a datum of awareness remarks:

> There must, then, I agree, be individuation. But how is this possible if the immaterial substances in question cannot, as the thought of them would seem to imply, 'be individuated by spatial relations'? This problem, I must now add, does not worry me a great deal, and it never has. It has always seemed evident to me that everyone knows himself to be the being that he is in just being so. We identify ourselves to ourselves in that way, and not in the

last resort on the basis of what we know about ourselves. The reaction to this is sometimes to retort that we seem to be running out of arguments, and we must surely make our case by argument. This is a trying situation for a philosopher to have to meet; quite clearly he does not want to seem unwilling to argue. But argument is not everything, we have also to reckon with what we just find to be the case, we cannot conjure all existence into being by argument and we cannot, as I hope does not sound pretentious, argue against reality.[18]

It may be, as Terence Penelhum has remarked, 'that such a doctrine has no content, and just amounts to an empty assertion that our problem really does have an answer'.[19] It may be, as Godfrey Vesey and Sydney Shoemaker think, that in so reasoning Lewis in effect construes 'I' as a proper name when it is not, and when in reality it functions more like 'here' such that 'I' no more names a person that 'here' names a place.[20] On Lewis's account, even if I suffer amnesia, I do not lose the direct sense of self-identity – my direct awareness of self – of which he speaks. There just is this direct self-awareness. Vesey asserts that such a self-identification is an illusion, and so cannot give meaning to talk of personal immortality.[21] There are perfectly non-deviant uses of 'here' where 'here' does not name a place. As Vesey puts it:

Suppose that, *although I am quite lost*, I say *to myself* 'I know where I am, I'm here'. This use of 'here', although completely uninformative, may nevertheless *seem* to be a significant, non-empty use. It borrows a facade of meaning from the informative uses. Similarly, an empty, soliloquizing, use of 'I', may 'borrow a facade of meaning from the informative, interpersonal, uses'.[22]

Suppose I am suffering from amnesia and I remember Lewis's doctrine that 'Everyone knows himself to be the being that he is in just being so', so, fortified by that, I know who I am: 'I am I'. I just find it to be the case in immediate experience that I am I. This is just something, the Cartesian story goes, we find to be so in a self-disclosure or in self-awareness. But if we recall that 'I', in standard contexts, is no more used to name a person than 'here' names a place, we should recognise the emptiness of Lewis's remark that 'Everyone knows himself to be the being he is in just being so'. It is like saying

'Everyone knows where he is, in that he can say, "I'm here" and not be wrong'.[23]

Perhaps, as J. L. Mackie thinks, things are not quite that simple (in philosophy they usually are not).[24] However, even if the above arguments about emptiness do not go through there is, I believe, a simpler objection to such an account. Suppose we grant that there is this dumb or brute self-awareness (perhaps 'inarticulate' is the better word) giving one some kind of inchoate self-identity. I am directly aware of myself in a manner similar to the way in which I am directly aware that I am thinking – like the having of a sudden thought – or having a pain. But this brute datum (if that is what it is) is just that: it does not itself carry the heavy *interpretive* weight that Lewis in effect puts on it, namely that the self of which I am aware is *immaterial* (disembodied). That is clearly an *interpretation* of the experience to which there are alternative interpretations and one would (*pace* Lewis) have to argue for that alternative. (Argument cannot stop where Lewis wants it to.) One could not rightly claim that it is just something found to be true in experience. Indeed to the extent that we do not understand 'immaterial thing', 'immaterial individual', 'disembodied person', we might think *that* interpretation is a non-starter in being only a putative interpretation.

Be that latter point as it may, what we have here, in claiming that we are directly aware of ourselves as not just a self, as something I know not what which has thoughts and feelings and initiates actions, but also as a disembodied agent, is in reality an *interpretation* and not just a datum of experience, just as much as when I say that the pain I feel is the stimulation of my C fibres I do not just report my experience but interpret it. Both are interpretations of experience. They are not direct data of experience. And if we say, misleadingly I believe, that all experiences are interpretations, then we must recognise that there are degrees of interpretiveness and grades of theoreticity. There cannot be the direct way to immortality that Lewis seeks, not even as an enabling doctrine. 'I am immortal' cannot be a matter of direct awareness in the way 'I am tired' is.

It is a rather common belief among many analytical philosophers (A. J. Ayer, Peter Strawson and Bernard Williams among them) that the very idea of a disembodied person is incoherent, for reference to a body is a necessary condition for establishing the identity of a person and for ascribing identity through time to a changing person. We indeed characteristically appeal to memory as well in determining whether a person at a later time was one and the same person as at some earlier time. But when memory and bodily criteria conflict bodily identity takes pride of place. Suppose, to take an example, Hans dies and it is alleged that his spirit lives on. However, because having a body is a necessary condition for making ascriptions of personhood, we can have no way, even in principle, of ascertaining whether there is really a disembodied Hans who is the same person as the ruddy-cheeked Hans we used to know. The very idea of a '*bodiless individual*' seems to be unintelligible.[25]

If we try to substitute memory as the primary criterion for personal identity we will fail, for we need to be able, for there to be memories at all, to distinguish between real and apparent memories, between Mildred's thinking she remembers cashing the cheque and her actually remembering it. Only genuine memories guarantee identity, not merely apparent ones. Actually remembering that I am a professor of philosophy at the University of Calgary guarantees my identity, only thinking I remember it does not. But for these to be real memories as distinct from apparent memories the events thought to be remembered must actually have occurred *and* they must have happened to the person remembering them. Memory cannot constitute personal identity or, more plausibly, be the fundamental criterion of personal identity for it presupposes that such identities have been established, that we can determine who it is that has the memories. So memory will not do the fundamental work. The only alternative – or at least the only other argument alternative – for in any fundamental way establishing personal identity is having the same body (bodily continuity).

However, are there not at least conceivable happenings that would loosen our attachment to bodily identity as a necessary condition for establishing personal identity and not only show that people, like Locke's Cobbler and the Prince, could 'exchange bodies' but that they could also exist without bodies at all? The following story is designed to show that bodiless existence is a *logical* possibility. Suppose I am a rather credulous fellow and I live in a house with a spouse, two children, my aged mother and two dogs. The house initially is a perfectly normal house, but then one day strange things, sometimes in front of us all, start happening. Lights inexplicably go on and off, doors open and close and chairs move in unaccountable ways. The happenings cannot be traced to any member of the family, to the dogs, to neighbours, to friends, or to agents whom we ordinarily would regard as people, or to the wind, or to anything like that. Suppose I, the credulous one, hypothesise that the house is haunted by a poltergeist to the considerable amusement of the more skeptical members of the family. But then suppose my son, age 16, begins to receive premonitions of what is going on. He can predict accurately when a door is going to open, a light go on, a chair at the table will move and the like. He says an invisible person, *S*, has talked to him. Pressed he retracts 'talked' – no one else hears it and no tape recorder catches it. He now says rather that 'talked' is a groping way of saying *S* lets him know like thoughts popping into his head. But this, whatever it is, goes on with considerable accuracy for some time. My son (for example) says *S* told him that *S* is going out in the garden and sure enough the backdoor to the garden opens and closes.

Suppose, after a time, *S* comes out of the closet, so to say, and gives my son to understand that *S* is lonely and wants to belong to the family and to be accepted. After dinner, Sarah, as *S* tells my son she wants to be called, communicates to him that she is going to wash up, take care of the fireplace, and turn the thermostat down in the evening and up in the morning. We see, with no body around making it happen, dishes go from the table to the dishwasher, matches striking against the grate and regularly lighting the fire at the desired time and just before I get to it I see the thermostat go up in morning and down in the evening set to the required day-time and night-time temperature with no discernible hand moving the thermostat. Sarah, as we now have started to call *S*, lets my son know that she is beginning to feel like a member of the family. She lets him know she will be on the watch-out for us and guard us. Subsequently Sarah lets my son know that my daughter is in danger in the back yard, and indeed we rush out and discover she has fallen into the well, and at another time she warns us, again through my son, that my German Shepherd is in danger and again we rush to the back yard and find him confronted by a rattlesnake. The whole family becomes convinced, after such episodes, that Sarah is real, that she is an invisible person and a family friend. She might, if people want to talk that way, be said to have a 'subtle invisible body' that neither the family members nor the dogs can see or in any way detect, for example, no one ever bumps into her and she never steps on the dogs' paws. If such conceivable things did actually happen we might be led quite naturally and quite plausibly to use the name 'Sarah' and to think of

Sarah as a person, indeed to take her to be a person albeit a disembodied person. If such things really happened there would, it is natural to say, be at least one disembodied person.[26]

If things really were so to transpire would we be justified in calling Sarah a person? Well, it would be at least plausible to say Sarah met all of Daniel Dennett's suggested conditions for personhood, namely, rationality, intentionality, propriety as the object of a personal stance, ability to reciprocate such a stance, verbal communication and a special kind of consciousness.[27] She knows, to take the elements fitting her most problematically, concern for the well-being of the family, for example, her protection of my daughter and concern for the well-being of my German Shepherd as instanced in the rattlesnake event. This gives rise to gratitude and affection and Sarah reciprocates concern with other acts, for example, at Thanksgiving various mixings mysteriously go on in the kitchen done by none of the regular family members and by no visible hands and a lovely Indian pudding emerges. And we have seen how Sarah communicates, though it is perhaps stretching things a bit to call it *verbal* communication. Sarah also seems plainly to be aware of herself and her surroundings. We identify Sarah in identifying these happenings.

Could Sarah be identified with a normal human being known to have lived a normal life? Suppose in checking the records I discover that a previous owner several years back had had a shy and retiring daughter, also called Sarah, who had died while living in what is now my house. Suppose it is further discovered from accounts about her that she had a personality very like that of 'our Sarah' and that when we ask 'our Sarah' about that young woman Sarah says that she is that very woman and leads us in the attic to a hidden box of letters from that Sarah to her parents. Under such circumstances it would be reasonable to believe that our disembodied Sarah was that very woman. So it appears at least we have described what would have to be the case to become acquainted with a disembodied person and indeed a disembodied person who had formerly had a perfectly normal body. We have given verifiable, empirical sense to the concept showing that it makes sense to speak of 'bodiless persons' and that such a concept, bizarre as it is, is an intelligible one. It has what used to be called empirical meaning.

The first thing that needs to be said about this is that, conceivable or not, things like this do not happen. Some might say this is irrelevant because, after all, what is at issue is that such talk is intelligible and this only requires that disembodied individuals be consistently describable, not that there actually be the slightest likelihood that there really are such beings. There is not the slightest chance that there are people whose skin is naturally orange and hair naturally purple but the conception, like that of 'golden mountain' or 'wooden jetliner', is perfectly intelligible. Yet we do have some understanding here in the way we do not have for 'Procrastination drinks melancholy', or 'Reagan sleeps slower than Trudeau', but then again we must remember that intelligibility, and even more obviously coherence, admits of degrees and perhaps of kinds. When we think concretely about what causally speaking would have to be in place for there to be a wooden jetliner that actually could fly we see that such a conception doesn't fit in with anything else we know. In terms of what we know about the word, it just doesn't make any sense at all and the same is true of Sarah and of Locke's story of the Cobbler and the Prince. In that perfectly standard way these accounts are incoherent. They are just stories we can tell, like certain children's stories or certain science fiction. Part of their charm (where they have any) is that they couldn't happen, and our reason for our confidence that they couldn't happen is not that we have made careful inductive investigations like looking to see if there are magpies in New York State or if the quail are different in the east of North America than in the west. Rather, our source of confidence is that these things actually obtaining just does not fit with what we know or at least reasonably believe about the world. Just how could a wooden jetliner take off or fly at 500 miles an hour at 40,000 feet? How would it stand the stress, and so on and so on? The wood would have to be remarkably hard, very different indeed from anything we know to be wood. Such things just do not make sense and at least in this way Sarah doesn't make sense either. There are indeed more things in heaven and earth, Horatio, than is dreamt of in your philosophy. But in this context that is just empty talk. These things never happen and we would, to put it mildly, be extremely skeptical – and rightly so – of any claim that something like this did happen. People touched by modernity would not accept at face value the claim that my watch just disappeared into thin air as distinct from a claim that I had just lost it and could not find it. There cannot be wooden jetliners, Sarahs or Locke's phenomena, any more than there can be, as Evans-Pritchard was perfectly aware, Zande witchcraft substance.

However, the cobbler and the prince and Sarah aside, there are cases of alleged possession and mediumship and there is Sally

Beauchamp, Dr Jekyll and Mr Hyde, and *The Three Faces of Eve*. Some cases of this sort have actually been said to have happened by non-credulous people of intellectual and moral integrity and the fictional cases have a certain verisimilitude. But in these cases, if we look at them soberly and non-metaphorically, we need not, and indeed should not, say that we have, as for example in the Eve thing, three persons caged in one body. There are not three Eves but the one Eve has a multiple personality. We should speak in these cases of a plurality of *personalities* not of *persons*. This, as J. L. Mackie points out, is much more guarded and plausible a claim to make than to say there are, mysterious as it may seem, three different persons.[28] We need not invoke disembodied existence or even dualism to handle such cases. They are bizarre and puzzling enough anyway, assuming they are not fraudulent, without adding *unnecessarily* ontological puzzlement. Here is a good place to apply the old maxim about not multiplying entities or conceptions of entities beyond need.

   More generally, to return to the question about logical possibilities, we should take to heart David Wiggens's point that the concepts we use, and the particulars we identify and describe in using them, are not such that they can range over all at least putative logical possibilities. They are rather constrained by the nomological grounding of the sortal words we use.[29] We must not confuse what we can imagine or conceive with what is possible. We can *conceive* of an ice-cream cake at the centre of the sun, but such a state of affairs is *not possible*. For it to be possible the ice-cream cake, as the wooden jet, would have to have so changed that it could no longer coherently be called an ice-cream cake. In identifying any particular, say a candy bar melting in my pocket, this ability to identify and re-identify is closely tied up with our concept of what the thing in question is. We expect the bar to melt in my pocket, but the claim that it survived unmelted on the hot stove, let alone in the centre of the sun, is not a possibility that the concept allows for any more than our concept of what it is to be a wren allows for the possibility that it might fly at 60,000 feet and at the speed of 2000 miles an hour. Where we have a sortal concept it is constrained by the physical laws that apply to the exemplifications of those concepts. Copper cannot do just anything; rather it must obey the laws of nature which enable us to distinguish it as a substance. What in fact happens is the basis of all our concepts. It constrains the conceptual connections inherent in our use of language. Iron cannot melt in snow and the flesh and blood Sarah, who used to live in my house long before I lived there, cannot become a disembodied person. It *may* be that the idea of a 'disembodied person' is not contradictory – we *may* have (beyond mental pictures) understood my narrative of Sarah – but disembodied persons are neither physically nor, as some people like to talk, metaphysically possible.[30] We cannot rely on thought experiments – on various underdescribed fantasies – rather, as Wiggens puts it, we have to work back from the extensions to work out what is essential to something being the thing it is. 'For persons this extension is living, embodied, human beings'.[31] Person may not be a natural kind, but a human being – a human person – is. For our kind of natural kind, mind and character are dependent for their activities on a body in causal interaction with the world.[32] We have no coherent grounds for thinking ourselves to be immaterial substances or disembodied continuants incapable of destruction.

IV

This discussion has been metaphysical, somewhat arcane and, it seems to me, quaint. It is not the sort of thing that contributes either to the growth of knowledge or to salvation. It is, or so it seems to me, strange that people should be arguing about such things in our epoch. Yet argue they do. I think what fuels such talk is a deep human problem and I want now to turn to that. Such talk, to come at it at first indirectly, is at home against a religio-ethical background, as Pascal and Dostoevsky well saw, otherwise what we have are just some not very interesting metaphysical puzzles. After all, there is over personal identity and the like, as Derek Parfit and Thomas Nagel have shown, far more fascinating metaphysical conundrums, than the ones generated by such religious concerns, conundrums that we can, if we like doing that sort of thing, wile away our time with, if we are sufficiently leisured and undriven.[33] It is not the metaphysical puzzles about immortality but the human side of immortality that can be gripping and it is that, and that alone, that gives these arcane metaphysical investigations their point. Given our entangled lives, given the deep frustration of human hopes and aspirations, given the unnecessary hell that is the fate of many (40,000 people simply live on the streets in New York to say nothing of what goes on in Calcutta), it is surely understandable that we humans should ask 'Shall I live again?' and, noting the often utterly pointless suffering of the world, ask of those so suffering 'Shall they live again? Could there be "another world" in which they could live in some decency?'

We live in a world where 10,000 people, most of them quite unnecessarily, die of starvation each day, where people are horribly tortured and degraded and where the rich not infrequently live frivolous and expensive lives, living off the backs of the poor, and where in our part of the world Yuppidom reigns supreme. It is hard, given such a world, to just accept the fact of all those people dying in misery who have hardly had a chance to live. It is hard to accept the fact that they should just die and rot and that that is all there is to it. Of course, cognitively speaking it is easy to accept that, for what could be more obvious, but, morally speaking, it is very hard indeed to accept. The moral sense rebels at such a world.

It is easy enough for someone like myself, surrounded by a caring environment, living in comfort and having interesting work, which I can hope will have some significance, to accept the inevitability of death and my eventual utter destruction. It would be nice if it were not so and I could go on living as I am but that cannot be and others will continue after me. That is not such a hard cluster of facts to come to accept. Moreover, it is evident enough anyway.

The thing is to make something of the life I have. It can be a good and meaningful life and whether it is or not, in the circumstances in which I live, is not independent of what I do. And I can hope that I'll be lucky enough, without cancer or the like, to have my 'allotted time'. I would be frustrated if I do not and perhaps irrationally bitter, but, if I happen to be unlucky, it would just be something – and we have here the unforgettable example of Freud – to be, if I am capable of being reasonable under such circumstances, stoically accepted. But with luck nothing like that will happen to me or those close to me and I can live out my life in a meaningful and pleasant way and eventually die. What did Tolstoy get so exercised about?

I think Reinhold Niebuhr was right in turning with contempt from the egoism of healthy individuals, living what would be otherwise normal lives, having obsessive hang-ups about the fact that they will eventually die. For them to be so all important to themselves hardly inspires admiration. For those ageing Yuppies (perhaps former Yuppies is the right phrase), firmly situated in Yuppidom, who have such preoccupations, where there is no suffering or Strindbergian or O'Neillish laceration or self-laceration, their worries are not something to inspire much sympathy or concern. The temptation is to tell them to get on with it and stop snivelling. (Dietrich Bonhoeffer had a good sense of this.)

However, for the suffering, ignorant and degraded millions, living in hellish conditions, and who have unremittingly, through no fault of their own, lived blighted lives, the inevitability, and at least seemingly evident finality, of death is another thing entirely. This, though plainly there before our eyes, is what is so hard to accept. We do not have something here which is just, or perhaps even at all, a philosopher's puzzle or a neurotic's worry. The matter of blighted lives is a very real one indeed. Five hundred million children and adults suffer from malnutrition and 800 million live, or try to live, in extreme poverty. This remains true while globally one trillion dollars is given to military spending, a spending which is astronomically beyond the needs of anything, for the various great powers principally involved, that could even remotely count as defence. Yet the World Food Council concluded in 1984 that four billion dollars a year committed internationally until the end of the century, would ensure access to food and productive lives for the 500 million people most in need, and set on track a stable world food order where among the poorer nations basket cases would not constantly pop up. However, the brute facts are that a trillion dollars a year goes into doomsday military spending and even a comparatively paltry four billion can't be found to save people from starvation and malnutrition. (Here we are reminded of the world of *1984*.)

Thinking of the callousness of it all, the hypocrisy of many great nations, the placid acceptance of this by the masses, even though such a situation is totally unnecessary, is very sickening indeed. It is understandable, given that, that people despair of the world and that there, out of despair with our human lot, arises a hope for and even faith in immortality, an immortality that will give those (along with everyone else) who never have had anything like a decent chance in life another life that is worthwhile. This is not a matter of a kind of grubby individual craving for life eternal but a longing for a morally worthwhile life for humankind as a whole. (Has our individualism and egoism dug so deep that we cannot really believe that people are genuinely capable of such hopes?)

There is a stance within Christianity, though no doubt there are similar stances within Judaism and Islam as well, often associated with Irenaean universalism, which maintains that human suffering would be irredeemably tragic if our present earthly life were not followed by another in which the suffering of each individual could be made worthwhile for that individual.[34] Suppose, in pursuing this, we ask the famous trio of questions of Kant: 'What can I know?', 'What ought I to do?' and 'What may I hope?'. Think particularly of the last one, 'What may I hope?' and then think of (to put it gently) the unhappy world that we know – keeping in mind the facts that I have just described, facts which are but some salient members of a set of deeply disquieting facts. Hopes are hard to maintain against the persistence and pervasiveness of such facts. Max Horkheimer, who certainly was no defender of a theistic world perspective, well put it when he remarked 'moral conscience . . . rebels against the thought that the present state of reality is final'.[35] Still, in the struggles of our everyday life, our hopes for a realisation, or even approximation, of a truly human society, a society of human brotherhood and sisterhood, a just society or even a rational society, are constantly being defeated. We do not, in fact, given our economic and scientific potential, have something that even remotely approximates a caring society or a just society. (It is pure propaganda for a cabinet minister to speak – boast might be a more accurate word – as one recently did of there being equality and social justice in Canada. But that is standard issue for politicians in our countries.)

Such states of affairs led Kant, Lessing, and even Voltaire, to postulate immortality in order to make some match between our hopes and what is achievable in 'this world'. It is easy to satirise such Kantian postulations of 'pure practical reason' and it is utter folly, as J. L. Mackie has well argued, to try to argue from such *hopes* to *any likelihood* at all that such a reality will come to be.[36] However, as we know from Pascal and Dostoevsky, it may be rational in certain circumstances to have a belief or to cause a belief to come to be formed (if we can) which, viewed from a purely intellectual or cognitive perspective, is an irrational belief. If I am lost in the Canadian North, and if a firm belief that I stand a good chance of getting out is, as a matter of fact, essential if I am going to have any chance at all of getting out, though in fact my objective chances are pretty slim, then it is reasonable for me to come to have that false belief if there is some possibility that I can somehow come to have it in that circumstance. (Recall Pascal on holy water and Schelling's answer to armed robbery.)

Is it similarly reasonable, given the human condition, for me to hope for human immortality in the form of universal salvation for humankind even though the objective likelihood of anything like that being the case is extremely low? In responding to this question I am going to assume that the cognitive situation *vis-à-vis* immortality is as I have claimed and argued it to be. If the situation is not as bad as I argue it is, then we should perhaps, depending on just what we believe the situation to be, draw different conclusions. But suppose I have managed to tell it like it is, then should we continue to hope, or at least wish, for immortality?

Let me describe a scenario that understandably might push a person in the direction of Pascalian hope. Imagine this person, as a humane and sensitive person, reflective and reasonable, with a good education, coming of age in the west just after the First World War. Suppose she becomes a Marxist or an Anarchist, or some other kind of socialist, and says and feels, given what is then going on in the world, that now there is hope in the world. Now imagine her living through all the times in between up to our time (1987) and now, as a rather old person, though still with sound faculties and a humane attitude, she becomes, given the world she has seen and continues to see before her, utterly disillusioned with secular struggle (including, of course, political struggle), with being able to bring that hope into the world or even to bring into the world (small isolated pockets apart, for example, Iceland or Denmark) a tolerable amount of decency. It isn't that she now comes to think that religious revival will bring it into the world – a kind of moral rearmament with God in the driver's seat. Nothing, she now believes, will bring such an order of kindliness into the world. There can be, she believes, Brecht to the contrary notwithstanding, no laying the foundations of kindliness. She has simply given up on the world. The caring for humankind and the detestation of human degradation that launched her into political struggle is still there but she has utterly lost the sense that there is hope in the world, that there will be any lasting or large-scale remedy for these ills. She doesn't as a result become a reactionary. She still supports progressive causes, though, unlike a Marxist or an Anarchist – an E. P. Thompson or a Noam Chomsky – she will no longer, given her disillusion, throw her whole life into such activities, but, while continuing to support progressive causes, turns more and more to religious concerns and thinks and feels through the issue of immortality again.

Suppose, in thinking immortality through on the cognitive side, she comes to a conclusion very similar to mine. But, unlike me, she, keeping in mind Irenaean universalism, comes passionately to hope for immortality in the form of a hope for universal salvation for

humankind. Suppose further, facing non-evasively the odds, it becomes, not so much a *hope* (the odds are too dismal for that) but a
wish, but still a wish that persistently remains with her and guides her
life. Is this an attitude that it is desirable that we should come to share
with her? It is certainly undesirable if it comes to block our struggling
in the world, if it leads to a quietism in the face of evil: to being like
Martin Luther rather than like Thomas Münzer. If that is the upshot,
it is better to develop the set of attitudes that accepts that the human
situation is irredeemably tragic and that we, in such a situation, in
Camus's metaphor, should relentlessly fight the plague, knowing full
well that the plague is always with us, sometimes striking virulently
and at other times for a time remaining only latent, but always being
something that will return, after an uneasy lull, to strike again in full
fury. The thing to do is, acknowledging this, to unyieldingly and
relentlessly fight the plague. What we should do is to tackle the most
glaring ills or at least the ills we can get a purchase on, taking to heart
and accepting the fact that there will be no extensive or permanent
successes. We will have neither Christian nor Marxist eschatological
hopes, but, like Camus, we will accept stoically an irredeemably
tragic vision of the world. Doesn't this tragic sense of life square
better with a non-evasive human integrity than the religious turn?

Not necessarily and perhaps not at all if the religious person takes,
in a non-evasive way, a kind of Irenaean turn. Suppose she does not
stop relentlessly fighting the plague and doesn't fight it *because* of the
hopes/wishes she entertains for the afterlife, but fights the plague to
fight evil *and* does so while still wishing for a salvation for humankind, wishing for a fate which is not irredeemably tragic and where
human salvation is a reality. Isn't this way of reacting to life and to
the world more desirable than sticking with a bleak Camus-like tragic
vision, *if* so wishing does not lead to any self-deception about how
astronomically slight the chances for salvation are, and if it doesn't
weaken one's resolve to fight the plague or make one, in some other
way, less effective in fighting the plague? With some people it might
dull the native edge of resolution, but surely it need not. One can
doggedly fight the plague *and* have such eschatological wishes as well.
She can, that is, continue to fight and, utterly unblinkered, have the
wish that salvation could be our lot as human beings. So held, this
attitude seems at least to have everything the Camusian attitude has
and something more as well and thus, everything considered, it is a
more desirable attitude.

However, these are not the only alternatives. A Marxist, an Anarchist, or a revisionist socialist social democratic vision of things are not visions which are the tragic visions of an existentialist humanism or of a Freudian or Weberian view of life. If any of these forms of socialism can become and remain a reality – or can even firmly get on the agenda – and be the forms (different as they are among themselves) that Marx, Bakunin or Bernstein envisaged, or some rational reconstruction of them, without becoming like the later Stalinist *and* social democratic deformations of socialism (for example, on the social democratic side, the Wilson or Schmidt governments), then there could be hope in the world. There would be, in such an eventuality, the reasonable prospect of a decent world, or, more than a decent world order, a truly human world order where human flourishing would be extensive.

The person in our scenario turned away from such hopes because of the terrible historical events since the souring of the Russian Revolution, events such as forced collectivisation, the purge trials, the Second World War, the hegemony of Pax Americana, the Vietnam War, the rise of Islamic Fundamentalism (for example, Iran), the rise, both politically and religiously, of reactionary forms of Christianity and Judaism in American and Israel, persistent mass starvation, and the pervasiveness of doomsday war machines. She has seared into her consciousness the realisation that though we have modes of production capable of delivering plenty to the world, 10,000 starve each day, and even in the so-called First World many live, though often quite unnecessarily, very blighted lives indeed. The Russian Revolution did not spread to the west and we got instead, as Rosa Luxembourg anticipated, with the failure of its spread, on the one hand bureaucratic and authoritarian forms of statism which, if socialisms at all, are state socialisms of the worst sort and, on the other hand, matched with that we have forms of state capitalism bent on an imperialistic domination and a heartless exploitation of the world. We have, in *most* of the nations of the world, neither capitalism with a human face nor socialism with a human face. We are, that is, caught between two very unsavoury social systems indeed. The result is that we have, and quite unnecessarily, a pervasiveness of terror, a denial of autonomy and equality and massive exploitation and poverty. This picture, which *at most* is only slightly overdrawn, turns the person in our scenario, despairingly, to Irenaean universalism, to the hope, which for her, given her estimation of the probabilities, is little more than a wish, that there will, in an afterlife, be a universal salvation in which the sufferings of each individual could somehow be made worthwhile for that individual.[37]

What needs to be said here in response is that – given the turn of things historically, and given certain assumptions about human nature – however unlikely it may be that socialism on the necessary world-wide scale can be anything like the socialism of which Marx and Bakunin dreamt, it is still far more likely to become the case (to put it mildly) than is the religious eschatological dream. That is to say that something like this secular vision of the world could obtain is still vastly more likely than bodily resurrection or disembodied existence and the sustaining of Irenaean universalism. (Remember we might still have one or another of the first two things without having Irenaean universalism.) Neither the kingdom of heaven on earth nor the kingdom of heaven in a 'resurrection world' are very likely, but a kingdom of heaven on earth, of the two alternatives, is by far the least unlikely of two unlikely prospects. Moreoever, there is, with the former, though *perhaps* even here the chances are rather slight, some prospect of some *approximation* of it. The other's prospects are close to being nil. This being so, the desirable thing is struggle to make that hope in the world a social reality in all the ramified ways that need to be done. What may be unlikely there is at least much less unlikely than the Irenaean thing. It may be apple pie by and by for everyone but it is at least not in the sky.

However, again there is a response from the religious wisher for immortality somewhat similar to her response to the Camusian. Could one not have the socialist thing through and through without any evasion at all and still have this wish for a universal salvation that need in no way be a replacement for a deflect from the struggle for a classless society united in sisterhood and brotherhood where the conditions for both autonomy and equal liberty are maximised? There are reactionary atheists (for example, A. Rand and A. Flew) and there are religious Marxists or at least quasi-Marxists (for example, Gregory Baum and Dorothee Sölle). The latter have on their agenda the struggle for a classless society as much as those 'standard Marxists' who are atheists.

Marx and Bakunin were passionate atheists but there is nothing that is canonical to Marxism or Anarchism (libertarian socialism) that requires atheism, however plausible atheism may be on other grounds. Both atheism and socialism can be plausibly said to be part of the Enlightenment project. Still, that project is not such a seamless web that it is evident that one could not have socialism without atheism or atheism without socialism. There is a kind of conservative liberalism that goes well with atheism and some atheists are just plain reactionaries and there can be, and is, a socialism that is also religious. Perhaps the most coherent worldview would have socialism and atheism running tandem, but that that is so is not overwhelmingly evident. There is a lot of *lebensraum* for bracketing such considerations and in practical class struggles they can perhaps be ignored. Why divide comrades over a speculative matter that may not at all effect the struggle for socialism? Religion, of course, has indeed been an opiate of the people and a bastion of reaction, but, again, that is not intrinsic to its nature, though its pervasiveness is understandable ideologically.

I think the answer to my above question is that one could be consistently committed to a socialist transformation of the world and have, as well, Irenaean hopes for the salvation of humankind. One could, as some liberation theologians are, be through and through committed to the class struggle *and* have these wishes for an afterlife of a very distinctive kind. Where this is open-eyed, with an awareness of the fantastic and perhaps even incoherent nature of the belief, and is taken as a wish and not allowed to stand in the way of class struggles and other progressive struggles (struggles around racism and sexism), there is nothing wrong with such a wish.

I *suspect* that as a matter of psycho-sociological fact such an attitude will, though perhaps only in some rather subtle ways, stand in the way of liberation – solid liberation in the world – but to the extent that it does not and to the extent it neither wittingly nor unwittingly cooks the books as to the evidence, there is no reason for atheists like myself to criticise it as unreasonable or as in anyway morally untoward, though it is not an attitude we will share even though we recognise that even in a classless, non-racist and non-sexist world order there will be human ills: children born horribly deformed, terrible accidents, a loss of partner or child and the like. It is reasonable to expect that even ills of this sort will be less frequent in such a society with its developed productive forces (including its more developed science) and greater security and greater wealth more evenly distributed. Still, such ills will always be our lot. We can lessen their incidence and surround them with a new environment, but we can never eliminate them. They will always be with us. This being so, in some ways a certain kind of belief in immortality could 'answer' to that as no secular *weltbild* could. Atheists should not blink at that fact or try to obscure its force. They should only point out that, given everything we know, it is an idle wish humanly understandable though it be.

So why not add such a hope or at least such a wish to our repertoire? For me, to speak for a moment personally, the astronomical unlikeliness of such a conception answering to anything real, coupled with the equal unlikelihood of there being a God who could ordain a certain kind of immortality, for (as the Greeks and Romans show us) not just any immortality will do, makes such hopes merely idle wishes and as such nothing to make a matter of the fabric of my life. We have better things to do than to dwell on such idle wishes. Hume, I believe, had a remarkably sane and humane mindset here as did Freud. And Hume and Freud, conservatives though they were, as well as Marx and Bakunin, can remain, without any tension at all, heroes of a contemporary intellectual wedded to the emancipatory potential of the Enlightenment project, while being fully cognisant of the dark underside of it that, on the one hand, Adorno and Horkheimer and, on the other, Foucault, have in their different ways so well exposed. There are plenty of things in both Hume and Marx that no intellectually sophisticated and informed person could accept anymore, along with central things which, with a little rational reconstruction, can be seen to be both sound – or at least arguably sound – and important, and which have forged our contemporary understanding of ourselves and our world such that for a person who has taken things to heart none of the faces of immortality provide live options.[38]

Notes

1. Godfrey Vesey, 'Remarks', in Stuart Brown (ed.), *Reason and Religion* (Ithaca, New York: Cornell University Press, 1977) p. 306.
2. Soren Kierkegaard, *The Sickness Unto Death*, trans. Walter Lowrie (New York: Doubleday Anchor Books, 1954).
3. Antony Flew, 'Immortality', in Paul Edwards (ed.), *The Encyclopedia of Philosophy*, IV (New York: The Free Press, 1967) p. 142.
4. Peter Geach, *God and the Soul* (New York: Routledge & Kegan Paul, 1969) p. 29.
5. Thomas Nagel talks this way in his *The View From Nowhere* (New York: Oxford University Press, 1986) p. 23.

6. Vesey, op. cit., p. 306.
7. Derek Parfit, *Reasons and Persons* (Oxford: Clarendon Press, 1984) pp. 12–13.
8. Kai Nielsen, *Contemporary Critiques of Religions* (New York: Herder & Herder, 1971); Kai Nielsen, *Scepticism* (New York: St. Martin's Press, 1973); Kai Nielsen, *An Introduction to the Philosophy of Religion* (London: The Macmillan Press, 1982); and Kai Nielsen, *Philosophy and Atheism* (Buffalo, New York: Prometheus Books, 1985).
9. Antony Flew, *God and Philosophy* (London: Hutchinson, 1966) and Antony Flew, *The Presumption of Atheism* (New York: Barnes & Noble, 1976).
10. Antony Flew, 'The Burden of Proof', in Leroy S. Rouner (ed.) *Knowing Religiously* (Notre Dame, Indiana: University of Notre Dame Press, 1985) pp. 110–14.
11. Terence Penelhum, *Survival and Disembodied Existence* (London: Routledge & Kegan Paul, 1976); Terence Penelhum, 'Survival and Identity', in Mostafa Faghfoury (ed.) *Analytical Philosophy of Religion in Canada* (Ottawa, Ontario: University of Ottawa Press, 1982) pp. 35–53.
12. Penelhum, 'Survival and Identity', p. 47.
13. Ibid., p. 53.
14. Martin Hollis, *Invitation to Philosophy* (Oxford: Basil Blackwell, 1985) pp. 119–120.
15. John Hick, *Death and Eternal Life* (London: Collins, 1976) p. 193. See also Terence Penelhum's critical notice, *Canadian Journal of Philosophy*, IX (March 1979) pp. 141–62.
16. Hick, op. cit., p. 198.
17. Hywel Lewis, 'Immortality and Dualism', in *Reason and Religion*, p. 282. Sydney Shoemaker argues in the same volume that there is a non-Cartesian dualism which is not conceptually incoherent as he believes Cartesian dualism to be. Cartesian dualism, if sound, could support disembodied existence, but, as Shoemaker sees it, it is conceptually incoherent. Non-Cartesian dualism, he argues, is conceptually coherent but it does not support disembodied existence. However, even this battened down dualism with its talk of immaterial substances being related to material substances by a quasi-spatial relationship seems of doubtful coherence, as Shoemaker half admits in a footnote on p. 268.
18. Lewis, op. cit., p. 289. Thomas Nagel, without embracing dualism, in effect reveals the rational kernel behind such an impulse. Thomas Nagel, op. cit., pp. 13–37.
19. Terence Penelhum, 'Survival and Identity', op. cit., p. 51.
20. Vesey, op. cit., pp. 301–6 and Shoemaker, op. cit., pp. 307–11.
21. Vesey, op. cit., p. 306.
22. Ibid., p. 305.
23. Ibid., p. 305 and Shoemaker, op. cit., p. 311.
24. J. L. Mackie, *Persons and Values* (Oxford: Clarendon Press, 1985) pp. 15–27.
25. Penelhum, 'Survival and Identity', op. cit., p. 41.
26. This little tale is adopted from a tale by G. R. Gillett, 'Disembodied Persons', *Philosophy*, 61 (237) (1986), pp. 377–86.

27. Daniel Dennett, *Brainstorms* (Montgomery, Vermont: Bradford Books, 1978) pp. 267–85.
28. J. L. Mackie, op cit., p. 6.
29. David Wiggens, *Sameness and Substance* (Oxford, England: Basil Blackwell, 1986).
30. Gillett, op. cit., p. 384.
31. Ibid.
32. Ibid, p. 385. See, as well, Mackie, op. cit., pp. 1–27.
33. Parfit, op. cit., and Nagel, op. cit.
34. John Hick, op. cit., pp. 152–66.
35. Max Horkheimer, *Critique of Instrumental Reason* (New York: Seabury Press, 1974) p. 2.
36. J. L. Mackie argues this convincingly in his 'Sidgwick's Pessimism', *Philosophical Quarterly* (1976) pp. 326–7. For a more detailed argument for this see his *The Miracle of Theism* (Oxford: Clarendon Press, 1984).
37. There is a point I pass by here made forcefully years ago by Alasdair MacIntyre. The point is this: no matter what comes after in an afterlife the sufferings of people here and now are not thereby made worthwhile. Suppose an infant at birth is born with some horrible physical defect that causes him to be wracked constantly with terrible pain. After two years of such hell he dies and goes to heaven. How does the bliss of his afterlife at all make those terrible sufferings worthwhile? They are hardly a necessary condition for this bliss. See Alasdair MacIntyre, *Difficulties in Christian Belief* (London: SCM Press, 1956) and Alasdair MacIntyre, 'The Logical Status of Religious Belief', in Ronald Hepburn (ed.) *Metaphysical Beliefs* (London: SCM Press, 1957) pp. 168–205.
38. Kai Nielsen, 'Death and the Meaning of Life' in *The Search for Values in a Changing World* (New York: The International Culture Foundation, 1978) pp. 483–90 and Kai Nielsen, 'God and Coherence', in *Knowing Religiously*, pp. 89–102.

Response to Nielsen
John Hick

Let me say first where I agree with Professor Kai Nielsen. I agree with his implicit view that the belief in a life after death is not well established by parapsychology or other empirical evidence. If there is a further life beyond this one, the two phases of our existence are so separated that there is no communication across the boundary of death and therefore no empirical evidence within this life of the existence of the next. I do not make this negative statement with absolute conviction, as you may see from my own paper but for the sake of our discussion I shall join Nielsen in assuming it. I would only add that, from a religious point of view, the fact that we cannot look beyond our present mortal span, but have to live wholly within it, may well be an important aspect of the character of the universe as an environment in which moral and spiritual growth is able to take place.

But now points of disagreement. First, and not surprisingly, I do not agree that the existence of God – or as I should prefer to say, of an Ultimate Reality which is experienced within the theistic traditions as a personal divine presence – is impossible or improbable or that belief in God is accordingly irrational. I do not, however, maintain that the existence of God is probable: for I deny that the concept of probability applies here. I hold that the universe is religiously ambiguous in the sense that it is capable of being thought and experienced in both religious and naturalistic ways. To respond to it in either way, making that the basis of one's life, is to run an unavoidable risk. It is to 'live by faith', whether a religious or a naturalistic faith, within the assymetrical situation that if the religious belief basically corresponds with reality its truth will be verified in our post-mortem experience, whilst if the naturalistic faith corresponds with reality it will not be open to that kind of verification. I hold that those who, in this situation of ambiguity, experience the universe religiously, are entitled to trust their own experience and that of the larger stream of religious experience of which it is a part. On this basis it is, I suggest, entirely reasonable and rational for such persons to believe in God. This is, as will be evident, a modified version of William James's argument. I shall not pursue it further here because

Nielsen's paper does not focus primarily on the question of divine existence. But nevertheless it was necessary to give some indication of my reason for rejecting his dismissal of theistic belief as irrational and unworthy of an educated person today. To believe in the reality of God on the basis of an apparent experiential awareness of God is, I claim, a fully rational act of believing.

Secondly, I disagree with Nielsen's contention that life after death is objectively improbable and indeed improbable to an extreme degree. But before coming to this let me make the point that Nielsen works with too limited a range of options. He wants theists to believe either in resurrection in the sense of the raising of physical bodies from their graves, or in a naturally immortal immaterial soul. But this is bound to strike many contemporary theists as arbitrarily restrictive. I, for one, believe in an afterlife in neither of the ways that Nielsen allows, and feel therefore that his arguments pass me by. For the idea of resurrection does not *have* to be understood as a raising from the grave, or wherever, of a corpse which is somehow revivified in the process of being raised. The resurrection of the dead does not seem to have been understood in that way by St Paul (who speaks in I Corinthians 15 of the resurrection body as a spiritual and not a physical body), and it is only so understood today by theologically very conservative Christians – of whom there are admittedly many in our society, and a distinguished representative of whom will discuss the notion of bodily resurrection in his paper. I shall leave him to defend it as best he can. For my part I share Nielsen's view of it as highly implausible. The idea is indeed logically possible, and it was not implausible within the pre-scientific culture in which it was developed. But from the standpoint of a modern biblically and theologically critical Christian faith the raising of physical bodies is one of the elements of the tradition that has been filtered out in the evolution of Christian thought. An alternative understanding of resurrection is in terms of the 'replica' theory, the central principle of which has recently been importantly defended by Derek Parfit in his much discussed book *Reasons and Persons*, 1986. Should not this option be considered in any non-fundamentalist critique of the notion of resurrection? As a further complication of the options, we can conceive of being re-embodied, not in a form identical with or very like our earthly bodies, but in some quite other form through which the same basic personality is expressed. Likewise the idea of a soul which survives the death of the body does not necessarily entail an eternal and indestructible mental entity. It could be that the soul, if by this we mean the personal consciousness, outlasts the body, but is nevertheless not eternal. Again, there is the more complex eastern thought that a deeper aspect of us than the conscious self is expressed successively in a series of different empirical personalities until a perfected state of consciousness is achieved, the serial self thereby attaining to unity with the divine reality. On this view the present conscious 'I' is not immortal, but is nevertheless an episode within a very long process (far exceeding a single human life) which ultimately merges into the eternal divine reality.

But further, and more fundamentally, a believer in life after death on religious grounds is not obliged to make his/her belief stand or fall with a particular concrete way of conceiving it – as embodied or disembodied; if embodied, in this or another world, or space; if disembodied, in isolation or with a mind-dependent environment which might, as experienced, be more or less indistinguishable from a material world (as outlined in a famous article by H. H. Price); or again in some form which lies entirely beyond the range of our present concepts, but which will constitute a completely unexpected expression of the omnipotent divine love. This last option is probably the one that most thinking Christians today adopt. The afterlife for them is highly 'underdetermined'. That is to say, it is an expectation which is capable of being fulfilled in many ways, including ways which we cannot at present envisage. And why should not a religiously-based afterlife belief be open in this way? Why should not a basic conviction of the reality and love of God be accompanied by a sense of the symbolic character of the scriptural accounts of the life to come; so that one's anticipation of being brought to an ultimate blessed fulfilment is one that may be confirmed in ways concerning which St Paul says, 'eye has not seen, nor ear heard, nor the heart of man conceived, what God has prepared for those who love him' (I Corinthians 2:9). In his concentration upon the most simplistically literal construal of the idea of resurrection I detect in Nielsen's work at this point a desire that contemporary Christians should remain locked in pre-modern fundamentalism. Indeed Nielsen himself remarks that 'This discussion has been . . . somewhat arcane and, it seems to me, quaint . . . It is, or so it seems to me, strange that people should be arguing about such things in our epoch' (p. 19). It seems strange to me also. And I would recommend that he move his focus of interest forward to the options which engage more progressive religious thinkers today, such as Küng, Pannenberg and Badham.

Returning now to the question of probability, Nielsen will doubtless maintain that *any* form of life after death whatsoever, however spelled out, or not spelled out at all except as a presently unimaginable state, is enormously improbable. Let me propose a different starting point from his. Probability, when this is not a statistical concept, but amounts to the rather general notion of plausibility or likelihood, is relative to information or belief. Thus from an atheist standpoint life after death is very improbable. Given the atheistic presupposition, the idea of an afterlife is highly counter-intuitive and implausible. On the other hand, from a theistic standpoint it is very probable. For if we are the creatures of a loving God it is reasonably to be expected that God should make it possible for us to fulfil the potentialities of our human nature, potentialities which are not fulfilled for most people within the circumstances of this present world. Thus relatively to belief in God, belief in some kind of life after death is distinctly more likely than not. This is indeed something that Nielsen himself affirms (pp. 19–28), and in much of his last section he displays eloquently the basic logic of the afterlife belief, namely, that the affirmation of the divine is an affirmation of the ultimate goodness of the universe, from our human point of view; and the conditions of human life as a whole, round the world and through the ages, would be radically incompatible with that affirmation if human life terminates absolutely with physical death.

However, Nielsen also wants to insist that there is an objective sense in which life after death is enormously improbable. He speaks of its 'astronomical unlikeliness' (p. 28) and of its prospects being 'close to being nil' (p. 26). He even uses the expression 'the objective likelihood' (p. 22). Such language gives the strong impression of an objective degree of probability, or improbability; and it is this that I now want to question. The sense in which he means these expressions is, I think, revealed in his statement concerning belief in Good that 'It is a conception . . . that is beyond reasonable belief for a person in the twentieth century with a good philosophical and scientific training' (p. 7). The same holds, he urges, for the belief in a life after death. But it seems that he must mean by the person with a good philosophical training one who has arrived at the same atheistic conclusion as himself. For there are, after all, plenty of otherwise good philosophers who are both theists and believers in an afterlife. Likewise he must mean by the person with a good scientific training a scientist who shares – as indeed many do – Nielsen's naturalistic presuppositions. For after all there are not a few otherwise good scientists who do not share that metaphysical presupposition and who are both theists and either believers in or not deniers of an afterlife. In declaring so emphatically that the afterlife is fantastically improbable, is not Nielsen simply expressing its implausibility from the standpoint of his own atheistic and naturalistic faith?

Let me add a very brief note about one aspect of the naturalistic worldview which has been developed intensively during recent years, namely the mind-brain identity theory. During the last 20 or so years this has enjoyed a considerable vogue. But it has during the same period been as vigorously criticised as defended. Nielsen refers to one aspect of H. D. Lewis's critique of it. A more sharply focused critique, to my mind, is that of Richard Swinburne in various articles and now in his book *The Evolution of the Soul*, 1986. The issue is an open and hotly contested one in contemporary philosophy and it seems to me tendentious to award to one side of the debate the accolade of being the enlightened modern view. The identity theory may well take its place as one of the many exciting one-sided exaggerations which most philosophical dogmas have been.

But finally I want to welcome the rather remarkable openness of Nielsen's concluding constructive suggestions. This shows that he has not after all been wholly taken over by the obverse of Christian fundamentalism!

2 God, the Soul, and the Future Life

Paul Badham

The thesis of this paper is that belief in God, in the soul, and in the future life, should be seen as three interdependent beliefs, each of which relies on implicit assumptions about the validity of the two other beliefs for its own coherence.

As a description of current Christian awareness, this thesis is manifestly false. Most contemporary Christian intellectual apologists, at least in Europe, presuppose that belief in God can be emancipated from the other two beliefs. The characteristic contemporary emphasis is to stress that the Christian message is essentially concerned with the transformation of life in the here and now. And even those scholars who do maintain a future hope insist that it has nothing to do with 'mere survival', and that the distinctive message of the Christian faith speaks in terms of the resurrection of the body, and not of the immortality of the soul. For anyone wishing to commend Christian theism in an increasingly sceptical world there might seem good prudential reasons for separating the doctrines in this way. Belief in God is still intellectually respectable, while belief in a life after death is classified, even by the Journal *Theology*, as a 'fringe belief' in our society[1]; and as for the soul, the critical dissection of this concept is one of the earliest exercises given to a first year philosophy student in a British University. At first sight, therefore, my proposal must seem both false and foolish, and yet I persist in it for truth is not dependent on headcounts or expediency, but on what is or is not in fact the case. What I shall seek to show, therefore, is that when belief in God is isolated from the other two beliefs it becomes an exceedingly nebulous concept, and when belief in a future life is divorced from any concept of the soul it collapses into incoherence when the implications of what seems necessary for personal survival are spelt out.

Let us start with belief in God. According to the Epistle to the Hebrews 11:6 'The man who approaches God must have faith in two things, first that God exists and secondly that it is worth a man's while to try to find him'. This is from J. B. Phillips's translation.[2] Other translations speak of belief that God rewards those who search for him. In either case the point seems clear and true to human experience – living faith requires more than a bare acknowledgement of divine existence, namely a further conviction that God's existence makes a difference. It is quite possible to give assent to the proposition that God exists without in any sense being committed to a life of faith. A scientist like Paul Davies who believes that the 'New Physics' supports belief in God, but has no personal interest or commitment to religion, would be one example of this.[3] Likewise, though Bishop Hugh Montefiore thinks that the probability of theism is enhanced by recent developments in the natural sciences, he is 'not so foolish as to think that anyone actually makes an act of personal commitment to God' on such grounds.[4] As Montefiore points out, living commitment to God is always based on personal experience of God. Hence belief in the bare existence of God only becomes religiously or existentially significant when it is associated with supposing that some consequences flow from belief in God's reality.

In the past believers supposed that God's love manifested itself in this providential care of those who placed their trust in him. But though this view remains popular in much simplistic evangelical preaching and still has a few scholarly defenders,[5] most believers today acknowledge that this concept of God's action in the world 'died the death of a thousand qualifications' in the 'Theology and Falsification' debates of the 1950s.[6] The central thrust of the 'falsification' challenge, put most clearly by Antony Flew, was that a belief can only have content if it makes a difference whether the belief is true or false. Hence belief that God is love will only be a substantive belief if it affects the believer's life or understanding in some way. Yet believers and non-believers tend to have the same cluster of expectations about what will or will not happen in everyday life. And though some Christians claim to see God's providence at work in contemporary miracles of healing, no actuarial evidence appears available sufficient to persuade even the Churches' own insurance companies that such alleged instances of providential care make any observable difference to the believer's life-expectancy. Moreover double-blind clinical trials establish that spontaneous remission of illness is as common among those who pray as those who don't.[7] In practice, therefore, it seems that believers and unbelievers experience the same realities; and the claimed belief in God is in many cases vacuous, with no effect whatever on a person's life and expectations.

It is of course true that belief in a divine creator might be thought to meet the falsification challenge. One could hardly conceive of a greater empirical difference to reality than the existence or not of the entire cosmos! But, as I have already argued, belief in a creator, particularly when justified simply as a means of 'explaining' the 'big-bang' or the supposed 'anthropic principle' is, on its own, of no religious consequence. Only if one goes on from such a belief to the conviction that such a God might be concerned for, interested in, or able to communicate with, his creatures, does a belief in his existence become a matter of religious interest. The challenge posed in 'Theology and Falsification' was not really whether or not God exists, but whether or not God cares.

The only Christian responses to this challenge which took seriously the empirical findings behind it, were John Hick's postulation of 'eschatological verification'[8] and Eric Mascall's claim that Christian spirituality is based on an 'experimental awareness of God . . . which is not mediated by the senses'.[9] But to postulate an eschaton, or to speak of experiences not mediated by the senses, is to defend the reality of God, in the first case by asserting belief in a future life, and in the second by using language which may depend for its very intelligibility on some concept of the soul. To make any religiously significant claims for belief in God which can meet the challenge of contemporary empiricism seems to require that one be prepared to defend at least one of these unfashionable beliefs.

To explore why this is so, let us first look at the religious grounds for believing in God at all, and then go on to see the reasoning which led Hick and Mascall to their respective replies to the falsification challenge.

The foundation of all religious faith in a personal and loving God is, I suggest, the conviction that women and men of faith have had of entering into a lively relationship of love and trust with such a God. Certainly this seems true of the biblical writers. As John Hick points out 'they did not think of God as an inferred entity but as an experienced reality'.[10] And this also seems true of the faithful throughout the ages. When the twelfth century Abbot of Bec meditated on his experience of 30 years of monastic prayer and praise of God he wrote:

I have found a fullness of joy
that is more than full.
It is a joy that fills the heart, mind and soul,

indeed it fills the whole of a man,
and yet joy beyond measure still remains.[11]

To such a man it seemed literally unthinkable to suppose that God
was not a living reality. That was why he exclaimed 'Lord my God,
you so truly are, that it is not possible to think of you not existing'.[12]
St Anselm was not seeking to expound a bogus philosophical
argument, but to confess a truth about his own experience. And to
anyone who has ever had such an experience, or even an experience
sufficiently close to know what Anselm was talking about, this is
simply an experienced truth of personal biography. This sense of God
was something St Anselm had in common with all the major figures
of the Judaeo-Christian religious tradition. John Hick points out:

> If we consider the sense of living in the divine presence as this was
> expressed by, for example, Jesus of Nazareth, or by St. Paul, St.
> Francis, St. Anselm or the great prophets of the Old Testament,
> we find that their 'awareness of God' was so vivid that he was as
> indubitable a factor in their experience as was their physical
> environment. They could no more help believing in the reality of
> God than in the reality of the material world and of their human
> neighbours.[13]

Compared with the sense of certainty arising out of a direct encounter
with God, St Thomas Aquinas felt all his previous philosophical
reasoning about divine existence had been so much straw.[14] Likewise
St Augustine, writing to his friend Laurentius about how to gain an
understanding of the framework of Christian doctrine, insists that
more than books to load his shelves he needed a 'a great zeal to be
kindled in his heart'.[15] This sense of the supremacy of the personal
religious experience is not confined to the heroes of faith, but within
all branches of the Christian church it is acknowledged to be
supreme, as can be shown by reference to the hymns, prayers,
choruses or patterns of worship used in the differing traditions, as
well as in the concepts of conversion, dedication and vocation.
The supremacy of religious experience is important not only for
belief in God, but also for belief in a future life. For as Edward
Schillebeeckx says:

> the breeding ground of belief in life after death . . . was always
> seen in a communion of life between God and man . . . Living

communion with God, attested as the meaning, the foundation and the inspiring content of human existence, is the only climate in which the believer's trust in a life after death comes, and evidently can come to historical fruition.[16]

Within the biblical tradition it can be shown that the faith in a future life which developed in Israel during the inter-testamental period was profoundly shaped by a growing belief that each individual mattered to God and, if this was so, then the all-powerful God could be relied on to ensure that death did not ultimately triumph over that relationship, nor destroy for ever the loved individual.[17]

The stress on the importance of the individual person to God was further strengthened by the teaching of Jesus, and his constant use of the analogy of fatherhood to describe the human relationship to God. As a consequence of his teaching, and of the belief that God had raised him to new life, the Christian faith came into existence explicitly as a religion of salvation offering the first converts a sense of utter and joyful certainty about a life to come: 'an eternal weight of glory beyond all comparison' with our present earthly existence.[18] All the first Christians thought of heaven as their true home, and came to think of themselves as 'no more than strangers and passing travellers on earth'.[19] It was their absolute faith in a life beyond which enabled so many of the early Christians to embrace martyrdom with composure, and even with enthusiasm! Indeed St Ignatius of Antioch, on his way to death in the Roman amphitheatre, could even write 'I am yearning for death with all the passion of a lover',[20] so convinced was he that it was just the prelude to a glorious destiny. In the mission field too it was the claim to know of an eternal life that was perceived as Christianity's greatest attraction. Certainly according to the Venerable Bede it was this message that persuaded the Anglo-Saxons to embrace Christianity.[21]

Throughout the centuries the hope of immortality has been so interwoven with the Christian understanding of God that it has been the central mode of interpretation of other doctrines, and integral to the Christian sacramental system. Thus for St Athanasius, and the whole Orthodox tradition, the motive behind the incarnation was to confer immortality upon humanity: God became what we are so that we might become immortal as he is.[22] In Catholic and Protestant Christianity the death and resurrection of Christ was seen as vitally connected with the opening up of everlasting salvation. In the Church's sacramental system a Christian was said to become an inheritor of the kingdom of heaven at baptism and reference to God's everlasting kingdom was made at the most solemn moments of confirmation, marriage, ordination and absolution. In the holy communion service Christians are said to receive the 'bread of immortality' in the Orthodox liturgy, or the bread of eternal or everlasting life in Catholic and Anglican formularies. Finally, in the last rites the Christian receives the viaticum to nourish his soul for the journey through death.

However to show that a belief was, in the past, absolutely central to Christianity is by no means a sufficient ground for supposing it to be relevant today. As T. S. Eliot put it: 'Christianity is always adapting itself into something which can be believed'.[23] And it is easy to point to a whole range of doctrines, from an infallible Bible to a historical fall, which were only perceived as central but which has since been discarded by all but the most wooden of fundamentalists. Should we then join the young Schleiermacher in categorising the hope of immortality as part of the 'rubbish of antiquity' from which Christianity must be cleansed if it is to speak to the modern world?[24] That the 'father of modern theology' subsequently changed his mind on the central importance of this doctrine[25] does not in itself remove the possibility that his first thoughts were correct. What has to be shown therefore is not merely that belief in a life after death was, historically speaking, an important belief in earlier formulations of Christian doctrine, but, far more importantly, that it remains vital to the intellectual coherence of the Christian vision.

My basic contention is that, without belief in a future hope, the Christian doctrine of God becomes irrelevant because vacuous. It is no accident that when William James surveyed *The Varieties of Religious Experience* 80 years ago he found that for almost all believers then, God primarily mattered as the provider of immortality.[26] That God has ceased 'to matter' to so many contemporary intellectuals may well reflect, at least in part, an intuitive awareness of the emptiness of claims about God in a context where there is little emphasis on a future hope.

The challenge of 'Theology and Falsification' has already been noted. Let me stress its implications for the current debate by posing the direct question: If belief in life after death is excluded, is there *any* actual difference between the substantive beliefs and expectations of well-educated and informed believers and non-believers in God? Obviously a few minor differences can be noted. Believers are more likely to attend churches, to read sacred books, and to link their moral beliefs with New Testament stories. They may also hold different theoretical beliefs about the origins of the universe or the significance of the life of Jesus of Nazareth. But I suggest there will be no actual difference worth mentioning in what they expect to happen either to themselves or to the world, or in the valuation they give to human existence. Neither will expect God to act in any way within the world and both will expect their own personal existence to terminate after 70 or 80 years. In short, I claim that unless a Christian is willing to postulate a future life, any claim to believe in the fatherly care of an omnipotent God is without content.

On the other hand, if John Hick's hypothesis of eschatological verification is accepted there will be a real difference in attitude between the believer and unbeliever in God even though both may equally accept an empiricist's view of the nature of our present existence, and the autonomy of the order of nature.[27] Nevertheless, the fact that in Hick's view this life is a preparation for an eternal destiny alters the perspective from which the challenges and difficulties of life are seen. A real difference comes into view between the Christian and the atheist visions of life and the Christian claim is a factual one, in that it would be verified if it turns out that there is indeed a life after death.

Moreover, only in the context of belief in a life after death is it possible even to sketch a theodicy which could conceivably reconcile belief in an all-knowing, all-loving, and all-powerful God with the manifest evils of earthly existence. For, as John Hick has argued,[28] if there is a life after death, it becomes at least conceivable that the changes and chances of this world with all its potential for joy and sorrow, for good and evil, may make sense as an inevitable part of an environment in which persons can develop as free and responsible agents. As a 'vale of soul-making' the hardships and challenges of this life may serve a larger purpose; but if there is no soul to make, no larger purpose to serve, then the fact of suffering in general, and its random character in particular, simply makes nonsense of Christian claims about God's character and power. It should be stressed that Hick's theodicy does not in any way imply that suffering is in itself enobling or redemptive for the evidence would go flat against any so simplistic a view. But what this theodicy does say is that a real objective physical world governed by regular physical law, provides an environment more suited to the development of responsible agents than would an environment in which divine intervention consistently saved humanity from the consequences of its folly, or from the heartache and challenge implicit in any finite and physical existence. John Hick's arguments do not 'solve' the problem of evil, the extent and nature of which remains a persistent challenge to the integrity of Christian believing, but what Hick's work does make clear is that without a belief in a future life no approach to the problem of evil can even get off the ground. If death means extinction, then there is no question but that old age, suffering, disease and death will gain the ultimate victory over each and every one of us, and thereby bring to nothing the belief that each one of us is eternally precious to an all-sovereign God.

So far in my paper I have tried to provide documentation for two claims:

(a) that Christian faith in God is dependent on accepting the authenticity of the religious experience of entering a relationship with God, and

(b) That Christian faith in God has always been utterly interwoven with belief in future life, and that this belief is necessary to the intelligibility and coherence of Christian theism.

I now embark on my second task, and that is to explain why it seems to me that some concept of the soul seems a necessary condition for both claims. This is not a pleasant conclusion for any committed Christian to have come to, and I would very much welcome a refutation of my argument inasmuch as it is clear that the difficulties of expounding or defending a credible concept of the soul today are truly formidable. As one who wishes to believe both in God, and in a future life, I have no wish to set a stumbling block in the way of either belief. For though I think the concept of the soul can be made intelligible today, and indeed that there may even be empirical evidence to support belief in its reality, I am conscious that I am imposing difficulties on many who wish to believe in God and immortality, and yet are convinced that the case against the soul is unanswerable.

The starting point for my exploration of the concept of the soul is the fact, which I have already documented, that the religious grounds for belief in God are that men and women throughout the ages have believed themselves to have encountered God in prayer and worship, and to have had their lives transformed by such an encounter. This experience of being encountered by God is the living heart of religion, and yet as we noted earlier, Christian spirituality has always insisted that this experiental awareness of God is 'not mediated by the senses'. According to Vladimir Lossky, 'The divine light being given in mystical experience surpasses at the same time both sense and intellect. It is immaterial and is not apprehended by the senses'.[29] Lossky insists that all the greatest theologians of the Eastern Orthodox tradition stress the immediacy of the mystic's knowledge of God.[30] Eric Mascall, speaking for the western tradition, emphasises that 'a very impressive body of religious thought has affirmed the possibility and indeed the occurrence, of a cognitive experience which is not mediated by the senses'.[31] Paul Tillich has characterised this approach as the Augustinian-Franciscan solution to the philosophy of religion which asserts that God is knowable in himself directly.[32]

This understanding of the divine-human encounter is not something which is confined to the great mystics. The whole of Christian spirituality is permeated by it. Historically, the one indispensable element in a person wishing to offer himself for the Christian ministry in Catholic, Protestant and Orthodox traditions has been whether or not he felt 'inwardly moved' and 'truly called' to this ministry.[33] Almost all books on prayer insist on the importance of quieting the senses and of opening oneself up to God. They urge the seeking out of a place of complete quiet, closing the eyes and putting hands together. All such activities presuppose that the sense of the presence of God is only distracted if data from the senses continue to pour in upon the mind. Only when as far as possible one has closed off one's sensory input is one in a state where encounter with God is deemed to be likely.

This whole approach to prayer presupposes a dualist understanding of man as its necessary condition. For it asserts that God can make the reality of his presence felt other than through neural pathways. In other words, it implies that knowledge of God can be understood as communicated to us through some process akin to telepathy; direct to the mind and not via sensory stimuli. This is of immense importance for our consideration of the concept of the soul. In his brilliant defence of materialism, *Body and Mind*, Professor Keith Campbell argued that it was basic to his belief in central-state materialism that 'the brain is receptive only to information which arrives by neural pathways and so is confined to perception by way of the senses', hence 'if some people are receptive to the contents of the minds of another by some more direct means such as telepathy then those minds are just not brains'.[34] My argument is that this applies just as much to claimed instances of non sense-mediated awareness of God as it does to any alleged claims of telepathic rapport between other human minds, with the important difference that claims to communion with God are vastly more common, better attested, and more influential in human history than any claims to non sense-mediated communication between human beings have been. For as I have sought to show, this religious experiencing is at the root of the deepest Christian commitment, and the Thomist way of moving from the world to God represents a second reflective stage in the person's religious development. Of course some religious experience takes the form of considering the beauty of the world, or of worship, or of a sense of duty, and abstracting from these experiences to the notion of a transcendent God. But I suggest that the movement of thought from the world to the transcendent depends upon a pre-existing mystical-intuitive immediate awareness of God which can only be a reality if dualism is true.

This does not mean that Christianity should be concerned solely with the so-called 'inner life' of the human person. The witness of the Bible is that God is concerned for the whole of our humanity, and Jesus summed up the essential religious requirement as entailing a duty to love God with 'all your heart, and with all your soul and with all your mind and with all your strength . . . and you shall love your neighbour as yourself'.[35] Nevertheless, the Archbishop of Canterbury's Commission on *Faith in the City* was on shaky ground when it suggested that, in view of the difficulties of dualism, Christians should dispense with the notion of a personal relationship with God and focus entirely on the social and prophetic elements in the biblical message. According to the Commission:

> Few philosophers now allow for a separate component or 'soul', with which religion can be uniquely concerned, and modern philosophy encourages us to return to the idiom of the Bible, according to which, God addresses our whole person along with the social relationships amid which we live . . . The suggestion that religion is an entirely personal matter of the relationship of an individual with God should now be . . . unacceptable.[36]

This is one of the few instances I know of any quasi-official organ of Church tackling the difficulties of articulating Christian faith in a strongly anti-dualist ethos, but I suggest its solution to the difficulty, namely the abandonment of the idea of a direct and personal encounter with God has not considered sufficiently carefully the implications of doing this for the foundations of Christian belief, including the grounds on which the social gospel itself also rests. For in a strict sense it is simply not true that God *addresses* the whole person. We do not see God with our eyes, or hear him with our ears, rather as St Paul said 'spiritual things are spiritually discerned'.[37] We have no sense-experience of God. Hence, if a thorough-goingly materialist understanding of the human person is adopted, I do not see how the claims to 'encounter' or enter into a relationship of love with a transcendent and immaterial God can be considered. I would go further and argue that if the commission on *Faith in the City* is prepared to allow philosophical criticism of dualism the right to exercise a veto on the notion of a spiritual component in human beings, it ought to have noted that by, parity of argument, the concept of God also should be abandoned. Anthony Kenny correctly points out that 'most contemporary philosophers find immateriality problematic',[38] but this does not relate just to the concept of the soul, for if anything the difficulties are even greater with the notion of God, 'a non-embodied mind active throughout the universe'. Belief in God and the soul hang together not just because the religious grounds for belief in God are experiences which transcend our sensory equipment, but also because the two beliefs have a comparable logical status.

I now turn to the relationship between belief in the soul, and belief in a future life. We have already noted that the primary religious ground for belief in a life after death is the view that each person as a unique individual really matters to an all-powerful and ever-loving God. One essential logical requirement for the belief to be realised is that it should happen to the same person as the one whom it is claimed is the object of this love. On our everyday understanding of what it means to be a person, namely this present psycho-somatic entity of flesh, blood, bones and brain, the only logically possible future life would entail the literal raising to life again of the buried or cremated corpse and the restoration to healthy functioning of the very same organs. However, although belief in the 'resurrection of this flesh'[39] has had a long running in Christian history, an awareness of the numerous practical problems associated with its realisation have led virtually all contemporary Christians to abandon, or radically reinterpret this doctrine. Almost all Christians today who affirm belief in the 'resurrection of the body' believe that they will get new and somewhat different bodies to serve as vehicles for their self-expression and development in heaven. And the only bond of union between the present and future bodies is that they are to be 'owned' successively by the same person. This is the view explicitly taught by the Church of England Doctrine Commission of 1938, by the Catholic Bishops of Holland in their 1965 Catechism, and by nearly all contemporary theologians who continue to affirm a substantive belief in a personal life after death.[40] But, of course, the problem with any such reinterpreted understanding of a future life is that it has radically parted company with what I have described earlier as our 'everyday understanding' of what it means to be a person.

What almost all reinterpretations of bodily resurrection have in common is that the point of contact between the two 'bodies' is not physical. This is largely a consequence of an increasing realisation of how much our embodiment is part of an ever-recycling process of nature. For example, 60 per cent of our body-weight is water, and the water drunk in London will on average have passed through five other human intestines since it last fell from the clouds. Hence the material of which a person happened to be composed at the moment of death can in no sense be regarded as necessary to his ongoing self-hood. But if we discount numerical physical identity how can we be the 'same persons'? The only way is to argue that what constitutes our self-hood is not necessarily to be identified with our present embodiment. The favoured terms normally used by Christian writers in these circumstances are phrases like, 'the person', 'the essential part of what we are', 'the vital principle of our being', 'the pattern of what we are' or 'our moral and intellectual qualities'. The irony is that such terms, generally chosen in conscious preference to the term 'soul', happen to be the meanings which the Concise Oxford Dictionary gives to that expression. Hence, though many today deny the word, they find themselves wishing to affirm much that the word signifies.

I believe that whatever terminology is used, any attempt to spell out belief in future life today will in fact have to rely on an understanding of what it means to be a person who, historically speaking, was associated with the concept of the soul. For in the absence of any physical continuity, 'I' can still be 'I', only if it is possible to identify my self-hood with some non-physical principle of continuity. The word 'soul' is the historic term for this notion, and I think it can help to clarify discussion to use the expression, provided that it is understood that a modern exposition of the concept is not necessarily tied to all the ramifications associated with notions of soul in earlier worldviews.

The most essential element in the concept of the soul is that for each individual person his own sense of self-hood is associated ultimately with his being a thinking, feeling, willing subject. Of course, most of the time our sense of self-hood is also associated with our physical embodiment. No one should wish to deny that. Nor indeed should anyone wish to deny the intimate and precise relationship which the natural sciences in general, and neuro-biological research in particular, has established between our thoughts and feeling and particular brain states or hormone levels. Nevertheless, I think that for each individual the locus of her or his own sense of personal identity is more strongly associated with being the subject of the experiences she or he is conscious of having than of her or his present embodiment. Consider, for example, the claim some people make to have dreams in which the subject of the dream experiences has or is another body, answers to another name and exists in a different historical context from the dreamer. It is significant that the dreamer always identifies herself with the subject of those dream experiences. However, once we concede that in imagination or a dream, people do from time to time *identify themselves* with another name, body and life-style, it becomes clear that these things are not as essential to their own sense of self-identity as the sense of being an experiencing subject. More significantly, as we shall explore further below, is the fact that people who report out-of-the-body experiences always identify themselves with the alleged out-of-the-body subject, rather than with the unconscious body they think they have left.

But talk of the soul is not just a claim that our self-identity is most properly focused on the subject of our conscious experiences, it goes on to claim that that subject is capable of surviving bodily death. However, the soul can only do that if it is credible to suppose that it exists before death as something which can, at least in principle, be differentiated from the body, and be perceived to be integral to the thinking and willing subject. The evidence for this will always come from relatively unusual events, since contemporary dualists fully accept what the natural sciences teach about the one/one or one/many correlation between mental events and brain processes. Hence all the 'normal' data of human experiencing will be equally compatible with brain-mind identity and brain-soul interaction. What I suggest supports belief in the reality of the soul in this life are the data from religious experience we have already considered, and the data from telepathy to which I have alluded. The importance of exploring such phenomena carefully is indicated by Keith Campbell's acknowledgement that 'if even a single example of para-normal phenomena is genuine central state materialism is false'.[41] My own conviction which I have documented fully elsewhere[42] is that we have many such examples, and therefore that a dualistic understanding of humanity enjoys a fair measure of empirical support.

The most important evidence for the soul, however, comes from the experiences of people who have been resuscitated from a close encounter with death and who would undoubtedly have died but for modern medical advances. Although the majority remember nothing, those who do remember claim to have had a very distinctive set of experiences which are reported with near unanimity from young and old, educated and illiterate, and from every conceivable religious background. The most important feature of this experience for our present purposes is their claim that at the moment of apparent death *they* went out of their bodies and found themselves looking down with interest on the resuscitation attempts. After recovery they accurately described what was going on while they were unconscious and their perspective was from a point of view different from that of the body on the operating table. These findings are of absolutely crucial significance for the concept of the soul, for if a single out-of-the-body experience is correctly described as such, then the soul is a reality. If consciousness can, even for a moment at the brink of death, think-observe-and-remember from a different perspective from the physical brain, then brain and mind are not identical and consciousness can exist apart from the body. And if consciousness can exist apart from the body, then the soul is a reality and the most fundamental barrier across the road to immortality has been removed.

But what reply does one make to a whole generation of able philosophers who believe the concept of the soul to be mistaken? My own view is that many of their criticisms are addressed to views which are not held, or which need not be held, by a contemporary dualist. It is undoubtedly true that embodiment is central to most of our perceptions of what it means to be a person, and that any quasi solipsistic account of mental life has to be false. But dualism need not involve these kind of errors or the category mistakes so often attributed to it. In practice, a thorough-going interactionist dualist and an exponent of brain-mind identity will be in complete agreement about how they see the world 99.9 per cent of the time, even though as I have argued in this paper, great importance attaches to the areas of disagreement.

It is also important to stress that none of the world's major religions believe that a permanently disembodied soul is a realistic means of expressing a future hope for human persons. Hence philosophical criticisms of the notion of a permanently disembodied soul, and the limitations and unsatisfactoriness of such an existence are not relevant to what any of the world's religions claim. For the Catholic Christian the official teaching expressed by Pope John Paul II is that, 'the Church affirms that a spiritual element survives and subsists after death, an element endowed with consciousness and will, so that the "human self" subsists, though deprived for the present of the complement of its body'.[43] But clearly this is a temporary stage before the fuller realisation of the Christian hope in the resurrection of the body. Likewise in Islam the soul at death enters the mind-dependent world of Barzakh till the hour of resurrection.[44] And in the religions of the East the difficult concepts of rebirth or reincarnation testify to the view that any existence in a mental or 'bardo' state will be merely a temporary stage in the ongoing pattern of life.[45]

There remains the problem of the soul's origins and destiny. One of the major difficulties for belief in the soul today has been the notion that it requires one to specify a moment of 'animation' in which a metaphysical substance is inserted into the human embryo. I believe that John Hick's Eddington Memorial lecture *God and the Soul*[46] long ago established the vacuousness of such a notion. Why cannot Christians take more literally their widely-held understanding of this world as a 'vale of soul-making', in which we do not come into the world with our personhood already in existence, but where it gradually develops in response to the challenges and stimuli of life? This has the implication that initially, as the natural sciences indicate, the soul is shaped and influenced by the developing brain, but this need in no way diminish its potential for spiritual advance and development.

Finally may I conclude with a quotation from a recent defence of the soul by Professor Keith Ward of Kings College, London:

God is the true end of the soul, and in this sense, its goal, its proper purpose and true nature, lies beyond the physical universe. That is a strong reason for thinking that the subject which is embodied in this world may properly find other forms of experience and action, in contexts lying beyond this universe . . . Of course the soul depends on the brain . . . but the soul need not always depend on the brain, any more than a man need always depend on the womb which supported his life before birth. The most basic dependence of the soul is upon God, and it is in becoming conscious of the reality of God and learning to love and obey God, that the soul discovers what its true nature is. Belief in the dignity of the soul and the reality of God go together. And that is why belief in God is the essential basis of a genuine and rational respect for the dignity and sacredness of the rational soul and of human life.[47]

Notes

1. M. Hammerton and A. C. Downing, 'Fringe Beliefs among Undergraduates', *Theology*, 82 (690) 1979 pp.433–6.
2. J. B. Phillips, *The New Testament in Modern English* (London: Geoffrey Bles, 1958).
3. Paul Davies, *God and the New Physics* (London: J. M. Dent, 1983).
4. Hugh Montefiore, *The Probability of God* (London: SCM Press, 1985) p.3.
5. Vernon White, *The Fall of a Sparrow* (Exeter: Paternoster Press, 1985).
6. A. Flew and A. MacIntyre, *New Essays in Philosophical Theology* (London: SCM Press, 1955) chapter 6.
7. Peter Baelz, *Prayer and Providence* (London: SCM, 1968) pp.34–5, in which he summarises statistical evidence indicating that all available evidence appears to suggest that petitionary prayer has no observable efficacy.
8. John Hick, *Faith and Knowledge*, 2nd edn (London: Macmillan, 1967) chapter 8.
9. E. L. Mascall, *Words and Images* (London: Longsmans Green, 1957) p.43.
10. John Hick, *Arguments for the Existence of God* (London: Macmillan, 1970) p.102.
11. Anselm, 'Proslogion', chapter 26 (lines 739–43) in *Prayers and Meditations of St.Anselm* (Harmondsworth: Penguin, 1973) p.265.
12. Ibid., chapter 3 (lines 197–8) in *Prayers and Meditations*, p.245.
13. John Hick, *Arguments for the Existence of God*, op. cit., p.112.
14. Gerald Vann, *Saint Thomas Aquinas* (London: Hague & Gill, 1940) p.63.
15. St Augustine, *Enchiridion on Faith, Hope and Love,* chapter 6 (Chicago: Gateway, 1961) p.6.
16. E. Schillebeeckx, *Christ, the Christian Experience in the Modern World* (London: SCM Press, 1980) p.797.
17. Paul Badham, *Christian Beliefs about Life after Death* (New York: Barnes & Noble, 1977) pp. 13–17.

18. II Corinthians 4:17.
19. Hebrews 11:13.
20. St Ignatius of Antioch, *Epistle to the Romans*, chapter 7.
21. Bede, *A History of the English Church*, Book 2, chapter 13.
22. St Athanasius, *On the Incarnation*, chapter 54.
23. John Hick, *The Myth of God Incarnate* (London: SCM Press, 1977) p.ix.
24. F. Schleiermacher, *On Religion* (1799) (New York: Harper & Row, 1958) p.9.
25. F. Schleiermacher, *The Christian Faith* (1830) (Edinburgh: T. & T. Clarke, 1960) pp.696–720.
26. William James, *The Varieties of Religious Experience* (London: Fontana, 1963) p.498.
27. John Hick, *The Existence of God* (New York: Macmillan, 1964) pp.257ff.
28. John Hick, *Evil and the God of Love* (London: Macmillan, 1966) part 4.
29. V. Lossky, *The Mystical Theology of the Eastern Church* (London: James Clarke, 1957) p.223.
30. Ibid., p.224.
31. E. L. Mascall, op. cit.
32. Paul Tillich, *Theology of Culture* (Oxford: Oxford University Press, 1964) p.12.
33. Ordination Service in the Book of Common Prayer of the Church of England, 1662.
34. Keith Campbell, *Body and Mind* (London: Macmillan, 1970) p.191.
35. Mark 12:30.
36. Report of the Archbishop of Canterbury's Commission on Urban Priority Areas, *Faith in the City* (London: Church House, 1985) p.50.
37. I Corinthians 2:14.
38. Anthony Kenny, *The God of the Philosophers* (Oxford: Clarendon Press, 1979) p.127.
39. According to an account by Rufinus this was the form used in one of the earliest versions of the Apostle's Creed. Later versions substituted 'the' for 'this' (Rufinus, *The Apostle's Creed*, chapter 45).
40. Paul Badham, op. cit., chapter 5.
41. Keith Campbell, op. cit., p.91.
42. Paul and Linda Badham (eds), *Immortality or Extinction?* (New York: Barnes & Noble, 1982) chapters 5 and 6.
43. John Paul II, 'Man's Condition after Death' (1979), cited in J. Neuner and J. Dupuis (eds) *The Christian Faith in the Doctrinal Documents of the Catholic Church* (London: Collins, 1983) p.691.
44. Salih Tug, 'The Idea of Immortality and Death in Islamic Thought', in Paul and Linda Badham (eds) *Death and Immortality in the Religions of the World* (New York: Paragon House, 1987).
45. Cf. John Hick, *Death and Eternal Life* (London: Macmillan, 1976) chapters 18–20.
46. John Hick, *Biology and the Soul* (Cambridge: Cambridge University Press, 1972).
47. Keith Ward, *The Battle for the Soul* (London: Hodder & Stoughton, 1985) p. 149–50.

God and the Soul: A Response to Paul Badham

Kai Nielsen

I

Professor Paul Badham argues that 'Christian faith in God is dependent on accepting the authenticity of the religious experience of entering a relationship with God' and that the 'Christian faith in God has always been utterly interwoven with belief in a future life, and that this belief is necessary to the intelligibility and coherence of Christian theism'.[1] So far he would get extensive support from traditional Christians. Indeed he might of necessity get universal support, for to have such a set of beliefs may be partially definitive of what we mean by someone being a 'traditional Christian'. But dissent will begin within the traditional Christian community over Badham's third thesis, namely that the concept of the soul is a necessary condition for both the above claims so that to have a coherent Christian faith we must have a 'belief in God, in the soul and the future life', where these three beliefs are taken to be 'interdependent beliefs each of which relies on implicit assumptions about the validity of the other beliefs for its own coherence'.[2] As Badham is well aware, some traditional Christians will not go along with him concerning his belief in dualism and in a soul as an immaterial substance, but, while remaining as firmly anti-dualist as a materialist, some traditional Christians believe in bodily resurrection.

I have no desire to adjudicate this dispute between traditional or orthodox Christians. As I argue in my 'The Faces of Immortality', the choice between bodily resurrection and an immortal soul as a immaterial entity is the choice between a patently false belief and a probably incoherent one.[3] But my first concern with Badham's account is to argue that even if dualism is both coherent and true, and even if the soul is immortal and immaterial, the truth of these claims will not help him out in the slightest with his claimed non-sensory encounter with God or his claim that there is a mystical-intuitive immediate awareness of God. He may be right in claiming, as he does, that there can only be this awareness if dualism is true but

53

dualism could be true, as C. J. Ducasse and C. D. Broad saw long ago, and belief in God could still be utterly mistaken and, as J. E. McTaggart argued, again many years ago, we could be immortal even if there were no God, though again, as Ducasse argued, dualism could be true and it still could be the case that there was no independent existence, even for a short time, of an immaterial soul which is just to say that there is no immaterial soul. I do not want to suggest even for a moment that I think dualism is the least bit plausible. Indeed, work at the cutting edge of the philosophy of mind takes it to be an utter non-starter. (I refer here to the work, in certain important respects very different, of Hilary Putnam, Daniel Dennett, Paul Churchland, Patricia Churchland, Thomas Nagel and Derek Parfit.) But my bone of contention with Badham is that even if dualism were true, and in addition the soul was immortal and immaterial, his case for an immediate intuitive awareness of God would not be furthered.

I agree with Badham that Christianity is and ought to be a religion of salvation and not just some rather arcane metaphysics. The Christian concept of God is that of a caring God who loves and protects Her creation. 'Living faith', as Badham puts it, 'requires more than a bare acknowledgement of divine existence'; it requires, as well, 'a further conviction that God's existence makes a differen-ce'.[4] But, as I am confident that Badham will agree, that does require the affirmation of God's existence.

My trouble with Badham's account starts with his account of how we can know or come to be aware of God's existence. He tells us that our 'living commitment to God is always based on personal expe-rience of God'. A religiously significant concept of God, he goes on to claim, is of a God who is 'concerned for, interested in, or able to communicate with, his creatures'.[5] This leads him to speak of, what he calls, an 'experiential awareness of God . . . which is not me-diated by the senses'.[6] This we might have now or only after the death of our bodies in an eschatological verification. God, on such an account, is not an inferred entity but an experienced reality with which, if we have faith, we will enter into a trusting and loving relationship. People of faith, he tells us, have 'the sense of living in the divine presence'; they share an awareness of God that is so vivid that this experience is an undubitable factor in their experience. They have, he tells us, a direct encounter with God that carries with it a sense of certainty. Moreover, in traditional Christianity, the God we are said to encounter is also the God who promises us everlasting life and, at least if we are faithful, a life of everlasting bliss in heaven.

However, this alleged encounter with God or awareness of God is a very strange one. It is said to be a mental awareness that is not mediated by the senses. After all we surely do not understand what it would be like literally to see or hear God. But our awareness of God is not like that. It is a kind of mental experience that surpasses at the same time both sense and intellect. It is something which is immaterial. God, that is, makes 'the reality of his presence felt other than through neural pathways'.[7] Our movement 'of thought from the world to the transcendent depends upon pre-existing mystical-intuitive immediate awareness of God which can only be a reality if dualism is true'.[8] 'Spiritual things', as St Paul avers, 'are spiritually discerned'. (I Corinthians 2:14). This experience is said by Badham (following E. L. Mascall) to be cognitive but non-sensory. God, on this account, is knowable in himself directly.[9] To be aware of God, to have an encounter with God, it must be the case that we have such a non-sensory awareness and for this to be possible, Badham tells us, we need an immaterial self or soul.

Like most contemporary philosophers, I find the very concept of *immateriality* problematic: the immaterial self as well as God. (The problematicity of that immaterial self is not in the slightest lessened if it is only momentarily disembodied in going from one body to another. It is what it could be in just that short-lived independence that is problematic.) However, in this first section I will assume that both of these concepts, though puzzling, are coherent. My trouble here is with someone in the world, dualism or non-dualism, encountering God, as God has come to be conceived in the developed strands of Jewish, Christian and Moslem theism, that is, a concept of God that is no longer a cosmic Mickey Mouse. On such a conceptualisation, God, to use Richard Swinburne's unexceptional characterisation, is taken to be 'a person without a body (that is, a spirit), present everywhere, the creator and sustainer of the universe, able to do anything (that is, omnipotent), knowing all things, perfectly good, a source of moral obligation, immutable, eternal, a necessary being, holy and worthy of worship'.[10]

I will argue that such a putative reality could not be directly encountered or could not be something of which we are directly aware. Such a God is, as a creator and sustainer of the universe, transcendent to the universe as well as being an infinite individual.

Now if we are in the universe, immaterial or not, we could not, logically could not, encounter or be directly aware of something transcendent to the universe. We ourselves, material or immaterial, would have to be out of the universe to so encounter or so to be aware of what was 'beyond the universe'. But Badham places us squarely in the universe, as indeed we are, and still claims such an awareness. But then if we encountered God or were aware of God, God herself would be in the universe.

Suppose we say, to counter this, that, given the above definition of God, God is somehow also immanent as well as transcendent, and let us assume for the nonce that we can make sense of that. God, being everywhere, like smoke in a smoke-filled room, is immanent as well as transcendent and it is in her immanency that we are aware of God and encounter God. We know God in her immanency but not in her transcendency. But then we could hardly have anything like a religiously adequate knowledge of God for it is God in her transcendency that is vital to grasp.

Perhaps? But it still could be replied that we have gained an experiential foothold here in directly encountering God as an immanent reality who is everywhere. However, if she is literally everywhere – there is no place at all where she is not – we cannot encounter her for we cannot identify her. For to identify a person, or an individual, is to be able to distinguish that person or individual from some other person or individual, but that which is literally everywhere is not so distinguishable and thus not identifiable. But we cannot be aware of or encounter, sensorily or non-sensorily, what we cannot identify.

Someone might respond, in effect conceding a lot, by saying 'Drop the part about being everywhere and only conceive God – as creator and sustainer of the universe – as being transcendent to the universe'. We would, of course, then have trouble with God being caring or in any way acting in the world, but let us set that aside and go back to the claim that spiritual things discern spiritual things spiritually. Let us further say, to avoid the above difficulties, that we do not experience God in this life but that we experience God – encounter and become aware of God – in the next life when we, as purely spiritual beings, or spiritual beings with a 'spiritual body', are transcendent to the universe ourselves. We live by faith now without an awareness of God, but after death we will, so to say, meet God face to face, as two transcendent beings, two spiritual beings, one infinite, one not, meeting each other, both residing outside the universe.

There are a number of distinct criticisms to be made of such a conception. God, whether inside or outside the universe, is said to be both a person and an individual who is also infinite and omnipresent. If God, as spiritual person, an individual, outside universe, is said to be infinite and omnipresent, then again she is not identifiable and if she is not identifiable she cannot be encountered and we cannot be aware of her for we cannot pick her out as a person, and thus, an individual, distinct from other individuals. Being finite, immaterial or partly immaterial persons ourselves will not help us one bit, for we still will not understand at all what it is we must encounter to encounter God and become aware of her existence. We do not understand, for example, how something could be both infinite and an individual. We do not understand what it would be like to meet an infinite individual. That combination of words doesn't even make sense.

If it is said, in turn, I am being too literal here, I will respond that Badham talked as if he were speaking, or at least trying to speak, literally. If we resolve to speak metaphorically or analogically then we must, if we are to get anywhere at all, explain how this works, explain what our metaphors are metaphors of, and show how we are saying something that has some family resemblance to what in a stumbling way we were trying to say above, taking the words in their plain senses.

However, even if the criticism, raised in the paragraph before the one immediately preceding this paragraph, could be somehow met, the amended position ascribed to Badham would still not give him what he wants. He wants to show how we, if we have immaterial souls, can now, as embodied persons in a dualistic universe, by a movement of thought from the world to the transcendent, be aware of God now given that we are finite and fragile creatures in a very material universe. Speaking of beings such as ourselves in our earthly conditions, he wants to give an account of how, for some of us now, as persons of faith, we could now really have an awareness of God that was so vivid that that awareness was an indubitable factor in our experience. Indeed, he wants to claim that it is for them as indubitable a factor as their very physical environment. (We see here again the old quest for certainty. Even in our fallibilistic age, after Peirce's devastating assault on Cartesianism, it still dies hard.)

If my arguments above have been sound there could be for us here and now no such an awareness of God. To say that after we die we can come to have such an awareness does not help us now to show that our faith is rooted in a vivid awareness of the reality of God. Even if dualism is true and beyond that we are immaterial beings or can have, if only for a short time, a disembodied existence, it has not been shown that we can encounter God or understand what it is to experience God. We can, and some of us do, have religious experiences, experience *perhaps* best understood on a Durkheimian or a Feuerbachian or a Freudian or a Frommian interpretation. However, be that as it may, without at all denying the reality of that experience, *qua* experience, we can know that it cannot be understood as an experience *of God* where 'God' is construed in anything like the normal way. If 'God', by contrast, is construed in a Spinozist, Tillichian, Phillipian, or Braithwaitean way, then perhaps we can speak of the experience of God, but, with these reductionisms, even atheistic humanists, nay even Marxists, can be led gently into belief, for then there is nothing of substance that distinguishes the atheist from the religious believer. We can all gather around the tribal campfire together.[11]

II

I assumed above that it made sense to say that there can be bodily death and that that notwithstanding we could live on as spirits (as immaterial beings) and that, for a short time at least, we could have an utterly disembodied existence. It is a bit of philosophical orthodoxy, at least in analytic circles, that immateriality is problematic. I am in that respect part of that orthodoxy. I shall argue briefly, what I argue in detail in my 'The Faces of Immortality', that belief in the disembodied existence of persons, whatever we might want to say about numbers, is incoherent. I shall be concerned here to meet Badham's particular arguments.

Badham concedes that the 'difficulties of expounding or defending a credible concept of the soul today are truly formidable' but he presses on none the less for he takes such a belief to be a religious necessity.[12] He thinks the concept of the soul can be made intelligible and that there actually is some empirical evidence for the claim that we have souls and these souls are immortal. Suppose I am substantially mistaken in what I have argued in the first section and we can be aware of God. Well, it is clear enough that we cannot see God with our eyes and hear him with our ears. God must be spiritually discerned, if he is to be discerned at all, in a way that requires at least dualist assumptions about a non-material encountering faculty. Because our bodies are constantly going through changes, Badham thinks that the material of which a person happens to be composed can in no sense be regarded as necessary to his ongoing self-hood. What, however, is essential is not some particular stuff he has at a particular time but the having at any time of *some* such particular stuff, linked together in a causal history with other bits of particular stuff that were had at an earlier time by him and with the particular memories that a particular embodied person has. To say that the person is 'the essential part of what we are' or 'the vital principles of our being', 'the pattern of what we are' is perhaps fair enough, but it does not say much until filled in. These things are compatible with an utterly materialistic way of looking at things. Badham takes the word 'soul' to be a term for 'some non-physical principle of continuity' of persons. But I do not see how this can be, for, as is well known, one can be a dualist, as Ducasse was, without believing in immortality or even thinking it is a coherent concept. Memories, on a dualist account, are non-physical and they provide a non-physical principle of continuity. But memories are experiences persons have. That they provided a principle of continuity, if they do, for saying that a certain embodied being, while changing extensively in her bodily make-up over time, is the same person, does not at all show that that person is or could be disembodied. It does not show us that there is a kind of being, a kind of individual, that we call a person that could exist in a disembodied state. It at best only shows us that embodied beings could have non-material properties. Of course, our own sense of self-hood is associated with being a thinking, feeling, willing subject. But that does not show, or even indicate, that we understand the concept that we are disembodied spirits who have those experiences, or even that we understand how those experiences can be given a dualistic interpretation. It is not at all evidence that we have a sense of what it is to be a 'we' without a body. But to say this is not to say that we just think of ourselves as bodies in motion. That we have all kinds of strange notions in dreams shows nothing pertinent here for dreams need not make sense, need not be consistent or coherent and indeed frequently are not. (That they make Freudian sense is another matter.)

Badham has done nothing to show that we are persons capable of surviving bodily death, or that our self-hood is constituted by immateriality. He has not even shown that these puzzling notions make sense. Even if our sense of self-identity is intimately linked with things like memories, it does not show that this establishes our identity so that it can be correctly said, just in virtue of memories and the like, that this is Hans, Pierre or Nadine.

It may be the case, though I doubt it, for it sounds to me like bad scientific methodology, that a single example of para-normal phenomena being genuine, would establish that central state materialism is false. But that would only take us to dualism, not to immortality. Badham has not clarified the concept of disembodied existence sufficiently for us to have reason to think we have or could have any evidence either for disembodied existence or against it.

All the same he presses on with giving us what he takes to be evidence. He thinks telepathy gives us some evidence but the most important evidence, he claims, comes from 'the experiences of people who have been resuscitated from a close encounter with death and who would undoubtedly have died but for modern medical advances'.[13] For some people, though not for the majority, of all age groups and from all educational and social strata, and from different religious backgrounds, some report that at the moment they were near what appeared to be their death, they had a sense of going out of their bodies and finding themselves looking down with interest on the resuscitation attempts. Moreover, and this is surprising, that 'after recovery they accurately described what was going on while they were unconscious and their perspective was from a point of view different from that of the body on the operating table'.[14]

Badham takes these findings, as he puts it, as being of 'absolutely crucial significance for the concept of the soul', for, as he continues, 'if a single out-of-the-body experience is correctly described as such, then the soul is a reality'.[15] These experiences, if they have been correctly described, show, he attests, that 'consciousness can exist apart from the body'.[16] And thus 'the most fundamental barrier across the road to immortality has been removed'.[17]

The catch is in his 'has been correctly described'. What is evident enough is that some people will honestly avow that they have had experiences that they will describe in that way. But that they will talk this way, that they will interpret these experiences in this way, does not mean that this interpretation is the correct descriptive-interpretive account of these experiences or even, in such a context, that it will be the most perspicious account of those experiences. Post-positivist philosophy of science has taught us that all data, even the best data, underdetermines theory. That is to say, there will always be the possibility, and frequently the reality, that the 'same data' will be equally compatible with different theories, and that it will never be the case that we can just read off which theory, if any theory, is the correct theory from the data. Moreover, as Richard Rorty has shown us, if not Wittgenstein before him, there is no such thing as nature's own language, and there is no such thing as an utterly neutral description of the world.[18] If, on the one hand, we think the concept of disembodied existence makes sense, and if we are inclined to believe in, or at least hope for, its reality, we will be likely to interpret such data as evidence for disembodied existence. If, on the other hand, we think that the concept of disembodied existence makes no sense or that there being any disembodied beings is extremely unlikely, then we will interpret the data differently. Perhaps we will seek to explain it in terms of telepathic powers, suggestibility, overworked imagination after such a dreadful experience, and the like. If we think the occurrence very improbable, or, even more so, if we believe and have powerful arguments for believing that a belief in disembodied existence is incoherent, we will say, and reasonably so, even if we do not have a good alternative explanation for it, that that cannot be the correct description of what went on because it does not make sense to just speak of consciousness existing where it is not the consciousness of some person who is conscious, and we do not understand what it would be for a person to be disembodied. We have rather some anomalous phenomena for which we cannot, for a given time, give a proper account. But that happens all the time in science as its history attests. If there are good theoretical arguments for thinking that the concept of an immaterial soul is problematic and indeed quite likely incoherent and, given other things we know or reasonably believe, it is highly unlikely that there is any such thing, then some anomalous data, such as the data that Badham adduces, should be treated as just that.

III

Badham also claims that belief in immortality in some form is a *religious* necessity at least for Christians. Surely this is how traditional Christians saw it and surely he is right in following Anthony Kenny in arguing that, if immateriality is problematic, that makes both God and the soul problematic as traditionally conceived.[19] But he also insightfully quotes T. S. Eliot as saying, 'Christianity is always adapting itself into something which can be believed'. As Paul Tillich and John Robinson have pointed out, throughout the history of Christianity the way God has been conceptualised has changed – one might even argue that it has evolved – to meet the way we humans have come to understand the world. With what Max Weber has characterised as the steady, and he believed irreversible, disenchant-ment of the world, we may have reached the point where many of us (particularly if we are intellectuals) can no longer take the God of Christian *theism* or belief in the soul as credible, but, if we are to believe in God at all, we will have to believe in Spinoza's God or Tillich's God, as the ground of being and meaning, or some utterly reductionist account such as we find in plain form in Hare and in Braithwaite and in an evasive form in Phillips and Dilman.[20] All these conceptions of God would go with an utterly naturalistic framework, and with them we could, as did the young Schleiermacher, treat 'immortality as part of the rubbish of antiquity from which Christian-ity must be cleansed if it is to speak to the modern world'.

However, the God of Christianity is a caring God and Christianity is a religion of salvation. Without a belief in immortality how could we believe in either of these things? Moreover, as Badham puts it, people 'throughout the ages have believed themselves to have encountered God in prayer and worship and they have, as a result, had their lives transformed'.[21] This experience of being encountered by God is, he claims, 'the living heart of religion'.[22] But, again in the face of the incoherency or unbelievability of the traditional concep-tions, such notions can be de-mythologised. Being encountered by God can come to be seen as symbolic talk for a categorical commit-ment to love and care for one's fellow and to relentlessly struggle against the plague. The sense of Christianity as a religion of salvation can be captured by a sense of hope in the world that the lives of human beings can be transformed, first in the direction of decency and later into a human emancipation, where, for the first time in history, there will be an extensive human flourishing. It will take from the Christian message those elements 'essentially concerned with the transformation of life here, and now'.[23] The hope for the future would not be an eschatalogical hope, but a hope for a new world in which an order of goodness and justice would prevail, and in which human beings in an order of equality would flourish. To believe in the providential care of an omnipotent God does not require, *pace* Badham, the postulation of immortality. It comes just to a belief, on this de-mythologisation, that such a truly human society with such deep human flourishing will come to prevail. Indeed, belief here may be principally trust or perhaps even just plain hope. And that is plainly in accordance with Christianity as a religion of salvation. It does not, *pace* Badham, deprive the belief of content.

Badham, I am confident, would claim that such a de-mythologisation would not give us an adequate theodicy. Without belief in immortality we are just stuck with the manifest evils in the world. Even if we will eventually get a just and humane social order, it will not make up for the ills some have suffered and, if, as Badham puts it, 'death means extinction, then there is no question but that old age, suffering, disease and death will gain the ultimate victory over each and every one of us, and thereby bring to nothing the belief that each one of us is eternally precious to an all-sovereign God'.[24] But even, as traditional belief has it, an omnipotent God cannot do that which is logically impossible. If belief in immortality really is incoherent, it is logically impossible for it to obtain. It is logically impossible for God to make us immortal. But it does not count against God's providence or his omnipotence that he cannot, to speak anthropomorphically, redeem our suffering by affording us eternal life. But that providential care can manifest itself in coherent ways. It will not all take, or try to take, the turn of traditional Christianity. If there comes to be, against the pervasiveness of evil that is now in the world, a truly human order where the needs and interests of everyone are answered to in an equitable way so that there is extensive human flourishing, we can call that, if we want to talk that way, a firm manifestation of God's providential care. Those who want to use such vocabularies can go on doing so and in doing so make sense out of some things at the heart of Christianity. That such talk is identical, in all but name, to an atheistic humanism that can also be a Marxism only shows that Eliot is right. Christianity can always adapt itself into something which can be believed. We do not need, to make sense of it, as a religion of salvation, to crucify our intellects and make belief in immortality one of the conditions for religious adequacy.

Notes

1. Paul Badham, 'God, the Soul, and the Future Life', pp. 36–51 in this volume.
2. Ibid., p. 43.
3. Kai Nielsen, 'The Faces of Immortality', pp. 1–30 in this volume.
4. Badham, op. cit.
5. Ibid., p. 38.
6. Ibid., p. 38.
7. Ibid., p. 44.
8. Ibid., p. 45.
9. Ibid., p. 46.
10. Richard Swinburne. *The Coherence of Theism* (Oxford, England: Clarendon Press, 1977) p. 110.
11. Kai Nielsen, *Contemporary Critiques of Religion* (New York: Herder and Herder, 1971); *Scepticism* (New York: St. Martin's Press, 1973); and *Philosophy and Atheism* (Buffalo, NY: Prometheus Books, 1985).
12. Badham, op. cit.
13. Ibid., p. 49.
14. Ibid., p. 49.
15. Ibid., p. 49.
16. Ibid., p. 49.
17. Ibid., p. 49.
18. Richard Rorty, *Consequences of Pragmatism* (Minneapolis, Minn: University of Minnesota Press, 1982).
19. Anthony Kenny, *Faith and Reason* (New York, NY: Columbia University Press, 1983).
20. I discuss these forms of evasion in my *God, Scepticism and Modernity*, (Ottawa, Ont: University of Ottawa Press, 1988).
21. Badham, op. cit.
22. Ibid., p. 43.
23. Ibid., p. 36.
24. Ibid., p. 43.

3 The Idea of Reincarnation
Joseph Prabhu

I should like in this paper to explore the idea of reincarnation as a metaphysical and moral notion shedding interpretive light on our experience. I shall argue that it provides a plausible and coherent account of our moral and spiritual life. Being concerned with its appeal at a general philosophical level, I shall not go into an exegesis of the idea as articulated in different philosophical and religious systems. Rather, I will borrow freely from these contexts to construct a version of it, that in its generality seems to me worth considering as a view about the nature and destiny of human life, and specifically about the evolution of consciousness.

I shall begin first with an argument defending the probability of survival of consciousness beyond physical death as against the extinction of all life at death. Next I shall argue that there are good reasons why survival should take an embodied rather than disembodied form. I shall contend further that these reasons are pointed to by the character of our moral experience, and provide in turn a perspective from which to look at our lives. Then I shall take up the question of empirical evidence. Finally, I shall address some of the objections made against the idea and attempt to show that they are not decisive. The overall result of these investigations is to suggest the plausibility of a different view of life from that which seems to hold in our empirical-scientific culture.

Let me begin with the argument for survival. The fact of our moral consciousness, argues Kant, is the guarantee of personal immortality. The highest good must consist in the union of virtue and happiness. The orientation of the ethical will is towards virtue, while that of the sensuous will is towards happiness. But between virtue and happiness no causal relation exists empirically, while ethically no teleological relation can be permitted either. And yet our fundamental moral conception is one of ultimate justice, expressed in the thought that virtue alone is, in the final analysis, worthy of happiness. While we cannot, of course, use this eudaemonistic conception as a basis of morality, it still serves as a high-order, 'transcendental' postulate, if morality is to be meaningful at all. This demand of our moral consciousness is not satisfied by the experience of empirical life, where virtue often requires renunciation of wordly happiness and where vice often goes along with success and the temporary happiness therefrom. If, therefore, moral consciousness requires such ultimate justice, without which it lacks completeness, and if such justice is not to be found in empirical life, it follows that we have to go beyond the limits of such life and postulate another order of existence, which Kant called 'immortal life', in order to make such a union of virtue and happiness both final and permanent. What is important about this argument for our purposes is that it is the demand of morality itself, as Kant conceives it, that points to the conceptual necessity of a life beyond death.

My argument for survival has the same form as Kant's, though a more phenomenological content, which I maintain points towards both post-existence and pre-existence. It is not just the abstract requirement of moral faith that entails an extension beyond empirical life. Rather it is the concrete texture of our moral lives that suggests the need to go beyond the parameters of a single earthly life. The seriousness of our endeavour to shape our lives according to ideals of truth, wisdom, love and compassion, and all that they entail in terms of the development of virtue, together with the sense of inadequacy in our actual achievement, warrant the presumption that a single life cannot be all that we are destined to have. To grant that would make a mockery of our moral experience. It would mean that the very real possibilities of moral purification that we discern on the path from ego-centredness to reality-centredness, to use Hick's expression, would for most of us, who do not achieve full enlightenment in this life, be forever unfulfilled. But these moral and spiritual possibilities are not imaginative fantasies; they are real, both as regulative guides without which our moral lives would lack direction, and as ideals that we, to varying degrees, fulfil.

I am emphasising more phenomenological and developmental aspects of morality by conceiving it in terms of the education of moral consciousness oriented to complete and transparent self-knowledge. In doing so I take a different view of morality, and specifically of its relation to religion, than Kant. Whereas he in some sense reduces religion to morality by basing his analysis on the primacy of duty, I, by contrast, wish to see morality in terms of the demands of spirituality and of spiritual self-knowledge. The movement from ego- to Reality-centredness is primarily a movement of self-consciousness and freedom, in the sense of *moksa*, ultimate spiritual liberation. Till such time as there is misidentification of who we really are, we are destined to remain bound to the world of *samsāra*, which in Sanskrit means 'passing through intensely', where the passing through refers to the embodiment of spiritual consciousness in a series of bodies. By contrast, when self-consciousness does not tie itself to its empirical masks or personae, but is able to see through them and use them for its self-education till it recognises its true spiritual nature, it is free of the samsaric realm and of reincarnation.

It is obvious that this view, which I have sketched very briefly in order to provide a context within which to locate the idea of reincarnation, is dependent on a certain conception of Ultimate Reality and of the human spirit's participation in it. Again I am forced to be brief in order to focus on the question of reincarnation itself. *Saccidananda* is how much of Indian philosophy describes Ultimate Reality, being (*sat*), consciousness (*cit*), and bliss (*ananda*). It is beyond the scope of this essay – and indeed of most human lifetimes – to unpack the full content of this notion. Let me just say that reality is seen as being completely and thoroughly spiritual, with all its modes and appearances being, in the final analysis, good. The fundamental assumption of an empirical-scientific mentality that the world is morally neutral, is thought in this perspective to be limited. Within this limited context, explanation of the world in purely empirical terms has a relative truth and appropriateness. It is certainly proper to explain mechanical, chemical, and biological realities in respectively mechanical, chemical, and biological terms, without invoking moral or spiritual categories. But when one wants to see the world as a whole, or when one wants to investigate realities of a different order, these categories are no longer appropriate. Kant recognised this in his attempt to keep theoretical and practical and teleological reason apart, and to recognise the primacy of practical reason. He does so, however, in the thrall of Newtonian physics, which he thinks provides the true explanation of the natural world. It is because of this that he is forced to shrink morality to a narrow deontological conception of duty derived from the rational will alone. But Kant cedes too much to Newtonian physics and to the epistemologies and philosophy of mind built on it. The Indian view is different from Kant's in thinking that questions of the meaning and purpose of the universe, which Kant with his epistemological strictures felt he had banished from the realm of pure reason, are in fact perfectly intelligible questions, but intelligible in terms of moral-spiritual rather than physical categories. Physical causation itself is placed within a larger and more comprehensive spiritual causation.

What are the alternatives? A naturalist may say that these speculations are baseless, when the facts of natural science establish that everything that we can plausibly call personality ceases at the time of physical death. If one ignores the results of psychical research, or at least suspends judgement about them as being problematical, one is compelled to say that in the nature of the case natural science cannot pronounce on what is clearly beyond its domain. It is a strange step from this recognition to argue that just because natural science, as presently constituted, cannot in principle give an answer to the question of life after death, that the very question ought to be dismissed. The price of this dismissal, however, is greater than just the nullity of its speculation about a possible afterlife; what is more damaging is that it leaves unexplained the deeper moral impulses of this life. We may grant that there is for both the naturalist and the believer in an afterlife, the incentive to achieve as much moral goodness as one can within the span of a lifetime. The difference is, however, that the very attempt to do this brings into sharp focus the vaster reaches of goodness, that for most of us cannot be attained in a single life-span. It is this inner, dynamic aspect of goodness which is part of the experience of a great many people, that is simply denied, implicitly or explicitly in the naturalist's position.

Suppose we grant that our moral consciousness establishes a strong presumption of post-existence. We still have to argue that pre-existence is intelligible and probable. I have dealt above with moral aspiration and what it points to prospectively. But it is a fact that moral aspirations themselves differ greatly between people. It is also a fact that hindrances to the fulfilment of such aspirations, rooted in the character of people, differ significantly. In truth, these hindrances determine the nature and extent of moral response. So, how can we explain the patent inequalities of people in this matter, not to mention inequalities in other sorts of ability, in circumstances and opportunities? One line of explanation may be that these inequalities are the result of the agents' own actions in this life. But in many cases, this will not do, because people have not lived long enough to have naturally achieved such abilities or disabilities. How, for example, can one account for the advanced spiritual evolution of a Krishnamurti, while still in his early twenties, and at the other end of the scale the depravity of a Richard Ramirez, the California criminal, at the same age?

To this question believers in reincarnation provide a thoroughly causal answer: those of unequal abilities are such only by virtue of their own actions – the principle of *karma*, or the moral law of cause and effect. Therefore, since their actions in this life are insufficient to account for their abilities, the latter are due to actions in a prior life. This is, of course, a completely different answer from the orthodox Christian view that God creates each human soul *ab initio*, which saddles God with the responsibility for inequalities. But the implications of this ascription are at the very least problematical for a traditional conception of God as all-good and all-powerful. The Indian view makes each agent herself responsible via her *karma*. This may not solve 'the problem of evil' in any ultimate sense, but I shall argue later that it sees the problem quite differently from the Judaeo-Christian perspective.

While, of course, the notion of *karma* is logically distinct from that of rebirth, the two ideas are run together, because in combination they provide a more powerful explanation for the inequalities that plague existence. It is worth examining both the principle of *karma* and the associated notion of rebirth, in order to get clearer about what precisely is being asserted and what the rationale for it is.

In maintaining that one's moral nature is entirely determined by one's own actions, rather than the adventitious operations of fate, chance, or divine grace, the *karma* theory provides a thoroughgoing application of causation to the moral and spiritual world and with it the notion of complete personal responsibility for one's present character and dispositions. As for the operation of *karma* itself, it is important to define what seems to me to be the important insight, and separate it from various accretions that have grown around the notion, which have given rise to many misunderstandings, some of which I will consider later. I have consistently emphasised that the workings of *karma* apply to the moral and psychological realms, to the interior life of a person, where her basic dispositions and attitudes are an exact product of what she has wanted and done in the past. This is not at all to deny that these dispositions are also acquired as a result of contingent choices made in this life and that these choices were in part influenced by heredity and environment. There is no claim made that *karma* is the exclusive cause of all that happens to us. The theory does not deny the role of both heredity and environment in explaining the moral and psychological traits of an individual, but if it is to have any punch, it has to claim, as indeed it does, that *karma* is the critical factor in explaining a person's moral make-up. How can this arguement be made? The idea is that these other factors serve as instrumentalities for the operation of *karma* in a manner that permits a great deal of flexibility, such that there is no rigid one to one correlation between certain kinds of acts and their consequences. Karmic laws state tendencies rather than inevitable consequences. The general principle is that morally good acts tend to produce suitably good consequences, while morally evil acts do the opposite.

What is the force of 'suitably'? It is not just a principle of retribution to be understood in conventional terms of reward and punishment, but far more a principle of continuity and of spiritual growth designed to wean consciousness away from its ignorance and false self-identifications. Thus, let us suppose that a person has hankered after wealth and has oriented his life's actions around its acquisition. Let us assume further that he has been successful at this and has enjoyed considerable worldly success. It is difficult to specify what exactly the karmic consequence of this attitude is. He may be reborn either as a poor person or a rich one, once more or a number of times, till the lesson of non-attachment to wealth is learned. It is possible that the experience of poverty may help him to achieve the 'poverty of spirit' which the Christian gospel talks about or alternatively that it may make him hanker after wealth even more, in which case another karmic cycle is initiated. On the other hand he may be reborn rich, but with life circumstances this time showing the hollowness of such wealth in relation to his desire for happiness. The only thing worse than having our desires not granted is having them granted says Oscar Wilde. But whether our desires are granted or not, the main point of the karmic principle is the education and evolution of consciousness. That presupposes, of course, a principle of continuity, such that past lives will have a future effect, but given that the effect is to be seen in moral and spiritual terms, its exact empirical embodiment is difficult to predict, and in any case is a secondary question.

It may be claimed that all this is vague and far-fetched and that heredity and environment and present life choices are sufficient to explain psychological and, perhaps, moral traits. Against this is the patent evidence of similarity in hereditary and environmental influences producing different psychological traits. Thus, H. H. Newman, who has made a special study of twinning and of identical twins in particular, observes:

In describing several pairs of these strange twins, writers have commented upon their lack of close similarity. Such twins have been regarded as the only kind of twins that are beyond question derived from a single egg and therefore surely identical in their hereditary make-up. One would expect such twins, since they have not only a common heredity but a common environment (for they must be in the same environment all the time), to be even more strikingly similar than pairs of separate twins that are not so intimately associated. The fact is, however, that Siamese twins are almost without exception more different in various ways than any but a very few pairs of separate one-egg twins. One of the most difficult problems faced by the twinning specialist is that of accounting for this unexpected dissimilarity of the components of Siamese twin pairs'.[1]

This difference is surely due to a third factor other than heredity and environment, and while this by itself does not establish the presence of a karmic factor, it may possibly point in that direction. So, too, do the cases of geniuses or child prodigies, whose accomplishments cannot be accounted for in terms of heredity or environment.

In the second place I think it is important to reiterate that what the *karma* theory is designed to explain is the spiritual status and evolution of an individual, and while these are undoubtedly conditioned by the above-mentioned factors, they are so, neither exhaustively nor even primarily. The claim is that spiritual forces are indeed shaped and moulded by the empirical, but that they have a degree of autonomy, expressed in dispositions which are only analysable by laws that are *sui generis*.

Granted that rebirth may be a possibility, does this appear more reasonable than disembodied survivors? In answer to that question I wish to make clear the rationale behind the idea of reincarnation and show its plausibility. Here, too, I shall abstract from the variety of justifications offered in different systems and come up with a general one.

There are two main reasons for embodiment, one metaphysical and the other ethical and they are closely related. The metaphysical thesis is that human life, and more generally the life of the soul in the samsāric realm, must be seen as a psycho- physical unity, so that both pre- and post-existence must be in a body and a body which expresses the inner character of an individual. In contrast to the Greek notion of the immortality of the soul in a disembodied state, Indian and Christian escatologies affirm the essential role of the body, though in different ways.

In the Indian scheme an evolutionary movement is postulated beginning at the most elemental level, where the *jīva* or soul passes through a series of increasingly complex bodies, until at last a human one is attained. Up to this point, the soul's evolution is straightforward and automatic in its upward ascent. This automaticity ceases, when chemical, biological and organic life reaches the human level where, depending on the actions performed, the soul can either ascend or descend in the evolutionary scale. This set of alternatives betokens the reaching of self-consciousness and with it responsibility for one's choices. But even though at the human level one may retrogress, the nisus and dynamic of the whole movement are upwards towards self-conscious identification with the Absolute. The moment this identification is complete, the whole samsāric realm is transcended and karma and rebirth are finally overcome.

This metaphysical doctrine points to its ethical counterpart. The body can be conceived as the soul's necessary self-externalisation, and externalisation necessary for self-consciousness and its intentional nature. Thus, as self-consciousness becomes more spiritual in terms of its deepening identification with the Absolute, the conception of the body changes from a gross, materialistic one, where the primary modality is absorption in sense-gratification, to a centre of pure energy radiating the energy of the Divine, as Jesus did as his transfiguration of the mountain and the Buddha at his enlightenment under the Bodhi tree. Once this enlightenment is complete, however, the whole realm of *samsāra* and bodies is transcended in a state of Pure Consciousness, which is not intentional at all, and is not conscious 'of' anything including itself.

The body, then, serves as the stage on which the ethical and spiritual drama is played out, with the action being controlled by the director, the *ātman* or true self, to varying degrees depending on the co-operation of the actors, the moral and psychological traits of the individual. Sometimes the actors can become egotistical and wilful, in which case the vision of the director is obscured. At other times, they can serve as living instruments of his design and express his purpose transparently. If the *jīva* provides the thread of 'inner' continuity, the body is the arena in which its psychic life is acted out, and it is only in the acting out and the articulation through the body that self-awareness is attained. Prior to that the soul exists as a bundle of potentialities, some of which are actualised in a particular manner. We can make the point clearer by a change of image. A novelist may start out with only the faintest glimmer of the eventual book, a scene, a character, a mood perhaps. What these amount to only become clear in and through the writing, in the process of which she may become aware of what she really wants to say. In a similar fashion the body serves as a self-articulation of the soul. Sometimes the expression may not be appropriate to the inner state, as in my earlier example of the person identifying the desire for happiness with the greedy acquisition of wealth. Gradually through trials and errors made visible in the body, the soul is educated to identify true happiness with the Absolute and not with any partial or limited instantiation of it.

If the purpose of embodiment, then, is to enable the soul to educate itself and thus evolve, the mode in which this education proceeds is through justice in a law-abiding moral universe. As you sow, so shall you reap, if not in this life, then in some future one. But as mentioned before, it is a justice that is not simply retributive but rather a discipline of natural consequences designed to impart moral knowledge. And for this purpose too, bodily experience is necessary, as the place where such consequences are made visible. When misfortunes befall us, which we feel we in no way deserve, because of no wrongdoing on our part in this life, which we can detect, or 'when bad things happen to good people' to use the title of Rabbi Kushner's book, it is not God, or our neighbour, or some cruel fate that is to be blamed. They (that is, misfortunes) may serve as a reminder of some wrongdoing or weakness that we may well have forgotten, or may have been too insensitive even to recognise. Or, if that is not the case, as for example, in children or infants stricken with illnesses or handicaps, the belief is that this is the consequence of some crime committed in a previous life. This belief is neither fanciful nor vacuous, as is often alleged. I think it is a common part of our experience to encounter within ourselves some weakness or temperamental flaw or alternatively, some skill or facility that we cannot satisfactorily account for by the pattern of our present lives. We cannot, of course, know for sure that the actions of a previous life are responsible for this, but the belief is a reasonable one, especially when placed in the context of a more comprehensive belief in a moral universe. There is then no bitterness about life, but rather a calm acceptance of what it has to offer, of joy or of sorrow, aware that both are given us to draw the soul upwards toward God.

It may be argued that the viability of the argument from justice requires a certain memory of our past lives, without which it seems to lose its point. I shall tackle that particular objection later, but at this stage let me say that the argument requires only that one's own actions have consequences on one's life and that one's present actions do not satisfactorily explain one's present condition.

With these explanations I come now to the question of empirical evidence. What evidence, you may ask, is there that any of these speculations are true? There is now a considerable amount of scientific data garnered according to the strictest standards. Ian Stevenson's investigations are the best known. Five volumes of his case histories have thus far been published, while the number of reincarnation-type cases now in his files totals over two thousand. His research has revealed a number of instances where the details people, usually small children, give of their past lives could not possibly have been done in their present lives, details whose accuracy was largely verified, when investigated. Nor is it true, as some have suggested, that these cases are mainly to be found in cultures, where the belief in reincarnation is prevalent. In July 1974 Stevenson's colleague at the University of Virginia, J. G. Pratt, carried out a census of Stevenson's cases and found that of the 1339 cases then in Stevenson's file, 'the United States has the most, with 324 cases (not counting American Indian and Eskimo) and the next five countries in descending order are Burma (139 cases), India (135), Turkey (114), and Great Britain (111).'[2]

Most of the time Stevenson has gathered his information from children between the ages of two and four, though occasionally older, who spontaneously offered information about their previous lives and personae in the course of conversation. He prefers children to adults as subjects because of the obviously greater difficulty in controlling subconscious influences from information adults have been exposed to, as also the more pronounced tendency to indulge in fantasies, imaginative inventions and other forms of psychological projection.

Among the most frequently observed characteristics in these cases are the possession of a skill not taught or learned, including knowledge of a foreign language to which the person has not been exposed in this life; names of people whom they claim to have known previously, places where they lived and incidents in these lives, all of which Stevenson found to be about 90 per cent accurate; a phobia for objects and circumstances associated with their previous deaths; and an ability to detect changes in people and surroundings in the places of their former lives.

Now Stevenson is most scrupulous in asserting that he has uncovered possible evidence for reincarnation and not definitive proof.

He himself has explored a number of alternative hypotheses to explain his data, from fraud and fantasising to clairvoyance, telepathy and mediumistic possession. Again it is beyond my scope to go into the plausibility or otherwise of these hypotheses, because I would have to examine each individual case in detail. Suffice it to say that Stevenson, who does not explicitly profess a personal belief in reincarnation, said in an interview in 1974, looking back on his own research,

> what I do believe is that, of the cases we now know, reincarnation – at least for some – is the best explanation that we have been able to come up with. There is an impressive body of evidence and it is getting stronger all the time. I think a rational person, if he wants, can believe in reincarnation on the basis of evidence.[3]

Needless to say, in spite of the fact that his research is respected by his peers, his findings and conclusions can hardly be said to be accepted by the scientific establishment at large. This is only to be expected, because a reincarnation hypothesis goes against the beliefs of many reared in a materialist or physicalist culture. Within these assumptions, the scope of observation, experiment and reality-testing is going to be restricted, while the limited data uncovered by these methods in turn reinforces these narrow assumptions. This problem of the theory-ladeness of all data and of what counts as evidence is well known from discussions in contemporary philosophy and history of science. Data alone will not dislodge a set of theoretical assumptions, because data that does not fit a theory will usually be explained away in some fashion or another.

That, however, is not my problem. I have not offered the idea of reincarnation as an empirical hypothesis though given my openess to it, I am impressed by the evidence. My tack in this paper has been different, concerned more with the significance of reincarnation than with its empirical status. I have tried to argue that it makes sense of our moral experience, as part of the evolution of consciousness towards complete and transparent self-knowledge. Within this framework the notion of *karma* expresses the internal law of our moral life according to which actions produce consequences which are strictly proportional to their moral nature. Thus, it is our actions alone that are responsible for our fate. This notion, in turn, requires the idea of rebirth, because the consequences of action may spread over many lifetimes and conversely, starting at the other end, our present status may not be explainable in terms of the actions of this life combined with the forces of heredity and environment. The particular form in which I have tried to couch my argument for rebirth has been as a kind of transcendental deduction based on a phenomenological analysis of our moral experience.

I want to proceed now to three objections which are often made against the notion of reincarnation:

1. that it does not really offer a solution to the inequalities and natural evils that pervade existence,
2. that a belief in reincarnation is likely to produce a fatalism or at least passivity, and finally,
3. that the claim of evolution in moral education is undercut, if in fact we lack memories of our previous lives, which most of us do.

Let me begin with the first objection, which is that the theory does not really tackle the problem of inequalities, but instead simply pushes it back to an indeterminate stage of existence. Hick puts it this way:

> For we are no nearer to an ultimate explanation of the circumstances of our present birth when we are told that they are consequences of a previous life if that previous life has in turn to be explained by reference to a yet previous life, and that by reference to another, and so on in an infinite regress. One can affirm the beginningless character of the soul's existence in this way; but one cannot then claim that it renders either intelligible or morally acceptable the inequalities of our present lot. The solution has not been produced but only postponed to infinity.[4]

Now, much depends on how exactly we define the problem that we are attempting to solve. The assumptions behind Hick's argument are taken from a western and predominantly Christian perspective, where the problem of natural evil is thrown back on God and we are faced with the conundrum of how an all-good and all-powerful divine creator can escape responsibility for his creation. Many streams of Indian philosophy see things differently. The Ultimate Reality, *Saccidananda*, is seen more as an impersonal process, an eternal moral order that comes into its own in and through the realm of *samsāra*, which too is eternal. Why the Ultimate Reality goes through this process is a mystery, at least to those in the samsāric realm. But the evolution of consciousness gives us some clues.

Goodness is to be conceived primarily in terms of spiritual knowledge, while evil is seen essentially as ignorance. Knowledge in the dynamic sense of knowing, or coming to know, can be construed as the overcoming of such ignorance. Just as it is not possible to talk about knowledge without also talking about ignorance, so also 'good' and 'evil' are seen as correlative terms. Indian philosophy in general is far more accepting of evil seen in gnostic terms than western thought, which sees it in largely moral terms, tends to be. It is relativised as a phase that is constantly being overcome, rather than being absolutised as a thing in itself. There is no expectation, therefore, of God's creating a perfectly good world. The Divine is conceived much more as a immanent process of progressively more transparent self-consciousness. Human beings participate in and tially constitute that divine process, so that when it comes to evil, there is no external agency to be blamed.

It is true, to return to Hick's argument, that by saying the soul always and eternally has a character and a set of dispositions, we are in fact not offering a solution to the precise set of concerns that Hick has in mind. But the Indian is satisfied with the thought that if he pushes back far enough he will be able to see how his own choices, from among the possibilities presented, alone produced his present situation. No doubt some were disposed to make better choices at that stage, but the inequity of the conditions that produced the different choices, some better and some worse, matters less in an infinite time framework than the conviction that one alone is responsible for one's present state. After all, everyone has a chance to learn from their mistakes and the difficult situations they find themselves in; the fact that it may take longer for some than for others matters little in an infinite time span. And so, if 'the solution has only been postponed to infinity', the Indian is not as worried about it as Hick is.

These last remarks set the stage for the second objection, namely, that if what we are is conditioned by our past actions, then we are fated to bear their consequences, good or bad, and there is nothing we can do to change our lot. And, indeed, this is how it is often understood. But this is false. To say that one is conditioned, is not to say that one is determined, even by the consequences of one's own actions. This becomes clearer when we attempt to analyse an action and its fruits. Every act of ours has a double result, which we may term its direct and indirect results. The direct result is the pain or pleasure, which follows upon the act depending upon its nature. The indirect result is the tendency that is created to repeat the act again if it was pleasant and to avoid it in the future if painful (which is a negative way of expressing the first proposition, to the extent that the act of avoiding something painful can itself be conceived as a pleasurable act). The 'necessity' inherent in the law of *karma* applies only to the direct result – there is no way of avoiding the immediate consequences of what we do. Where the indirect result is concerned, we may grant that we are predisposed to perform the act again, but we have a measure of freedom in succumbing to that predisposition or resisting it.

Wherein does this freedom consist? Not in trying merely to repress this tendency, but rather by understanding its operation and the circumstances in which it comes to fruition, and then by initiating a different set of circumstances. Let us consider the example of a cigarette smoker trying to give up the habit. Nothing will erase the direct result of smoking – the physiological consequences. But the tendency to continue smoking can be checked both by not giving in to the tendency and by producing circumstances in which that tendency simply cannot be expressed, till such time as it withers away from neglect.

This psychological point has moral significance. While our tendencies do indeed predispose us to act in certain ways, to give in to them is not to be truly self-determining, but in fact to be determined. Self-determination consists in directing and regulating our tendencies as they tend to express themselves in action. Thus, far from being fatalistic in its implications, the *karma* theory is optimistic: our past actions may have produced our present state, but in the measure of freedom that we enjoy, we can direct our present actions towards the betterment of our moral nature in the future. The attitude is expressed in a much quoted Sanskrit saying:

Fortune comes to a person, who is as energetic as a lion, but cowards think that it is the gift of Fate. Let us overcome this Fate by our power and make all possible personal endeavours; no blame will attach to us, if our best efforts do not succeed.[5]

By thus orienting our actions towards moral progress, one may grow

indifferent to what happens in the present, as the inevitable consequence of past karma which is behind us now as we face the future.

This point leads to the third objection: the question whether we
can benefit from the just retribution involved in *karma*, if we have no
memory of our previous lives. Leibniz, in discussing this with one of
his correspondents, writes, 'What good would it do you, sir, to
become king of China on condition of forgetting what you have been?
Would it not be the same thing as if God at the same time he
destroyed you, created a king in China?'[6] But it depends what we
mean here by 'memory'. If we mean by that the preservation of a
comprehensive span of memories describing our situation, then
surely that condition is too strong for establishing identity. None of us
finds his sense of identity weakened by the fact that he has no
memories of the first years of childhood. That our conscious identity
in that case is established by spatio-temporal continuity is true, and,
of course, that distinguishes a previous life that we cannot remember
from circumstances of our present life that we have forgotten. But we
may point to a weaker but still intelligible sense of 'memory', where
continuity of memory is established through the persistance of
dispositions and tendencies. The fact that the circumstances of our
present life may not satisfactorily explain our skills, traits or
weaknesses, forces us back, if we accept the principle of *karma*, to a
consideration of previous lives. That we may have no conscious
memory of them is not fatal, because all that the *karma* theory asserts
is that past lives will have an effect on the present. If this is so, we
may grant that we are in fact different persons in different lives, while
still holding on to dispositional continuity carried in the
soul. 'Personality', after all, is a mask, and what matters is the
continuity of the spiritual consciousness underlying it, rather than the
identity of the masks it assumes at various times. Huston Smith
expresses it well; his words can serve as a fitting conclusion to this
essay:

Our word 'personality' comes from the Latin *persona*, which
originally meant the mask an actor donned as he stepped onto the
stage to play his role . . . This mask is precisely what our personalities are . . . The disturbing fact, however, is that we have lost
sight of the distinction between our true selves and the veil of
personality that is its present costume . . . We have come completely under the fascination of our present lines, unable to
remember previous roles or to anticipate future ones. The task is to

correct this false identification. Turning his awareness inward, [man] must pierce and dissolve the innumerable layers of the manifest personality until, all strata of the mask at length cut through, he arrives finally at the anonymous actor who stands beneath.[7]

Notes

1. Quoted in K. N. Jayatillike, *Karma and Survival in Buddhist Perspective* (Kandy: Buddhist Publication Society, 1969) pp. 55–5
2. J. Gunther Pratt and Naomi Hintze, *The Psychic Realm: What Can You Believe?* (New York: Random House, 1975) quoted in Sylvia Cranston and Carey Williams, *Reincarnation: A New Horizon in Science, Religion and Society* (New York: Julian Press, 1984) pp. 49–69, from which a good deal of the information in the paragraph is taken.
3. Ibid., p. 68. The original source of the quote is Alton Slagle, 'Reincarnation: A Doctor Looks Beyond Death', *Sunday News*, New York, 4 August 1974.
4. John Hick, *Death and Eternal Life* (New York: Harper & Row, 1980) p.309.
5. Yajnavalaya-Smrti, I, pp. 349–51, quoted in S. Chatterjee *The Fundamentals of Hinduism: A Philosophical Study* (Calcutta: Dasgupta, 1960) p. 87.
6. Leibniz, *Philosophische Schriften*, edited Gerhardt, IV, p. 300.
7. Huston Smith, *The Religions of Man* (New York: Mentor Books, 1959) chapter 2.

I wish to thank Scott Aebischer for a helpful discussion of some aspects of this paper.

Karma and Rebirth in India: A Pessimistic Interpretation
Ariel Glucklich

Can *karma* and *saṁsāra* (moral causation and transmigration) serve as general conceptual models for metaphysical theories which are not grounded in a specific cultural context? This seems to be the broadest issue entailed by Professor Prabhu's paper, which advocates a resoundingly affirmative position. For Prabhu, as for John Hick, *karma* is an accurate paradigm for the hypothesis that the soul journeys through several lifetimes, from engrossment in materiality to perfect enlightenment: 'The movement from ego to reality-centredness is primarily a movement of self-consciousness and freedom, in the sense of *moksa* ultimate spiritual liberation'.[1] *Karma* and *saṁsāra* are exportable Indian models for such an upward movement, which culminates in an identification with the Absolute.[2]

Prabhu does not develop an argument for the evolution of consciousness along the lines of any specific Hindu or Buddhist *karma* theory. His argument, thus, should not be gauged on historical or textual grounds. Instead Prabhu extrapolates a number of central, perhaps essential, features of various *karma* theories to make intelligible an optimistic and spiritually progressive interpretation of rebirth and moral causation. These include the proposition that good or evil acts inexorably produce corresponding consequences (*phala*) that must be experienced, if not in this life, then in future births (*punarjanma*). In the next pages I shall show that historical and textual precision aside, even the most abstract and theoretical components of *karma* and *saṁsāra* render a soteriologically optimistic interpretation of *karma* highly problematic.

The idea that our present predicament may be explained by reference to moral causality and our actions in previous births is orthodox, but constrained by severe internal and external inconsistencies. This is true both empirically and conceptually. The various *karma* theories formulated in India, are neither the exclusive, nor the most often-cited explanations for present circumstances. Classical

Hinduism presents a wide array of competing 'theories', including divine acts (*divya-kriyā*), fate (*daiva, diṣṭa* and so on), time (*kāla*), death (*mṛtyu*), nature (*prakṛti*), mechanical (or empirical) causes, and others.[3] All explain, in a variety of ways, such events as illness, premature death, poverty, or for that matter, sudden good fortune. Recent anthropological studies have revealed that low caste members seldom explain their birth, which is a moral predicament, in karmic terms.[4] Indians are far more satisfied in claiming that their formerly high-ranking ancestors were tricked and victimised into losing status.[5] Specific misfortunes and illnesses are attributed to agencies that one can manipulate for therapeutical purposes. In fact, the moral, rather than magical implications of disease are far less appealing to those who are suddenly stricken. *Karma* it seems, is the last explanation that a Hindu is likely to invoke, though perhaps it is also the last to be abandoned.

Of course, the veracity of a metaphysical theory does not hang upon the reluctance of individuals, or even communities, to apply it in their lives. Still, sociological observation is not entirely irrelevant because *karma*, as a moral soteriology, derives its potentially universal appeal from the manner in which it is said to satisfy existential dilemmas. Therefore, its psychological rejection by those who take *karma's* veracity for granted, is a significant methodological limitation.

Far more significant and damaging problems arise when we consider the internal logic of *karma* theories, even 'evolutionary' ones. Interestingly, both Hinduism and Buddhism developed progressive karmic schemes, that is, theories in which successive births generally represent an upward movement toward greater spiritual merit and final liberation. The best instances, perhaps, are Buddhist. In his *Acts of the Buddha* (XIII.58), Aśvaghosa attributes Buddha's ability to withstand Māra's assaults to the merit acquired by actions over innumerable lives.[6] The Śākyamuni Buddha emerged out of his mother's womb after having undergone an enormous number of previous births. Through these he had perfected his store of merit to the point where, as an infant he could take the vow not to be born again.[7] 'Progressive' *karma* is one of the central implicit assumptions underlying the *bodhisattva* tradition. One takes the vow to become a *bodhisattva* realising that the process entails thousands of successive lifespans: 'Those sons and daughters of good family who come to hear this Perfection of Wisdom must have fulfilled their duties under the Jinas of the past, must have planted wholesome roots under (those) Tathāgatas, and must have been taken hold of by good spiritual friends'.[8]

The psychology and metaphysics of moral causality and rebirth are worked out in great detail by the philosophical texts of the major Buddhist schools.[9] In fact, I submit that a precise extension of *karma* as a metaphysical and moral model to our own range of experiences cannot be accomplished without a familiarity with such works as Vasubandhu's *Abhidharmakośa*.[10] A reasonable argument for past and future lives needs to be developed in this context, which is consistent with theories of the self (*ātman* or *anātta*), the ontological status of reality (*abhidharma*), the nature of dependent co-origination (*paticcasamuppāda*), and other cognate theories. None of these arguments are based strictly on the 'moral consciousness' which requires 'ultimate justice' in the face of a morally imperfect world.[11] But there are graver logical problems still, even within the 'progressive' *karma* tradition, such as the one embodied in the *Jātaka*, or stories of the Buddha's previous births.[12] Consider the 'Matakabhatta-Jātaka' for instance:[13]

The story tells of a Brahmin who was preparing for the *Śrāddha* sacrificial offering to his ancestors. He commanded his students to take a goat, the sacrificial victim, to the river, bathe and anoint it, then put a garland of flowers around the animal's neck. As these preparations were taking place the goat suddenly remembered its previous birth and began to laugh. Then it started crying. When brought before the Brahmin the goat explained:

> I too was a Brahmin who sacrificed a goat on behalf of my ancestors. As a result I have been damned to five hundred births as a goat, each life terminating with a sacrificial beheading. This is my 500th birth and today I will finally be able to terminate this suffering and return to a human existence.

The frightened Brahmin promised that he would on no terms allow the goat to die on that day, having already consecrated it for the sacrifice. The goat replied: 'Weak is your protection, Brahmin, and strong is the force of my evil-doing'. So, although the Brahmin and his students closely guarded the goat, when the animal stretched out its neck to graze beneath a boulder, lightning struck the rock which fell and decapitated it.

The narrative raises a number of logical and ethical issues:

A. What is the precise relation between an act and its consequences in a future life? If a Brahmin undergoes five hundred births as a goat for one sacrifice, how many hundreds of thousands of animal lives must he experience to expiate for one lifetime of sacrifices and other rituals, occasional lies, nasty thoughts, and so forth? After these lives, does he return to a *status quo ante*? But pertaining to which precise existence? Moreover, let us assume that as an animal one is not a moral agent and thus accrues no additional *karma*. He only burns the negative merit which led to a birth as an animal. A hypothetical original status is then restored, but how is it possible to say that spiritual progress has been made? The goat in our story considers itself lucky merely to resume life as a Brahmin (to kill goats yet again?). This is all based on the assumption, universally accepted except in extraordinary circumstances, that we cannot recall our previous births.

B. Imagine that for habitually kicking your dog you are reborn as a leper.[14] Not once but ten times. Each life you lead as a leper you acquire additional merit (good *karma*) and additional demerit. Hence, each of these ten lives produces yet additional births. Even if through remorse you tend to act morally as a leper, you are still producing additional births that must be lived before you can resume the second then third lives as a leper, and so forth. Regardless of the precise sequence of lives, and regardless of the moral qualities of life, the process, like nuclear fission, is nearly endless. *karma* becomes a horrifying mechanism to perpetuate an unending lateral movement, which Indians call *saṁsāra*. Even under the best of circumstances there is little here to rejoice. As one Upaniṣad puts its, 'Considering sacrifice and good works as the best, these fools know no higher good, and having enjoyed their reward on the height of heaven gained by good works, they enter again this world, or a lower one'.[15]

C. Equally devastating, how can we exercise absolute moral control over our life in a world populated by constantly and indiscriminatly interacting karmic nexuses ('individuals')? Was the Brahmin condemned to be responsible for the goat's death by his (the Brahmin's) own acts or by the act of the goat (formerly a Brahmin), as the story indicates? If the latter, how can that be morally more satisfying than the quirks of fate? If the former, then moral conduct clearly has no bearing on karmic destiny:

Once informed, the Brahmin did the right thing (for whatever reason) and cannot be held karmically responsible for the consequences. Wendy O'Flaherty has characterised *karma* as the metaphor for the effect that individuals have on the life of others.[16] As an absolute generalisation, this may be extreme, but even granted the autonomy and karmic efficacy of our moral judgements and actions, it is theoretically and practically impossible to act in a manner that is completely free of other people's *karma*. Thus, while *karma* may be valid as a general natural principle, it is useless to attempt to chart individual karmic progress.

Finally, all major Hindu and Buddhist philosophical schools share one fundamental premise: *karma* and *saṁsāra* can never act as conditioning factors or causes for spiritual liberation. On the contrary, as the *Naiṣkarmyasiddhi,* an Advaita Vedānta work, puts it, *Avidyā* (ignorance) is the failure to understand that there is but one Self. Its seed is *saṁsāra*, its destruction is liberation (*mokṣa*), and this result comes from understanding the sentences of the Upaniṣads. The result does not come from action, since knowledge and action are incompatible'.[17] If *saṁsāra* is to serve as any generalised paradigm, it must be a metaphor for our perpetual ignorance of the true nature of reality, as Hick puts it, ego-centredness. The central feature of Indian philosophy is that action (*karma*) and insight are contradictory because it is action, and the impetus to act (*mithyājñāna*-false awareness) which bounds us in perpetual rebirth.

In Buddhist terms the matter is put differently. *Prajñā* or wisdom is the ability to penetrate the 'own-being' (*svabhāva*) of reality by cutting through the darkness of delusion.[18] This is a major step in the right direction. A Buddhist will cultivate such insight, and will follow the rigorous path of *dharma*. But he is still subject to the process of dependent co-origination, he is still within the realm of conditioned reality. To be sure, he becomes enriched, refined, his mind expands and his awareness deepens, but the Buddhist, as long as he aspires for the idea of Liberation, will still be reborn. Ultimately the path to *nirvāṇa*, the absolute non-conditioned reality, becomes open only when one turns his back on all conditioned things (*dharmas*), even the very thought of 'attaining' *nirvāṇa*:

Because it is so very clear,
It takes longer to come to the realization.

If you know at once candlelight is fire,
The meal has long been cooked.[19]

In sum, *karma* and *saṁsāra* are astonishingly fertile metaphors for
the dynamics of a corporeal self that acts and undergoes experiences
within the world. However, as metaphysical and moral theories that
may be utilised to rationalise future births they are logically problematic. As optimistic religious teleologies they would have to be
thoroughly 'de-Indianised'. We may be highly impressed by the
evidence which Ian Stevenson marshals in support of rebirth, but we
cannot ground the conceptual framework for his and other's hypotheses on the Indian doctrines of *karma* and rebirth.[20] Thus, the mere
fact of rebirth has little bearing on our pursuit for reality-centredness.

Notes

1. Joseph Prabhu, 'The Idea of Reincarnation', (working paper) pp. 66–7.
2. Ibid, p. 67.
3. Cf. J. Bruce Long, 'The Concepts of Human Action and Rebirth in the
   Mahābhārata', in Wendy Doniger O'Flaherty (ed.) *Karma and Rebirth
   in Classical Indian Traditions* (Berkeley: University of California Press,
   1980) p. 40.
4. Cf. Lawrence Babb, 'Destiny and Responsibility: Karma in Popular
   Hinduism', in Charles F. Keyes and E. Valentine Daniel (eds) *Karma,
   An Anthropological Inquiry* (Berkeley: University of California Press,
   1983) pp. 163–81; Kathleen E. Gough, 'Caste in a Tanjore Village', in E.
   R. Leach (ed.) *Aspects of Caste in South India, Ceylon and North-West
   Pakistan* (Cambridge: Cambridge University Press, 1960) pp. 11–60.
5. Babb, op. cit., p. 166.
6. E. B. Cowel, trans, *The Buddha-karita* SBE 49 (Oxford: Clarendon
   Press, 1894) p. 145.
7. Ibid., p. 6 (I.34).
8. *Lotus Sūtra*, quoted in Diana Paul, *Women in Buddhism* (Berkeley:
   Asian Humanities, 1979) p. 107.
9. Cf. Edward Conze, *Buddhist Thought in India* (Ann Arbor Paperbacks,
   1967) pp. 121–58; James P. McDermott, 'Karma and Rebirth in Early
   Buddhism', in W. O'Flaherty (ed.) *Karma and Rebirth* op. cit., pp.
   165–92.
10. The doctrinal distinction among schools is often critical as when the
    Visuddhimagga of Buddhaghosa speaks of an instantaneous transfer of
    consciousness to a new embryo (*patisandhi viññāna*), while Aśvaghosa

speaks of hells (*niraya*) and heaven (*devā*). Vasubandhu discusses other forms of an intermediate state (*antarā-bhava*).

11. Prabhu, op. cit., p. 69.
12. E. B. Cowel (ed.) *The Jātaka, or Stories of the Buddha's Former Births* (London: Luzac & Company, 1957).
13. Ibid. pp. 51–3.
14. Cf *Manu Smṛti*, XI.53.
15. *Muṇḍaka Upaniṣad*, 1.2.10.
16. W. O'Flaherty, 'Karma and Rebirth in the Vedas and Puranas', in O'Flaherty (ed.), *Karma and Rebirth*, op. cit., p. 29.
17. Karl H. Potter, *Encyclopedia of Indian Philosophies,* Advaita Vedānta up to Śaṃkara and His Pupils (Princeton University Press, 1981) p.531.
18. Buddhaghosa's *Visuddhimagga*, op. cit., XIV.7.
19. Zenkei Shibayama, *Zen Comments on the Mumonkan* (New York: Harper & Row, 1974) p. 67.
20. Ian Stevenson, *Twenty Cases Suggestive of Reincarnation* (New York: American Society for Psychical Research, 1966).

4 Life After Death, Parapsychology, and Post-Modern Animism
David Ray Griffin

In this essay I discuss the metaphysical possibility of life after death, and the empirical evidence for it, on the basis of a position I call 'post-modern animism'. Animism is something we have all, as moderns, been taught to reject. In the first part of the essay, I point out some of the problems with the anti-animistic starting point of modern philosophy, thereby suggesting that it is time to give a hearing to animism after these three modern centuries during which it has been taboo. I then briefly describe a post-modern form of animism. In the second part, I explain how this position overcomes the modern prejudice against the possibility of life after death, and hence against even looking at the evidence for it. In this second part I also mention some ways in which parapsychological phenomena provide indirect evidence for life after death. In the third part, I look very briefly at some of the direct evidence for life after death.

MODERN ANTI-ANIMISM AND POST-MODERN ANIMISM

Modern thought and sensibility discourage belief in life after death because the modern worldview does not allow for it. Most modern thinkers would say that belief in life after death is discouraged by modern thought because it is empirical, insisting on evidence for our beliefs, and that there is simply no good evidence for the survival of bodily death. However, most people who reject belief in life after death are not even familiar with the evidence there is for it, so that they cannot possibly judge whether it is good or not. The modern denial of life after death is much less of an empirical than an *a priori* metaphysical claim. Modern thought has, on the basis of an *a priori* claim that the human personality could not possibly survive the death of its physical body, discouraged people from even considering the evidence for such survival. In most academic circles, even to look open-mindedly at the evidence leads to a loss of reputation.

'Modern' is used here as a technical term to refer to thought and sensibility that is based upon the modern worldview of atheistic, reductionistic, mechanistic materialism. More precisely, this is the second version of the modern worldview. The first version of the modern worldview was supernaturalistic, dualistic mechanism. The problems inherent in this worldview led to its collapse into the second version, which has become increasingly dominant in westernised intellectual circles since the eighteenth century.

The common element in the two versions of modernity was an anti-animistic, mechanistic view of nature. Nature was thought to be composed of bits of matter which were devoid of (a) the power to perceive or experience in any sense, (b) the power of self-movement or self-determination, and (c) the power to act or be acted upon at a distance. This threefold denial of power to the elementary particles composing nature constituted the main planks of the mechanistic programme. Nature was inanimate. Each unit of nature was portrayed as a passive entity that could be moved, like a part of a watch, only by contact. Because each unit was devoid of the power of self-movement, it could only be moved from without; because it was devoid of the power of perception, it could not be moved by something at a distance, but only by the force transmitted by some contiguous entity. Accordingly, nature in its entirety was a machine.

This mechanistic view of nature required that the *natural world* could not be equated with the *world as a whole* if certain empirical facts were to be accounted for. Since we human beings perceive, and exercise self-determination or self-movement, there has to be something with this twofold power. Hence the existence of the soul. Since there is motion in nature that is not caused by us, and since motion is not inherent to matter, there must be something with the power to have imparted motion to matter. Hence the existence of God. Furthermore, matter did occasionally seem to be acted upon at a distance, such as in some of the extraordinary events reported in the New Testament and the lives of the saints. Since this kind of causality could not happen naturally, it had to be due to a supernatural agent, who could interrupt the laws of nature. This could occur, it was believed, since God had created matter *ex nihilo* and imposed the laws of motion upon it. That which has been freely imposed can be freely interrupted. God was not the soul of the world. Hence nature was not an organism, and the world was in no way necessary to God. God was the external creator of nature as a machine.

Because of problems inherent in this supernaturalistic dualism, it soon evolved into atheistic materialism. Whereas Descartes and Newton both held that the human soul or mind moved its body, and that the body in turn influenced the mind, the total difference in kind between material and spiritual substances made this interaction difficult to conceive. As long as supernaturalistic theism seemed unproblematic, the mind-body problem could be solved by appeal to God's omnipotence, as it was, for example, by Descartes, Leibniz, Malebranche and Thomas Reid. But this supernaturalism became increasingly implausible for a variety of reasons (such as the problem of evil, the decline in belief in miracles, and the evidence against supernatural inspiration of the Bible); supernaturalistic theism was soon replaced by deism, then by complete atheism. The mind-body problem could no longer be solved by appeal to God. For this and other reasons, a more or less fully materialistic doctrine of the human being emerged, according to which the mind or soul was not a distinct, active substance. Fully materialistic positions have thought of the mind or soul as identical with the brain, that is, with certain of its functions. Half-way between dualism and identism has been 'epiphenomenalism', according to which the mind or soul is a non-efficacious by-product of the brain. It has the power to perceive, but not the power to initiate any movement, at least in the physical world. In any case, with the decline of dualism, the soul was no longer conceived to be a full-fledged actuality.

This mechanistic materialism, while apparently avoiding the problem of mind-body interaction, creates several problems of its own. In the first place, it does not really avoid the mind-body problem. It regards the physical world, including the cells of our brains, as wholly devoid of experience, and regards our own conscious subjectivity as a quality that has emerged out of the complex organisation of physical cells. But how subjectivity can 'emerge' out of wholly objective things is as mysterious as how subjects and wholly objective things can interact. The alleged emergence of something that is something for itself out of things that are merely objects for others is *different in kind* from all the other examples of emergence which are used an analogues (such as the emergence of wetness, or feathers). In the second place, mechanistic materialism generally claims to be an empirical philosophy, yet it denies many of the most fundamental presuppositions of our experience. We presuppose that we are partially free while it says that our experience and behaviour are totally determined by antecedent causes. We presuppose that there are certain objective values, that some things are really better than others, while it denies that there are any objective values, at least that we can know that there are. We also presuppose the existence of an external world, the past, and of causality, but it says that the only type of perception we have is sensory perception, which gives us no knowledge of these things (as Hume and then Santayana even more clearly saw). This sensationalist, materialistic philosophy also leads to an *a priori*, unempirical rejection of all phenomena that seem to involve non-sensory perception or any other form of influence at a distance.

There are several reasons for questioning the modern view of matter as insentient and inanimate. The first reason has just been summarised: it leads either to dualism or to materialism, both of which are philosophically indefensible. A second reason is that, as recent historical studies have shown, the anti-animistic philosophy was adopted for sociological and theological reasons, not on the basis of empirical evidence.[1] In the third place, once dualism and supernaturalism were rejected, the movement in the world could only be explained if matter were self-moving. In any case, there is increasing reason to think of the ultimate constituents of nature as animate, in the sense of self-moving, energetic things. The billiard-ball model of atoms has been exploded. The convertibility of matter and energy in fact implies the rejection of the view of matter as passive. If we think of the ultimate units of nature as analogous to our souls or minds in being self-moving things, it is natural to think of them as perceiving things also. It is hard to conceive of a self-moving thing that is devoid of an 'inside', of experience, altogether.

The philosophy of Alfred North Whitehead and Charles Hartshorne provides the basis for a post-modern animistic philosophy. This viewpoint differs from most pre-modern animisms in three ways. First, the power of perception and self-movement is not attributed to things such as rocks, lakes, and suns. A distinction is made between individuals and aggregates of individuals. Only true individuals are self-moving, perceiving things. Most visible things hence are not animate (although their constituents are). The only visible animate things (aside from the universe as a whole) would probably be animals which, as their name implies, have an *anima* which gives the organism as a whole the power of perception and self-movement.

A second way in which this post-modern animism differs from most pre-modern forms is that radically different levels of *anima* are assumed. To have experience is not necessarily to have *conscious* experience, let alone *self-consciousness*. Most of the experiences in the universe are unconscious. Also, an organism's power of self-determination can be extremely limited. The organism can be almost totally determined by the past, so that its degree of self-determination is negligible for most purposes.

In the third place, whereas all pre-modern animisms (except Buddhism) thought of the basic units of the world as enduring souls, post-modern animism takes the basic units to be momentary experiences. The ultimate units are 'occasions of experience'. This distinction is important with regard to the question of causal interaction. When the basic units were thought of as enduring souls, it was hard to understand how the within of things could affect the outer, perceivable world. Most animistic or panpsychist philosophies held to parallelism, according to which the inside and outside moved along in parallel with each other, but without influencing each other. Since our inner experience of free self-determination was hence said not to influence the outer world, these philosophies were ultimately deterministic (for example, Leibniz, Bernard Rensch, Sewell Wright). In post-modern animism, a unit is first an experiencing subject exercising self-determination, then an experienced object exercising efficient causation. Hence, the efficient causation of individuals is based upon some degree or another of self-determination. Also, the more power of self-determination exercised by an experience, the more efficient causation it exerts.

Four features of this post-modern animism must be emphasised before applying it to the issues of parapsychology and life after death. One crucial feature is that the human mind or soul is *numerically distinct* from the brain but *not ontologically different* from the cells making up the brain. This is hence *non-dualistic interactionism*. It is important to distinguish interactionism from dualism. In most discussions of interactionism, both by advocates and by critics, this distinction is not made. This is in part because the most famous form of interactionism was Cartesian dualism. Descartes said that the mind was not only numerically distinct from the brain (the brain was one thing, the mind was another), but also ontologically different (the brain was one *kind* of thing, the mind was *another kind*). The ontological dualism was what created problems for interactionism. The collapse of dualistic interactionism led to non-dualistic identism, in which the brain and mind are said not only to be ontologically similar (the same *kind* of things) but also numerically identical (the *same thing*). It is its numerical identism that makes this form of non-dualism untenable. Because modern thinkers have assumed that the basic units of nature were insentient, they for the most part have ignored the fact that there is a third, mediating position: non-dualistic interactionism. Since the cells composing the brain are sentient, they are not ontologically different in kind from the experiencing mind. But the mind is not numerically identical with the brain. The mind is one thing, while the brain is another thing – or, more precisely, an aggregate of billions of things. The mind or soul is a temporal society of very high-level occasions of experience, each of which unifies the myriad data received from the many brain cells into a subjective unity of experience. Each cell is a temporal society of medium-level occasions of experience, doing the same thing on a lower level.

A second feature of this post-modern animism that must be emphasised here is that sensory perception is not the basic form of perception. Every individual, whether it has sensory organs or not, perceives its environment, in the sense of taking influence from other things into itself. Even *our* experience is not fundamentally sensory. For me to see the objects in front of my face presupposes that my soul has perceived my brain cells, thereby receiving the data from the outside world that have been transmitted through the optic nerve. Those data have been transmitted up the optic nerve by a series of non-sensory perceptions. Sensory perception is a very high-level, specialised type of perception which may or may not occur; non-sensory perception is going on all the time, in us and in all other individuals.

A third feature of this post-modern animism especially relevant to our topic is that various *animas* or souls have various degrees of power. As indicated earlier, higher-level individuals have more power to determine themselves and more power to exert upon others. An amoeba has more power than an atom, a canine soul more power than an amoeba, and a human soul more than a canine. Also, some human beings evidently have more soul-power than others. Some are hence more transcendent over the power of the past and the contemporary environment than others; some also have more power than others to influence their bodies, for example, in bringing about psychosomatic illness and health. Hence, the epiphenomenalistic doctrine that the soul is a passive by-product of the body is even less true for some human beings than it is for others.

A fourth and final feature of post-modern animism to emphasise involves its view of divinity. Its naturalistic theism distinguishes it from both atheistic naturalism and supernaturalistic theism. God is the soul of the universe, that unity of experience and agency which makes the universe a unity. To call this theism 'naturalistic' means that the fundamental relations between God and the world are natural features of reality, belonging to the very nature of things, not arbitrary features, based upon divine volition. Therefore, the most general principles according to which the units of nature, including the units of human experience, operate are not principles that can be arbitrarily suspended from time to time. The crucial difference from classical theism is that all creative power is not thought to belong to God alone. Creativity, or power in the most general sense (more general than the physicist's 'energy'), belongs equally to God and to a realm of finite beings. God influences all finite events, but totally determines none of them, since they are influenced by all previous finite events as well, and also have their own power of self-determination. Hence, the relative autonomy of the world is not based upon a voluntary self-limitation on the part of divine omnipotence, which could be suspended now and then; it is an inherent feature of reality. If extraordinary events happen, they are not 'miracles' in the sense of events in which the normal worldly causation is replaced by direct divine causation. 'Extraordinary' cannot mean 'supernatural'.

I turn now to the relevance of this post-modern worldview to the question of life after death.

Modern thought and sensibility discourage belief in life after death on the basis of three mutually-reinforcing claims: life after death is impossible; there is no evidence for it; and it is a bad thing to believe in anyway. The claim that it is impossible supports the claim about lack of evidence by ruling out all possible evidence in advance. The lack of empirical evidence is then used to buttress the claim about metaphysical impossibility. Also, since we usually like to make a virtue out of a necessity, the claim that it is impossible to believe in life after death leads us to say that we are better off to be rid of that belief anyway. Likewise, since we are also good at making the wish the father of the thought, the claim that it is better not to believe in life after death supports in turn the claim that it is impossible.

Post-modern thought and sensibility encourage belief in life after death, challenging the three claims on which modernity based its rejection. The post-modern worldview allows for the possibility of life after death. It thereby allows us to look seriously at the evidence for it, which turns out, surprisingly, to be rather good. On the question of the desirability of the belief, a post-modern sensibility recognises some truth in modernity's claim, but is more impressed by the undesirable effects of the *loss* of belief in life after death.

For the purposes of this paper I will presuppose a positive answer to this question of desirability. I deal only with the question of the possibility of a post-modern belief in life after death, and the question of evidence for it.

THE POSSIBILITY OF LIFE AFTER DEATH

Whereas the modern worldview rules out a non-supernaturalistic doctrine of life after death *a priori*, this *a priori* objection is overcome by post-modern animism in conjunction with some empirical evidence which it allows to be taken seriously.

Modern materialism, which implies the 'identist' view that the soul (or mind) is identical with the brain, obviously rules out any naturalistic belief in life after death: there is no soul to continue on while the brain decays. Some philosophers and theologians have claimed that materialistic identism rules out only 'immortality of the soul', but not life after death in the sense of 'resurrection of the body', which is, they claim, the authentically Biblical doctrine anyway. However, a literal resurrection of the material body – cells, molecules, atoms, and all – would require an act of God that would be supernaturalistic in the strongest sense of the term. Hence, materialism is compatible with belief in life after death only if it is part of a supernaturalistic worldview, which is to say, if it is not materialism at all. Materialism rules out God and miracles as firmly as it does a non-physical soul. As long as a materialistic worldview reigns, life after death will seem impossible.

Although modern dualism might seem to provide support for the possibility of life after death, it does not provide good support. Dualism agrees with the materialist's view of the human body, but insists that the human soul is something different in kind from the body. As such, it can be presumed to be naturally immortal. Or as most dualistic theologians would prefer to say, the soul's difference from the body allows God to conserve it in existence after the body's death without the supernaturalism that would be entailed by resurrection of the body. However, dualism could provide a basis from which to defend life after death only if dualism were itself defensible, but it is not. Because the idea of interaction between two different types of substances, material and spiritual, is unintelligible, dualism tends to self-destruct into materialism. Also, in an evolutionary context, dualism entails that a sentient soul was created out of inanimate, insentient matter. This implies a supernatural creative act different at most in degree from that required to resurrect the physical body.

Furthermore, the dualistic argument by itself proves either too much or too little. If the human soul is taken to be immortal simply by virtue of being an active, experiencing thing, the dualist argument would seem to prove the immortality of the soul of chimpanzees and dolphins, and even cats and rats, which is usually more than the dualist theologian wants to prove. If the rat soul is not thought to be immortal, then the mere fact of having a soul, in the sense of an active, perceiving centre of awareness, does not by itself mean immortality. To support human and only human immortality the dualist could return to Descartes's extreme dualism, according to which only the human being has a soul and other 'animals' are devoid of *anima*, being merely insentient machines. But this absolute dualism between humans and other animals is hardly credible, especially in an evolutionary age. Or, the dualist can agree that other animals have souls, but say that God chooses to sustain only the human soul's post-mortem survival, or that God added something extra to the human soul to make it immortal. But if the dualist position requires these special acts of God, beyond the initial conjoining of sentient soul to insentient matter, its doctrine of the human soul's immortality seems to require as much supernatural divine activity as does the doctrine of the resurrection of the body.

Besides being inherently indefensible, and requiring considerable supernaturalism, modern dualism generally fails in other ways to provide good support for the immortality of the soul. In so far as it accepts the sensationalist epistemology, according to which the soul perceives the world beyond itself only by means of bodily sensory organs, modern dualism implies that a disembodied soul, even if it could exist, could not perceive anything else. That solipsistic mode of existence would not be much to write home about – which brings up another problem. Besides sensationalism, modern thought has accepted what can be called 'muscularism', by which I mean the idea that we can act on the world beyond ourselves only by means of our voluntary nervous system, primarily our muscular system. Accordingly, modern thought implies that, even if the soul could somehow exist apart from its body, it would not be able to influence anything beyond itself, which is a state few of us would anticipate with enthusiasm. Besides its sensationalism and muscularism, modern dualism tends to be epiphenomenalistic, or at least at the epiphenomenal end of the interactionist spectrum. The soul is thereby portrayed as having so little power that its active existence apart from the body is inconceivable.

Modern liberal theology, in so far as it accepts the modern worldview, but rejects the idea of supernatural interventions by God, cannot convincingly support a belief in life after death. The modern worldview, as its supernaturalistic founders intended, cannot support the belief in life after death apart from a supernatural act of God. Also, apart from supernaturalism, the incoherence of dualism leads it toward materialism, which makes life after death even more inconceivable.

Because of its difference from modern materialism and dualism, post-modern animism allows life after death to be affirmed on a naturalistic basis.

Because the soul is not numerically identical with the brain, *contra* materialism, the soul can in principle be thought to live after the death of the body.

Because the soul is not ontologically different in kind from the brain, that is, from the cells making up the brain, the numerical distinction between the brain and the soul does not raise the dualist's insoluble problem of interaction. Hence, animistic interactionism, unlike dualistic interactionism, is not subject to collapse into materialistic identism.

Because the soul's perception of the world around it is not only, or even primarily, sensory perception, a soul separated from its physical body's sensory apparatus could still be capable of perception. While in the body the soul's perception of the outside world by means of its bodily sensory organs presupposes the soul's perception of its body itself, especially its brain, and this perception is not sensory. Also, the present moment of the soul perceives its past moments, a type of perception that we call 'memory', and this perception is not sensory.

The soul's direct perception of God, through which it learns of the reality of moral and aesthetic norms, as well as enjoying 'religious experience' in the stricter sense, is not sensory experience.

These considerations suggest that a soul existing apart from its body could at least remember its past experiences and have new experiences of God. In a state freed from fresh stimulation from a physical body, the perception of both God and one's own past might be considerably more intense than it had normally been before. In this situation, reviewing its past in the light of a numinous experience of the Holy One, the soul might well transform itself quite radically. Indeed, reports of near-death experiences generally speak of a life-review and of being in the presence of a numinous reality.

Furthermore, post-modern animism provides a basis for believing that a discarnate soul could continue to have fresh experiences of other finite beings. It suggests that we *directly* perceive all beings in our environment, not just those that are spatially contiguous with us. Hence the soul, besides directly perceiving its own body, also directly perceives other bodies and other souls. This perception usually does not rise to consciousness, being blocked out by our more intense perception of our own past, our own body, and the sensory data about the surrounding world supplied by the body's sensory organs. However, these other parts of the world are always being perceived, and there is no reason in principle why the soul could not become consciously aware of them. That exceptional type of perception to which the term 'extra-sensory' is usually applied is exceptional *not* because it involves non-sensory perception, since non-sensory perception is going on all the time. It is exceptional only because someone has become consciously aware of the objects of a type of perception that remains at the unconscious level most of the time.

The evidence from parapsychology supports this viewpoint.[2] In the first place, both controlled experiments and responsible reports of spontaneous phenomena over the past hundred years provide overwhelming evidence for the reality of extra-sensory perception (ESP). The two major forms, telepathy, meaning the direct perception of the contents of another soul, and clairvoyance, meaning the direct perception of other physical objects or situations, are about equally supported, both experimentally and spontaneously. (Technically, 'clairvoyance' means having visual-like images of objects, and would be distinguished from, say, clairaudience; but 'clairvoyance' is commonly used to refer to any knowledge of physical things acquired without sensory means.) In the second place, there is some evidence for the view that telepathy and clairvoyance are occurring all the time, and that it is only *conscious* extra-sensory perception that is extra-ordinary or paranormal. (Parapsychologists would therefore be much more likely to find the long-sought regularly repeatable experiment if they would turn away from conscious ESP, to which 99.9 per cent of the effort has been devoted, and concentrate instead on tests for unconscious ESP.)

In a post-incarnate state the soul's extra-sensory perception would take the place of sensory perceptions as the major source of knowledge about the surrounding world. Once the soul was not receiving sensory data from its body, its non-sensory perceptions might become much more conscious, regular, and reliable. There is also the possibility, much supported in occult and religious literature, including St Paul's letters, that we have more than one 'body', so that the soul's separation from its physical-biological body would not necessarily leave it *completely* 'disembodied'. Another, subtler body might provide some means of perception. Whatever the merits of this view, it does not seem necessary to the possibility of perception apart from the biological body.

Besides undermining the sensationalist argument against disembodied perception, post-modern animism and parapsychology also provide an answer to the 'muscularist' objection that a discarnate soul, even if it could exist and perceive, could not act, at least not so as to exert causal influence on anything beyond itself. In an animistic framework 'perception' and 'causal influence' are simply two perspectives on the same event. What is causal influence from the perspective of the cause is perception from the perspective of the effect. The soul is able consciously to influence the body's muscular system only because the bodily cells of this system perceive the conscious aims of the soul for its bodily parts; the soul unconsciously affects the body in so far as the bodily cells perceive its unconscious feelings. Likewise, the body influences the soul in so far as the soul perceives the feelings of its various bodily cells. To be perceived *is* to exert causal influence. Hence, if it is possible for souls in a discarnate state to perceive each other, which was established above, it is by definition possible for them to influence each other.

This philosophical deduction from the animistic viewpoint is empirically supported by psychosomatic and parapsychological evidence. Psychosomatic studies show that the soul's influence on its body is not limited to the muscular system; the bodily cells in general seem to be responsive to the soul's aims and other feelings. Phenomena such as stigmata show how strong the soul's influence on its 'involuntary' system can be. But, since we are inclined to take the soul's influence on its body for granted, seeing it as somehow built into the nature of things and in any case as an example of causation between contiguous things, the evidence for psychokinesis is more important. Psychokinesis is influence exerted by the soul (psyche) on material things outside the body without the mediation of the body. Since most of the founders of parapsychology (or, to use the more general term, psychical research) were dualists, psychokinesis has been radically distinguished from 'thought-transference', which is simply telepathy from the perspective of the sender. From an animist (or panpsychist) standpoint there is no difference in kind between thought-transference and psychokinesis (so we do not have to worry, as some dualistic parapsychologists do, whether to refer to the influence of the human mind on plants as telepathy – as the term 'plant perception' implies – or as psychokinesis; it is both). In any case there is well-documented evidence of the ability of the human soul to exert influence on inanimate things, such as dice, geiger counters, photographic film, weighing scales, cloud chambers, and living organisms such as bacteria and plants, as well as other human minds. This suggests that a soul existing apart from its physical body would be able to influence not only God and other souls, but also other things as well. (From an animist standpoint, any 'other things', however different they might be from the objects of our present sensory experience, would likewise be composed of units of experience.)

Evidence for out-of-body experiences[3] supports the above conclusion that the soul could perceive and act apart from its physical body, if it can exist apart from it, and possibly the belief that it *can* exist apart from it. People report perceiving things from a perspective more or less removed from the standpoint of their bodies, and seeming really to be there. They are also sometimes perceived by others, animals as well as humans, as being there at the time that they themselves seemed to be there. So there is evidence that they can at least influence human and animal souls who are at the places where they themselves seem to be, at some remove from their bodies. In some cases, they also seem to have brought about physical changes. The reality of their perceiving and being perceived from that out-of-body standpoint can be verified. What is notoriously difficult to ascertain is whether the soul is literally out of the body when it phenomenologically seems to the soul itself to be so, or whether it simply is exercising clairvoyant and psychokinetic power while imagining that it is out of the body. It is also difficult to know if this distinction makes any ultimate sense, that is, whether there is any difference between only *seeming* to be somewhere spatially removed from one's own body, while perceiving the world from that stand-point and producing effects there, and *really* being there. (This question involves the mystery of what 'space' is, and in what sense a soul or an individual experience can be said to be spatially located. In comparison with time, I for one find space – in so far as the two can be distinguished – much more mysterious.)

In any case, out-of-body experiences provide evidence for the twofold capacity of the soul to perceive and act without employing its bodily organism, and *some* evidence, of a less conclusive nature, for the capacity of the soul to exist apart from that organism, at least temporarily.

There is a sense in which the capacity of the soul to perceive without the body's mediation, and its capacity to exist without the body, are the same. To exist is to receive influences from other experiences, to make a self-actualising response to those influences, and to contribute influence to subsequent experiences. Nothing else exists that is more basic or more real than this everlasting reception, self-creation, and contribution of experiences. The soul and its experiences are not 'mental' things in distinction from 'physical' things which can exist apart from mental things but apart from which mental things cannot exist. That dualism between two different types of things is precisely what is rejected by post-modern animism. It is true that 'mentality' presupposes 'physicality'. But that distinction applies to each unit of which the world is composed. Each moment-ary unit of experience, whether it be a moment in the life-history of a human soul or of a cell or a molecule, has a physical and a mental aspect. The physical aspect is its reception of influences from previous units of experience. The mental aspect is its self-determining response to its physical aspect. Because a moment of human expe-rience has so much more capacity for free self-determination than does a moment of cellular or molecular experience, it has much more mentality. But it is not *fully* mental. In fact, there is a sense in which a moment of human experience is able to receive much more influence into itself than can those more lowly experiences. It is indeed precisely this greater capacity to be significantly constituted by direct influences from a wider range of other experiences which raises the possibility that the soul could continue to exist after it is no longer receiving influences from its bodily source of experience. This wider range of influences can perhaps constitute the physical base needed for the soul's continued existence. Hence, evidence for the extra-bodily influences on the soul is *ipso facto* evidence for the possibility of the soul's extra-bodily survival.

There is another dimension of post-modern animism that supports the possibility of the survival of the human *anima* apart from its body: the human soul has not only much more receptive power than other creatures, but much more power, period. It is because of the much greater self-actualising and contributory power of human souls that they are able to constitute a demonic power, strongly opposing the purposes of its creator. *This same quantum increase in power may also allow human souls to survive in the universe apart from the kind of body that was originally necessary to bring them about.* In other words, the power that allows us to be demonic also allows us to be angelic. There is truth in the mythological notion that the devil is a fallen angel.

The idea that the human soul has the unique power to survive apart from the body that first allowed it to emerge does not imply dualism. The human soul is only different in degree, not different in kind, from the souls of other animals. But it is possible for a difference in degree to bring about a radically new capacity, so radically new that it virtually amounts to a difference in kind. The human capacity for symbolic language constitutes such a difference. It *is* a difference in degree: the other higher animals are not devoid of a capacity for symbols (as distinct from mere signals), as had previously been thought. Nevertheless, the human capacity for language has been accompanied by an increase in self-actualising and contributory power of such magnitude that the effect of human power on the planet has been qualitatively different from that of all other species. (The recent realisation that this is a deeply ambiguous fact does not alter its truth.) In the same way, a difference in degree developed by the human soul some time in its evolutionary advance could have given it the unique capacity to survive separation from its body. In fact, I suggest that the human soul's unique degree of power to use language, its power for self-consciousness, and its power to survive apart from its body emerged at the same time – and in fact are one and the same power. If so, it was when human beings first asked, 'If a human being dies, will he or she live again?' that it was first true.

Because this idea of immortality does not require an ontological dualism between the human *anima* and that of other animals, it does not require any supernatural act of God. The emergence of the human capacity for language, self-consciousness, and survival is simply one more radical emergence brought about by the persuasive, evocative activity of God, not different in kind from several previous divinely wrought emergences in the evolutionary process. Each of these emergences has involved an incorporation of novel forms which were primordially located in the divine appetition. By whetting the appetite of the creatures for these forms, thereby incarnating these divine forms in the world, God has increasingly deified the world. The immortality of the human soul has been effected by its deification.

Because the immortality of the soul, meaning its natural capacity to exist apart from the physical body, is rooted in God's creative activity, the strong contrast often drawn between 'immortality' and 'resurrection' does not obtain. Both terms are needed. 'Resurrection' brings out the idea that the new life of the person beyond the body is rooted in God's creative activity – both God's past activity, in which the soul was sufficiently deified to make its post-mortem continuation a real possibility, and God's present deifying activity, in which new aims attract the soul into this new mode of existence. 'Immortality' brings out the idea that no supernatural divine action is involved, that the soul enters this new mode of existence on the basis of a fully natural, albeit divinely-rooted, capacity.

Each of these terms also has its false connotations. It is difficult to disassociate the term 'resurrection' from the idea of the resuscitation of the physical corpse, long decayed and dispersed. And the term 'immortality' suggests literally endless life – a billion trillion years would be only a beginning – whereas 'survivability' is all that we have evidence for, all that we can conceive, and all that, upon reflection, we can desire for ourselves and others – a journey that continues until this finite form of existence reaches fulfilment.

EVIDENCE FOR LIFE AFTER DEATH

For those who will examine it with the presupposition that it might be genuine, there is impressive evidence for human survival of bodily death.[4] This topic, which needs a book-length treatment in itself, can only be touched on here with irresponsible brevity.

Some of the most impressive evidence comes from near-death experiences.[5] Besides their out-of-body feature, they often involve encounters with a 'welcoming committee' which sometimes includes people of whose death the person did not previously know. Cross-cultural studies show that the series of events is very similar among people with vastly different cultural and religious beliefs, which suggests that this is a 'natural' phenomenon. Efforts to explain near-death experiences away pharmacologically or as an evolutionary adaptation have been unsuccessful. When approached with the presupposition that the soul *might* continue after the death of its body, studies of these reported experiences provide good reason to consider them authentic reports of what the first moments of that continuing journey is often like.

Apparitions of recently deceased persons are quite common.[6] They are especially impressive when information is learned through the apparition that can be independently verified and for which there had been no ordinary way of knowing – for example, that the person who appeared had died, and how the death occurred. There is no way of ruling out the possibility that the person to whom the apparition appeared had learned of the death of the other person through unconscious ESP, then produced a hallucination by which this knowledge could become conscious. (This explanation can also not be ruled out in near-death experiences of the 'welcoming committee' mentioned above.) However, such explanations can become so complex, especially in cases where the apparition appears to several people, as to lead one to conclude that a hypothesis based on survival is less implausible. Also, explanations requiring what is sometimes called 'super-ESP' presuppose that the soul has just those powers needed to make its survival possible.

Cross-correspondences in mediumship materials have provided some of the evidence most difficult to explain away.[7] In the most famous case, purportedly originating from the spirits of men who had been leading members of the Society for Psychical Research in England around the turn of the century, several people were independently receiving material through automatic writing. None of them knew that the others were receiving material during the same period, yet the various messages only made sense after they were combined. The episode appears, *prima facie*, to have been the result of a plan formulated by clever souls who knew the ways in which most mediumistic phenomena could be explained away.

Although reincarnation-type phenomena had long been despised among psychical researchers in the west, Ian Stevenson has recently produced impeccable and extensive studies, based on evidence from a wide variety of cultures, which have provided strong evidence that reincarnation at least sometimes occurs.[8] The evidence consists not only of verifiable memories of the experiences of previously existing persons, but also of physical phenomena correlating with the memories, such as birthmarks at the place on the body where the other person was shot or stabbed. Of course, alternative explanations involving extraordinary psychosomatic, extra-sensory, and psychokinetic powers are always possible. But if one is asking for the most plausible interpretation, and has a philosophy that in principle allows a reincarnational interpretation to be plausible, then the data provide some evidence for reincarnation as a form of the soul's continuing journey that at least sometimes occurs.

SUMMARY

In summary: the modern denial of life after death has been based less on evidence, or lack of evidence, than on the *a priori* conviction that it is impossible. This *a priori* conviction has followed from the outworking of the anti-animistic starting point of modern philosophy. Although originally part and parcel of a dualistic, supernaturalistic worldview, this anti-animistic view of nature eventuated in a materialistic, atheistic worldview. Being materialistic, this worldview forbad non-sensory perception, any other form of influence at a distance, and a mind or soul distinct from the material body. Hence, the belief that life after death might occur as a natural phenomenon, and any possible evidence therefor, were ruled out *a priori*. Also, being atheistic, this worldview ruled out the belief that life after death might be brought about supernaturally.

The emergence of a post-modern animism changes all this. Non-sensory perception and other forms of influence at a distance, through which evidence supportive of the possibility and actuality of life after death can be obtained, can occur naturally. The idea that the mind or soul is distinct from the brain does not imply an ontological dualism that would make mind-brain interaction unintelligible without appeal to a supernatural deity. Although the human soul is not ontologically different from the soul of other animals, it can be thought to have developed the unique capacity to survive apart from the biological body naturally, as a power that emerged in its evolutionary interaction with God.[9]

Notes

1. For the motives for the adoption of the mechanistic view summarised in the following paragraphs, see Carolyn Merchant, *The Death of Nature: Women, Ecology and the Scientific Revolution* (New York: Harper & Row, 1980); Eugene Klaaren, *Religious Origins of Modern Science: Belief in Creation in Seventeenth-Century Thought* (Grand Rapids: Eerdmans, 1977); J. R. Ravetz, 'The Varieties of Scientific Experience', Arthur Peacocke (ed.), *The Sciences and Theology in the Twentieth Century* (University of Notre Dame, 1981); Margaret C. Jacob, *The Newtonians and the English Revolution 1689–1720* (Cornell University Press, 1976); J. R. Jacob, *Robert Boyle and the English Revolution: A Study in Social and Intellectual Change* (New York: Franklin, Burt Publishers, 1978).

2. For the best overall survey of studies in a wide range of areas of parapsychological research, see Benjamin Wolman (ed.) *Handbook of Parapsychology* (New York: Von Nostrand, 1977). For the best accounts of recent work, see the series edited by Stanley Krippner, *Advances in Parapsychological Research*, especially vol. I, *Psychokinesis* (New York: Plenum, 1977), and vol. II, *Extrasensory Perception* (1978). For evaluations by capable philosophers, see Stephen Braude, *ESP and Psychokinesis: A Philosophical Examination* (Philadelphia: Temple University, 1980); C. D. Broad, *Religion, Philosophy and Psychical Research* (New York: Humanities, 1969); William James, *William James on Psychical Research*, Gardner Murphy and Robert Ballou (eds) (New York: Viking, 1960); Rene Sudré, *Parapsychology* (Secaucus, New Jersey: Citadel, 1960).

3. See D. Scott Rogo (ed.), *Mind Beyond the Body: The Mystery of ESP Projection* (New York: Penguin Books, 1978).

4. For surveys and evaluations of the various types of evidence, see F. W. H. Myers, *Human Personality and its Survival of Bodily Death* (London: Longmans, Green, 1903); Hornell Hart, *The Enigma of Survival: The Case For and Against Life After Death* (Springfield, Ill.: Charles C. Thomas, 1959); C. D. Broad, *Human Personality and the Possibility of its Survival* (Berkeley: University of California, 1955); C. J. Ducassee, *A Critical Examination of the Belief in Life after Death* (Springfield, Ill.: Charles C. Thomas, 1961).

5. See Raymond Moody, *Life after Life* (New York: Bantam, 1975); *Reflections on Life after Life* (New York: Bantam, 1977); and Karlis Osis and E. Haraldsson, *At the Hour of Death* (New York: Avon, 1977).

6. See Eleanor Sidgwick, *Phantasms of the Living* (Salem, NH: Ayer Co. Publishers, 1975); G. N. M. Tyrrell, *Apparitions* (London: Society for Psychical Research, 1942); and Celia Green and Charles McCreery, *Apparitions* (London: Hamish Hamilton, 1975).

7. See H. F. Saltmarsh, *Evidence of Personal Survival from Cross-Correspondences* (London: G. Bell, 1939).

8. See Ian Stevenson, *Twenty Cases Suggestive of Reincarnation* (University of Virginia, 1974); also the several volumes entitled *Cases of the Reincarnation Type*, the first volume of which was published in 1975.

9. The second half of this essay is essentially identical with the third and fourth sectors of 'Postmodern Animism and Life After Death,' which is chapter 6 of my *God and Religion in the Postmodern World: Essays in Postmodern Theology* (Albany: State University of New York, 1989). In that longer essay I treat also the question of the desirability of life after death.

The Soul in Modern Philosophy: A Response
Edward J. Hughes

In 'Life After Death, Parapsychology, and Post-Modern Animism', Professor David Griffin asserts that modern philosophy is anti-animistic (anti-soul). This attitude differs sharply from classical Greek or medieval Christian perspectives. Since modern philosophy is based on *a priori* metaphysical claims that take for granted the non-veridical nature of both religious and paranormal experience, his statement is difficult to seriously question. This bias has pragmatic import; for as Griffin correctly observes: 'In most academic circles, even to look open-mindedly at the evidence [for survival] leads to a loss of reputation' (p. 89).

This is a challenging accusation; for it questions the genuineness of philosophy's self-image as a discipline open to the radical exploration of presuppositions. Also, since reputation translates naturally into financial status, Griffin's charge implies that a subtle (unconscious?) pressure to avoid academic treatment of the issue intimidates those who would wish to explore the possibility of post-mortem survival.

This situation has a history which Griffin locates in the development over the last 400 years of the modern understanding of the concept of nature. The will to exclude the type of evidence for survival found in mystical and paranormal phenomena, experiences given significant ontological weight in cultures other than the modern west, emerges in the seventeenth and eighteenth centuries in the mechanistic world view common to Descartes, father of modern philosophy, and Newton, father of modern science. Griffin's article is post modern in its rejection of these assumptions. His thinking is heavily informed by the thought structures of process philosophy, which uses a highly specialised (some would say scholastic) vocabulary. It is therefore my purpose to present his ideas in more common language and then evaluate their significance for thinking about life after death.

In a mechanistic worldview nature was understood as an aggregate of bits of matter incapable of experience, self-movement or self-determination. In this model real work on portions of nature could only be done from without. Mind could not directly influence matter. Images taken from billiard behaviour and the grinding of gears predominated. There was, however, one exception to this rule, humanity. People experienced themselves as perceivers and movers, capable of self-determination. The perfect machine seemed to have a flaw; there was a ghost in the human portion. The inference then became necessary that something non-material was responsible for human activity, since a segment of nature was manifestly not capable of consciously directed activity.

If matter could only be acted upon from without, by that which was spatially contiguous, extraordinary or unusual phenomena such as telepathy, clairvoyance or healing at a distance had to be interpreted as supernatural by mechanistic thinkers within the Christian fold. Paranormal events reported in scripture were necessarily interpreted as violations of the laws of matter. The notion that these phenomena might be explained according to forces operating within nature was not available. One might contrast this position with that of the Hindu notion of *siddhis* or paranormal abilities explainable as intensifications of mental and bodily development within the orbit of nature, and therefore not supernatural. However, in the Christian instance the postulate of God resting outside his machine (creation) was necessary to explain paranormal phenomena, all of which fell now into the category of miracle. And in the doing of miracles God was *par excellence* the violator of his own natural laws.

In the world of the cosmic machine, soul and body (matter) were understood as two radically different substances whose interaction was difficult to comprehend. One might, like Descartes, surmise that a corridor existed in an area of the body that mysteriously bridged immaterial mind with measurable matter. In Descartes's case this proved to be the pituitary gland, an hypothetical location of brain/ mind interaction still taught in Rosicrucian circles. But another possibility existed. One could postulate an occasionalism wherein apparent causal relationships between body and mind were denied (Leibnitz and Malebranche). In such schemes mental and physical events are causally related only to themselves, not to each other. An apparent causal connection such as willing to move one's hands and bringing it to pass was explained by appealing to God's omnipotent ordering of a preordained psycho/physical parallelism. This approach, however, seems fantastic today given the ascendancy of the organismic view of mind/body interconnection. Also the common-sense theory of psychosomatic interaction which underlies psychiatric therapies has laid the axe to seriously considering occasionalism as a line option for the majority of modern thinkers.

Deism arose in the eighteenth century to supplant rational supernaturalism. God's role in miraculous interventions seemed arbitrary and the concept of miracle seemed contrary to the notion of a complete system of immanent law set in motion at the initial creation. The notion of a God who interacted with His creation became an intellectual liability. Not only were miracles in logical disrepute but the more common violations of a closed system experienced in the eruptions of grace in the life of prayer were discounted and explained away in psychological fashion. God thus became a *deus absconditus*, a hidden and inactive God, who was, from the viewpoint of experiential faith, no God at all. A God who could act neither on the material world nor in the souls of men seemed too unsubstantial for firm belief, and materialism with an attendant atheism won the minds of those committed to a scientific image of nature.

Yet problems accompanied the theory of mechanism. The system denied what seemed obvious to persons of common sense. For example, humans seemed at least partly free, transcendent over the web of mechanistic causality. Also certain ethical values appeared to many to have an objective status. The system, though, offered no reasons for holding that it is better to love than to hate, better to seek justice than power. Nevertheless, the ideals of love and justice continued to press home their demands.

Griffin offers a process model of nature in order to overcome the above limitations, and also to defeat the skepticism of Hume for whom neither the reality of causality nor the existence of an external world was capable of certitude. In the process model, largely taken from Whitehead, Griffin attempts to present a system of categories that is more faithful to common-sense perception, paranormal experience and religious encounter. It is unusual today to do philosophy in this manner; for a philosophy of grand systems has not seemed possible in the age of analysis. The style of most contemporary philosophy has to do with a minute analysis of the ways in which language works, and tends to stay within the boundaries of a specific problem, rather than reach out to a metaphysics that attempts to adequately describe the way in which the totality of things (including God) operates. Griffin is thus philosophising in the manner of Hegel or Leibnitz. It is not my purpose here to critique Whiteheadian metaphysics. Rather, I wish to understand the significance of Griffin's criticism of contemporary philosophy and assess his version of process philosophy's contribution to an understanding of post-mortem existence. Even if one finds building metaphysics in the grand style a quixotic task, one may yet find avenues of insight within the propositions and metaphors of the system.

Process philosophy is a species of panentheism, a version of reality that wishes to preserve the significance of both God and the world. Both realities are seen as necessary to the functioning of the other. Unlike deism, God is not banished to a supernatural inactivity; rather, God is that intelligence that is radically responsive to the self-actualising needs of all humanity. Further, God is that reality who is involved with providing each developing person, animal and thing with a goal, an ideal for his/her/its maximum unfolding, a type of lure that offers beings a sense for their next step of excellence. Given the fact of freedom, human beings (and sub-human creatures in less obvious ways) can resist the divine lure. Since the divine lure is the persuasion of a momentary *telos*, once rejected it no longer constitutes a proper goal, for the person has changed in the act of rejecting it, and will require a modified *telos*. God is thus not the elicitor of a predetermined human essence or nature; for the lures placed before us change with the circumstances that nature, God and human freedom set before us. God is infinitely responsive to aid in new conditions which are not fully his creation, but often the miscreations of human insensitivity and disobedience. As a presence with and in all things, God shares in the experience of his creatures and is enriched by taking into the divine life the memory of concrete actualisations of those ideal lures which bore fruit. Nature is necessary for the divine self actualisation and the divine is necessary for nature to reach beyond repetition into creative novelty.

Panentheism differs from supernaturalist theism in that God is not excluded from the world, external to it, inhabiting another realm. Yet it is not pantheism normally conceived, since God and the world are not identified, and God is not a synonym for an impersonal totality. Unlike the God of the mechanists, this God is not apart from the world and ensouls it as its persuasive, non-coercive architect.

In the process model the human organism is understood to have both a subjective and an objective pole. As the subjective pole, the mind is different from the brain. It is numerically distinct but not ontologically different. Neither pole is defined as a different substance, but each is an expression of a common life. The mind is not localised in a cranial spot, nor is it a ghost in the machine. Mind is understood as emerging out of highly organised patterns of brain cells.

Mind gives orders to the brain and the brain supplies information to the mind. They clearly interact. But this is not the interaction of two distinct substances or two radically different kinds of things. Though mind is a new emergent and has quite distinct properties from the brain, it can be described as a non-supernatural activity. Its interaction with the brain can be understood without the postulate of the unique creation and implantation of a spiritual substance. This is a theory of non-dualistic interactionism and possesses the strength of avoiding the pitfalls of both identism (brain equals mind) and dualism. Since brain cells also have an inner side, and have their own form of experience (subjectivity), they are not ontologically different from the experiencing mind (soul) which is the unified subjectivity of the interactions of billions of brain cells integrated at a vastly more complex level (see p. 93).

A number of features arise from the above model. One is that the soul is not a passive reflection of the body. Another is that the soul has access to a non-sensory perception in its perception of the divine lure, also in its experience of the past and anticipation of the future (neither is reducible to sensory perception, but rather accompanies experience), in its sensitivity to moral and aesthetic norms, in mystical phenomena, and so on. What is called extra-sensory experience is therefore not extraordinary in this model. Even ordinary experience that makes use of the senses is perceived in an extra-sensory manner by the mind reading complex electrochemical events. In a model where extra-sensory operations are common occurrences, room also exists for phenomena that are more usually listed under the ESP label.

The mind is not limited to the reading of electrochemical events; it is also influenced by the activity of other minds. A common claim made by those who appear to demonstrate ESP phenomena is that this potential exists in everyone. This may have some plausibility, given the frequency with which such phenomena occur in those who practice contemplative disciplines that detach the mind from the business of ordinary perception. This type of experience coupled with what Griffin calls the 'overwhelming evidence for the reality of extra-sensory perception', leads to the conclusion that soul to soul communication (telepathy) and knowledge of physical things without mediation of the senses (clairvoyance) are non-miraculous facts (pp. 98–9).

In a post-incarnate state extra-sensory perception would be the major source of knowledge about the environment. The discarnate would have access to a type of knowing that Griffin suggests may be occurring all the time, though unconsciously, and recommends that parapsychologists focus their testing on unconscious ESP (p. 99).

What is perhaps arresting to a reader not familiar with ESP literature is the ease with which Griffin accepts the reality of these events. The reason (apart from accepting the findings of researchers) is that Griffin holds that skepticism about well-documented phenomena occurs because of paradigm exclusivity. Because older epistemologies could not accommodate the data, they systematically excluded or explained them away. Griffin's post-modern animism therefore allows a resurfacing of what has become excluded knowledge.

Not all process philosophers would allow for Griffin's naturalistic supernaturalism. Whitehead remained ambiguous on the issue, while Charles Hartshorne rejects the possibility of subjective immortality, and interprets Whitehead's categories to allow only objective immortality. In Hartshorne's reading of process philosophy, only God is able to maintain a permanent developing subjectivity. God, enriched by the experiences of humankind (and subhumankind), maintains all experience in the divine memory. This is known as an objective immortality, in that all experience is remembered in God. Naturally those committed to a concept of either immortality or resurrection will find Hartshorne's vision of objective immortality a travesty of the traditional hope. In the Christian tradition, the words attributed to Jesus point to an afterlife joy beyond imagining. This explains the eschatological fervour that so frequently arises in Christian piety. Hartshorne's 'objective immortality' shorn of all experiencing human subjects is thin gruel indeed.

It is the strength of Griffin's paper that he corrects this deficiency in the process model and offers an interpretation that is a closer fit with religious experience. For whether one is speaking of a platonic intimation of eternity as the true human abode, or an out-of-body experience (OBE) in which one senses a radical transcendence of the flesh, or a mystical rapture in which one seems to apprehend reality (realities) above space/time, Griffin's model is phenomenologically more apt than Hartshorne's.

The central problem for Griffin's model is to make the notion that the soul is capable of surviving the death of its physical matrix appear reasonable. Since the soul is dependent on the complexity of the brain for its emergent life, the unravelling of its matrix in death would seem to demand its eventual demise. The word 'eventual' here refers to the possibility that a residual energy of sorts might allow the soul to continue for an indeterminate period of time after death, and perhaps in some instances even communicate with the living, while yet beginning its eventual decomposition.

However, contrary to models like the above one, Griffin would argue that to exist is to be in a situation of complex relationships. We are capable of development because of our total ambience which includes a large number of non-sensory relationships even while in the body. Death need not mean the ending of these relationships. We have noted several of these non-sensory experiences: memory, relation to ideal potentials, self-determination, sensitivity to the divine lure, ESP connections to other minds. Though physical perception often overwhelms these less obvious relationships, there is the possibility that the soul's continued openness to its non-sensory environment after death provides the ground for its continued existence. It is further possible that the experience of non-tangibles such as other minds, God and ideal possibilities becomes extraordinarily vivid in the discarnate state. This is, in fact, what the data concerning OBEs suggests, a vivid sense of the divine, the presence of other discarnates and an increased ability to evaluate one's faithfulness to life's ideals.

Studies of near-death OBEs suggest that those who have them are uniformly convinced of their veridical nature, regardless of the individual's conscious philosophy. It is curious that the ontological force of the experience convinces atheists, agnostics and believers of the reality of an afterlife. The experience is often described as 'more real' than waking reality. Participants look forward to the death experience in the future and seem to have lost anxiety about dying. Normal living seems subrated. That which is more intense is held to have greater value, meaning and reality.

In many traditional religious societies the response to such claims would naturally be affirmative. But in the academic west models of reality do not allow for a breakthrough of spiritual plane; and that which psychologically seems most indubitable is most rejected. The value therefore of the Griffin model is that it does not need to reject or reduce the more immediate reading of the data of OBEs. He holds that 'in a state freed from fresh stimulation from a physical body, the perception of both God and one's own past might be considerably more intense than it had normally been before' (p. 98).

Afterlife existence does not require special intervention on the part of God, nor does it require the notion that the soul is a stranger in the world of matter. The soul has emerged into a powerful self-reflective and determining agency through the creative evocation of God. As the most complex being within evolution, it is able to maintain its self-directedness in a post-mortem environment. The uniqueness of the human person as revealed in our self-reflective use of symbols indicates that God has successfully created a new order of being and deified a portion of nature, humanity. It is as if a flower emerged from the earth and upon separation from its stem realised that the sun and wind and air could continue to offer it the support needed to live on. This is a hopeful vision for humanity and one consistent with much paranormal data. However, one might question the size of the divide that Griffin has put between animal and human nature. Is the awakening of self-awareness sufficient to suggest a difference in kind so that humans survive death and animals do not. In the process system animals are also thought of as open to non-sensory perception. ESP studies also suggest that mind to mind exchange of information occurs in subhuman life.

Discarnate existence is not a ghostly life in the process model. To exist is to exert real force, and just as ESP phenomena occur in bodily form, they would continue to occur in out-of-body life. This raises many possibilities for religious reflection. If a saint could heal in an extra-sensory manner in this life, she or he might continue to be active in this world after death. The divide between heaven and earth would be narrowed. If psychokinesis, materialisations, clairvoyance and telepathy occur, they might indeed continue to occur. Saints, even dead saints, might continue to exert real force in Griffin's model, thus opening up a case for reconsidering the Catholic doctrine of the communion of saints, or, more generally, the notion that those who were spiritually powerful on earth continue to be so. This would apply regardless of the label, whether avatar, bodhisattva or messiah. Since power is conserved, and since there is continuity between development on earth and the discarnate state, any understanding of 'heaven' would be closer to the Catholic notion of a graded hierarchy of religious intensity, rather than a Protestant species of spiritual egalitarianism. In the Christian instance the Bultmannian mystification that Jesus arose into the gospel (rather than into an afterlife state), might be exposed as an unnecessary compromise with an outmoded modernist epistemology.

By arguing for a position in which souls interact between heaven and earth and in which God is the soul of the world, the process model satisfies the mythic need felt by many today to resanctify the earth, by creating images that justify the holiness of nature as the body of God. The significance of evolutionary cosmologies like Griffin's or Teilhard de Chardin's is that they allow religious sentiment to entertain the thought that more is going on in the play of natural forces than that described in elementary particle physics. They state that God is near, active and busy offering purpose in the sphere of ordinary life. They give an alternative vision to fideism and confessionalism and allow data that would commonly be categorised as supernatural to find a conceptual *modus vivendi* with naturalism. This permits both scientific and mythic concerns to be integrated.

Marxism, secular humanism and some activist forms of Christianity set their hopes on the future, on the upward thrust of historical forces. Mythic needs, often conflated with utopian sociological theories, are projected onto a coming kingdom of justice, leaving the cosmos (nature) bare of genuine religious significance. The strength of the process model lies in its ability to affirm the significance of both cosmos and history.

It is not uncommon in the history of religious thought to find traditional supernaturalism used to justify reactionary politics on the basis of a false eternalism. Ideology and mysticism have often been bed fellows, thus creating moral doubt in politically progressive intellectuals about the reality of religious experience. Since the divine is pictured as concerned with the future, Griffin's naturalistic supernaturalism is not susceptible to this danger. The will of God is not found in eternal laws, images or ideologies, but in the creative advance of humankind. This then is another dimension of postmodern philosophy: commitment to social change is compatible with the concerns of pietism, including a concern with post-mortem existence.

If post-modern philosophy is to successfully integrate excluded knowledge, it is important to understand the historical forces that make this task at present difficult to effect. Griffin has aptly documented the banishment of non-sensory data in the history of modern epistemology. This has been a significant influence, especially upon those touched by the university. But other developments are equally important in understanding why our age has rejected the validity of non-sensory information.

One factor lies in the modern commitment to democratic procedures in the realm of truth. Aristocratic culture is not as concerned about the availability of universal confirmation. There is greater readiness to accept that some persons perceive more of reality than others. But in the scientific west, in the conflict between logic and mysticism, democratic impulse has ousted the possibility of privileged insight. In India, medieval Islam or patristic Christianity, the rare vision was given a weight as great as the statistical visions of empiricism. Since the insights of Jesus or Gautama are manifestly privileged, they are in tension with both democratic and scientific modes of thought.

Another factor may be seen in the collapse of monastic life as a viable vocation for large numbers of people. This is in part due to the development of commercialism which is convinced that meditation bakes no bread. The endless jokes concerning navel gazing fill up the pages of American journals revealing the foundational biases of a business-built society. Monks were the professional full-time explorers of non-sensory reality. Today even the Catholic tradition is unable to supply the type of practiced spiritual guide that dotted the medieval religious landscape. The young of the west have turned east for that which was once a home-grown product. The collapse of feudal agrarian society that encouraged a ritualistic celebration of the stately rhythms of the seasons has led to a different conception of time. It equals money.

Feminist theology has something of importance to say concerning excluded knowledge in the west. Reason has long been identified in the popular psyche with masculinity. Reason is here understood as the rules of either science or logic; aesthetics is debarred, as is mysticism and paranormal knowledge. They are not 'hard' modes of knowing, in fact they are not knowledge at all. It was not always this way. Medieval monks often envisioned the mind as 'feminine' before grace, as receptive to truth rather than analytical. This would today be considered a 'soft' and therefore 'feminine way' to approach the issue of truth. Note that I am not suggesting that these 'hard' approaches to truth are incorrect. Rather my suggestion, which parallels Griffin's evaluation of modern philosophy, is that 'hard' approaches are incomplete, and that unconscious presuppositions determine which types of knowing we grace with the term 'truth'.

Theology also contributed to the demise of religious knowledge. The Reformation's emphasis on the sufficiency of faith for salvation led, especially after faith had been reduced to belief, to a rejection of spiritual empiricism in favour of scriptural systematics. Limited concepts of sanctification in some traditions and the substitution of ethics and moralism in lieu of religious encounter in others further impoverished the value of extra-sensory knowing. The most outstanding nineteenth century exponent of ethical Christianity, Albrecht Ritschl, was successful in demoting the truth value of religious experience in both pietism and mysticism. His influence continued indirectly in the writings of Karl Barth and permeated much of continental theology. A similar negative valuation can be found in the writings of Reinhold Niebuhr.

Technological thought has also contributed to the devaluation of non-sensory knowing. We rightly prize the power to control nature. Religious and paranormal information on the other hand is most difficult to control. And in terms of material achievement, the ability of a shaman to sense a danger to the community, such as a future flood, is simply not as impressive as the achievements of the Army Corps of Engineers.

If we are to regain a sensitivity to the reality of non-sensory facts, including that of life after death; if we wish to escape some of the problems of dualism while affirming many of dualism's strengths; if we want to affirm the benefits of a naturalistic view of the origin of mind from matter without rejecting the activity of God in the world or the reality of religious and paranormal phenomena; then Griffin's model is a strong candidate to plausibly meet these needs. It is the merit of his interpretation of process thought that it rises above the extinctionist interpretation and considers the data of religious life in a non-reductionist manner.

If Griffin's model or something like it should succeed in creating a post-modern philosophy, the nature of philosophy would alter. If the experience of the shaman and saint is not fully illusory, a philosopher would do well to prepare her/himself for glimpses of reality not found in propositions. Philosophy would again concern itself with *sophia*. The observation that Socrates was both shaman and dialectician would remind us of what we have lost.

5 The Resurrection of the Dead
Stephen T. Davis

I

One traditional Christian view of survival of death runs, in outline form, something like this: On some future day all the dead will be bodily raised, both the righteous and the unrighteous alike, to be judged by God; and the guarantee and model of the general resurrection (that is, the raising of the dead in the last days) is the already accomplished resurrection of Jesus Christ from the dead.

My aim in this paper is to explain and defend this basic view of resurrection. There are many ways it might be understood, of course, and perhaps more than one is coherent and, even from a Christian point of view, plausible. I shall defend one particular interpretation of the theory – an interpretation advocated by very many of the church fathers, especially second century fathers, as well as by Augustine and Aquinas.

It may help to clarify matters if I first provide a brief map of where we will be going in this paper. After introducing the topic I will discuss in turn what I take to be the three most important claims made by the version of the theory I wish to defend. Then I will consider one typical aspect of the traditional theory that has important philosophical as well as theological ramifications, namely, the notion that our resurrection bodies will consist of the same matter as do our present earthly bodies. Finally, since the version of the theory I wish to defend envisions a period of existence in a disembodied state, I will defend the theory against some of the arguments of those contemporary philosophers who find the notion of disembodied existence incoherent.

II

Now there are several ways in which the basic concept of resurrection sketched in the opening paragraph can be fleshed out. One option is to understand the nature of the human person, and hence the nature of resurrection, in a basically materialist or physicalist way. Perhaps human beings are essentially material objects, perhaps some vision of identity theory or functionalism is true. Now I am attracted to this option, and hold it to be a usable notion for Christians. But having defended elsewhere a physicalist conception of survival of death through resurrection, I will discuss it no further here.[1]

Another option is to collapse talk of resurrection into talk of the immortality of the soul. A closely related move (and a popular one in recent theology) is to interpret resurrection in a spiritual rather than bodily sense (if this in the end differs significantly from immortality). Such a view will doubtless be based on some version of mind-body (or soul-body) dualism. Let us define dualism as the doctrine which says that (1) human beings consist of both material bodies and immaterial souls; and (2) the soul is the essence of the person (the real you is your soul, not your body). It then can be added that the body corrupts at death and eventually ceases to exist but the soul is essentially immortal.

It is surprising (to me at least) that so many twentieth century Christian thinkers are tempted toward some such notion as this. For it is quite clear, both in scripture and tradition, that classicial dualism is not the Christian position. For example, the biblical view is not that the soul is the essence of the person and is only temporarily housed or even imprisoned in a body; human beings seem rather to be understood in scripture as psycho-physical entities, that is, as unities of body and soul. And the notion that the body is essentially evil and must be escaped from (an idea often associated with versions of classical dualism) was condemned by virtually every orthodox Christian thinker who discussed death and resurrection in the first two hundred years after the apostolic age; the Christian idea is rather that the body was created by God and is good; the whole person, body and soul alike, is what is to be saved. Finally, the biblical notion is not that we survive death because immortality is simply a natural property of souls; if we survive death it is because God miraculously saves us; apart from God's intervention death would mean annihilation for us. Thus Irenaeus says: 'Our survival forever comes from his greatness, not from our nature'.[2]

It would be interesting to discuss this option further, and especially to ask why so many recent and contemporary Christian theologians are drawn toward it, how they might distinguish 'spiritual resurrection' from immortality of the soul, and how they might defend the theory against criticisms such as those just noted. However, I will not do so in this paper. As noted above, my aim here is rather to explore and defend a third way of understanding the traditional Christian notion of resurrection, a theory virtually all (but not quite all) of the church fathers who discussed resurrection held in one form or another.[3] I will call this theory 'temporary disembodiment'.

This theory of resurrection is based on a view of human nature which says that human beings are essentially material bodies *and* immaterial souls; the soul is separable from the body, but neither body or soul alone (that is without the other) constitutes a complete human being. Thus Pseudo-Justin Martyr says:

Is the soul by itself man? No; but the soul of man. Would the body be called man? No, but it is called the body of man. If, then, neither of these is by itself man, but that which is made up of the two together is called man, and God has called *man* to life and resurrection, He has called not a part, but the whole, which is the soul and the body.[4]

What this theory says, then, is that human beings are typically and normally psycho-physical beings, that the soul can exist for a time apart from the body and retain personal identity, but that this disembodied existence is only temporary and constitutes a radically attenuated and incomplete form of human existence.

I call the theory temporary disembodiment because it envisions the following scenario: We human beings are born, live for a time as psycho-physical beings, and then die; after death we exist in an incomplete state as immaterial souls; and some time later in the eschaton God miraculously raises our bodies from the ground, transforms them into 'glorified bodies', and reunites them with our souls, thus making us complete and whole again.

Now temporary disembodiment has several theological and philo-sophical assets. For one thing, many Christian thinkers have seen a comfortable fit between it and the view of human nature expressed in the Bible and in the Pauline writings particularly. The apostle seems to hold that human beings consist both of material bodies and immaterial souls, that the body is not merely an adornment or drape for the soul, and is indeed good, since it can be the temple of the Holy Spirit (I Corinthians, 3: 16–17; 6: 19–20), and that the soul is in some sense separable from the body (II Corinthians 5: 6–8; 12: 2–3). What the body does is provide the soul with a vehicle for action in the world and expression of intentions and desires; and the soul provides the body with animation and direction.[5]

For another thing, the theory seems a neat way of reconciling the traditional view that the general resurrection does not occur until the eschaton with Jesus's statement to the good thief on the cross, '*Today* you will be with me in paradise' (Luke 23: 43). The explanation (which naturally goes far beyond Jesus's simple statement) is as follows: The thief would be with Jesus in paradise that very day in the form of a disembodied soul, only to be bodily raised much later. The theory may also help resolve a similar tension that is sometimes said to exist in Pauline thought, with texts like I Corinthians 15 and I Thessalonians 4 pointing toward the idea of a future, eschatological, resurrection (with those who die beforehand existing till then in a kind of bodiless sleep) and texts like II Corinthians 5:10 and Philippians 1:23 suggesting the idea that death for the Christian is an immediate gain since one is immediately at home with the Lord. (How one can simultaneously be both 'at home with the Lord' and 'in an incomplete state' is a tension that perhaps remains in the theory.)

Finally, the problem of personal identity after death seems in one regard more manageable on this theory than on at least some others, for there is in this theory no temporal gap in the existence of persons (although there is a gap in their existence as complete, unified persons). There is no moment subsequent to our births in which you and I simply do not exist – we exist as soul-bodies or as mere souls at every moment till eternity.

III

There are three main aspects of temporary disembodiment that require discussion both from a philosophical and a theological perspective. Let me now consider them in turn. The first is the notion that after death the soul exists for a time, that is, until the resurrection, in an intermediate state without the body. The second is the notion that at the time of the parousia the body will be raised from the ground and reunited with the soul. And the third is the notion that the body will then be transformed into what is called a 'glorified body'.

The first main claim of temporary disembodiment, then, is that after death the soul temporarily exists without the body. This differs from physicalist concepts of resurrection on which the person does not exist at all in the period between death and resurrection. Temporary disembodiment need not be based on classical dualism as defined earlier, but is based on one tenet of classical dualism, namely, the claim that human beings consist (or in this case at least normally consist) of both material bodies and immaterial souls. (The soul is not said to be the essence of the person, however, and is said to survive death not because immortality is one of its natural properties but because God causes it to survive death.)[6]

Now almost all Christians believe that there is some kind of interim state of the person between death and resurrection. But beyond this point there are very many theological differences. Some, for example, think of the interim state as purgatorial in nature, and others do not. Some hold that spiritual change, for example, repentance, is possible during the interim period, and others do not. Some think the soul rests or sleeps, that is, is not active or conscious, during the interim period, and others do not. It is not part of my purpose in this paper to express an opinion on either of the first two items of disagreement. However, I will argue on the third that the soul is conscious in the interim state. The biblical metaphor of sleep (cf. Luke 8:52; I Corinthians 15:20) is not to be taken as a literal description. This is because it is difficult to make sense of the notion of a disembodied thing being in the presence of God ('Today you will be with me in paradise') if that thing is unconscious and thus unaware of the presence of God.[7] Furthermore, since sleeping is essentially a bodily activity, it seems incoherent to suggest that a soul *could* sleep.

The state of being without a body is an abnormal state of the human person. This is one of the clear differences between temporary disembodiment and immortality of the soul, for the second doctrine (at least in versions of it influenced by Plato) entails that disembodiment is the true or proper or best state of the human person. On the theory we are considering, however, the claim is that a disembodied soul lacks many of the properties and abilities that are normal for and proper to human persons. Disembodied existence is a kind of minimal existence.

Which properties typical of embodied human persons will disembodied souls have and which will they lack? Clearly they will lack those properties that essentially involve corporeality. They will possess no spatial location, for example, at least not in the space-time manifold with which we are familiar. They will not be able to perceive their surroundings (using the spatial word 'surroundings' in a stretched sense) – not at least in the ways in which we perceive our surroundings (that is, through the eyes, ears, and so on). They will not be able to experience bodily pains and pleasures. They will not be able to engage in bodily activities. Taking a walk, getting dressed, playing catch – these sorts of activities will be impossible.

But if by the word 'soul' we mean in part the constellation of those human activities that would typically be classified as 'mental', then the claim that our souls survive death entails the claim that our mental abilities and properties survive death. This means that human persons in the interim state can be spoken of as having experiences, beliefs, wishes, knowledge, memory, inner (rather than bodily) feelings, thoughts, language (assuming memory or earthly existence) – in short, just about everything that makes up what we call personality. H. H. Price, in his classic article 'Survival and the Idea of "Another World" ', argues convincingly that disembodied souls can also be aware of each other's existence, can communicate with each other telepathically, and can have dreamlike (rather than bodily) perceptions of their world.[8]

But Aquinas argues that the disembodied existence of the person in the interim state is so deficient that attainment of ultimate happiness is impossible. No one in whom some perfection is lacking is ultimately happy, for in such a state there will always be unfilfilled desires. It is contrary to the nature of the soul to be without the body, Aquinas says, and he takes this to mean both that the disembodied state must only be temporary, and that the true bliss of the human person is only attained after re-embodiment, that is, in the general resurrection. He says: 'Man cannot achieve his ultimate happiness unless the soul be once again united to the body'.[9]

IV

The second main claim of the theory that I am calling temporary disembodiment is that at the general resurrection the body will be raised from the ground and reunited with the soul. As the second century writer Athenagoras says:

> There must certainly be a resurrection of bodies whether dead or even quite corrupted, and the same men as before must come to be again. The law of nature appoints an end . . . for those very same men who lived in a previous existence, and it is impossible for the same men to come together again if the same bodies are not given

back to the same souls. Now the same soul cannot recover the same body in any other way than by resurrection.[10]

As Athenagoras stresses, the idea is that each person's selfsame body will be raised; it will not be a different and brand new body but the old body. Aquinas (echoing the argument of very many of the fathers) notes the reason for this: 'If the body of the man who rises is not to be composed of the flesh and bones which now compose it, the man who rises will not be numerically the same man'.[11] Furthermore, in the resurrection there will be only one soul per body and only one body per soul. As Augustine says: 'Each single soul shall possess its own body'.[12] Otherwise (for example, if souls split and animate more than one body or if multiple identical copies of one body are animated by different souls) the problem of personal identity is unsolvable, and the Christian hope that we will live after death is incoherent.

The fathers and scholastics insisted, then, that both body and soul must be present or else the person does not exist. 'A man cannot be said to exist as such when the body is dissolved or completely scattered, even though the soul remain by itself' – so says Athenagoras.[13] And Aquinas agrees: 'My soul is not I, and if only souls are saved, *I* am not saved, nor is any man'.[14] Thus the Christian hope of survival is not the hope that our souls will survive death (though on temporary disembodiment that is one important aspect of it), but rather the hope that one day God will miraculously raise our bodies and reunite them with our souls.

What is it, then, that guarantees personal identity in the resurrection? What is it that ensures that it will really be *us* in the kingdom of God and not, say, clever replicas of us? Aquinas argues as follows: since human beings consist of bodies and souls, and since both souls and the matter of which our bodies consist survive death, personal identity is secured when God collects the scattered matter, miraculously reconstitutes it a human body, and reunites it with the soul.[15] And this surely seems a powerful argument. If God one day succeeds in doing these very things, personal identity will be secure. It will be us and not our replicas who will be the denizens of the kingdom of God.

V

The third main claim of temporary disembodiment is that in the resurrection the old body will be transformed into a 'glorified body' with certain quite new properties. This claim is based primarily on Paul's discussion of the resurrection in I Corinthians 15, and secondarily on the unusual properties the risen Jesus is depicted as having in some of the accounts of the resurrection appearances (for example, the apparent ability of the risen Jesus in John 20 to appear in a room despite the doors being locked). In the Pauline text just mentioned the apostle notes that some ask, 'How are the dead raised? With what kind of body do they come?' His answer is an argument to the effect that the new 'glorified' or 'spiritual' body (*soma pneumatikon*) is a transformation of the old body rather than a *de novo* creation (much as a stalk of grain is a transformation of a seed of grain, that is, it exists because of changes that have occurred in the seed and can be considered a new state of the grain). Further, Paul argues, while the old or natural body is physical, perishable, mortal, and sown in weakness and dishonour, the glorified body is spiritual, imperishable, immortal, and sown in strength and honour. The first body is in the image of the man of dust; the second body is in the image of the man of heaven.

The term 'spiritual body' might be misleading; it should not be taken as a denial of corporeality or as a last-minute capitulation to some version of the immortality of the soul as opposed to bodily resurrection. By this term Paul means not a body whose stuff or matter is spiritual (whatever that might mean) or an immaterial existence of some sort; rather he means a body that is fully obedient to and dominant by the Holy Spirit. Paul says: 'Flesh and blood cannot inherit the kingdom of God' (I Corinthians 15:50). What enters the kingdom of heaven, then, is not this present weak and mortal body of flesh and blood but the new glorified body. This new body is a physical body (Paul's use of the word *soma* implies as much),[16] and is materially related to the old body (taking seriously Paul's simile of the seed), but is a body transformed in such ways as make it fit to live in God's presence. If by the term 'physical object' we mean an entity that has spatio-temporal location and is capable of being empirically measured, tested, or observed in some sense, then my argument is that the new body of which Paul speaks is a physical object.

Temporary disembodiment, then, entails that human souls can animate both normal earthly bodies and glorified resurrection bodies. Continuity between the two bodies is provided by the presence of both the same soul and the same matter in both bodies. Thus Augustine says:

> Nor does the earthly material out of which men's mortal bodies are created ever perish; but though it may crumble into dust and ashes, or be dissolved into vapours and exhalations, though it may be transformed into the substance of other bodies, or dispersed into the elements, though it should become food for beasts or men, and be changed into their flesh, it returns in a moment of time to that human soul which animated it at the first and which caused it to become man, and to live and grow.[17]

The matter of our present bodies may be arranged differently in the resurrection, he says, but the matter will be restored.

Many of the theologians of the early church and of the medieval period stress also the perfection of the glorified body. It will be free of every bodily defect. It will be immune to evil because fully controlled by the spirit of God. It will not suffer. It will not grow old or die. It will have 'agility' – which is presumably an ability like that of the risen Jesus to come and go at will, unimpeded by things like walls and doors. It will exist in a state of fulfilled desire. It will need no material food and drink, but will be nourished by the elements of the eucharist.[18]

VI

Is the picture of resurrection just presented coherent? Is it plausible? The main objections that have been raised against it in recent philosophy revolve around the problem of personal idenity. Some philosophers argue that so far as disembodied existence is concerned this problem cannot be solved. That is, they argue that if some immaterial aspect of me survives death it will not be me that survives death. Since the view of survival of death I am defending essentially involves a period of disembodied existence, I had best try to defend the view against these sorts of objections. But a prior problem must be considered first – whether the fathers and scholastics were correct in their strong claim (I will call this claim 'the Patristic theory') that if it is to be me in the kingdom of God the very matter of my original earthly body must be raised. Having discussed the point, I will then turn in section VII to the arguments of those philosophers who oppose the notion of disembodied existence because of the problem of personal identity.

Why did Aquinas and the fathers who influenced him insist that the same matter of my old body must be raised? Let us see if we can construct an argument on their behalf. Like many arguments in the area of personal identity, it involves a puzzle case. Suppose that I own a defective personal computer which I rashly decide to try to repair myself. Having taken it apart (there are now, say, 60 separate computer components scattered on my work bench), I find that I am unable to repair it. I call the outlet that sold me the computer, and the manager suggests I simply bring all 60 components to that office for repair. I do so, but through a horrible series of misunderstandings and errors, the 60 pieces of the computer are then sent to 60 different addresses around the country. That constitutes the heart of my story, but there are two separate endings to it. *Ending number one*: it takes three years for everything to be sorted out, for the pieces to be located and collected in one place, for the repairs to be made, and for the parts to be reassembled and restored, in full working order, to my desk. *Ending number two*: After three years of trying in vain to locate and collect the scattered pieces, the manager gives up, collects 60 similar parts, assembles them, and the resulting computer ends up on my desk.

Now I do not wish to raise the interesting question whether my computer *existed* during the three-year period. I am interested in the related question whether the computer now located on my desk is *the same* computer as the one that was there three years ago. And so far as ending number one is concerned, it seems most natural to affirm that the computer I now possess is indeed the same computer as the one that I possessed before. The computer may or may not have had a gap in its existence, that is, a period when it did not exist, but it seems clear that identity has here been preserved. And so far as ending number two is concerned, it seems most natural to deny that the computer I now possess is the same computer as the one that I possessed before. Furthermore, we would doubtless insist on this denial even if each of the 60 components the manager used to construct the computer I now possess was qualitatively identical to the 60 old components. What I now have is a qualitatively similar but numerically different computer.

Now I doubt that the church fathers often pondered personal identity test cases involving computers, and it is obvious that personal computers are different from human beings in many striking ways. But it was perhaps *the sort* of insight arrived at above that led them to take the strong stand they took on the resurrection. Only if God reassembles the very particles of which my body once consisted will it be me who is raised. Otherwise, that is, if other particles are used, the result will be what we would call a replica of me rather than me.

But despite the above argument, does it still not seem that Aquinas and the fathers in their strong stand have made the solution to the problem of personal identity more difficult than it need be? Even granting the point that some of the particles of the matter of which our bodies consist will endure for the requisite number of years, why insist that God must re-collect it, that is, that very matter, in the resurrection? For surely in the interim state it will be us (and not soul-like replicas of us) who will exist without any body at all; surely the fathers and scholastics insist on this much. Thus the soul alone must guarantee personal identity; what philosophers call the memory criterion (which is typically taken to include not just memory but all one's 'mental' characteristics and properties) must suffice by itself. Identity of memory, personality, and other 'mental' aspects of the person are sufficient conditions of personal identity. To admit this much is not necessarily to go back on the traditional notion that the soul is not the whole person and that the whole person must be raised. It is merely to insist that the existence of my soul entails *my* existence. Otherwise talk of my existence in the interim state is meaningless.

Now I do not claim that the Patristic theory is logically inconsistent. It is possible to hold that when I die my soul will be me during the interim period but that it will no longer be me if my soul in the eschaton animates a body consisting of totally new matter, even if the new body is qualitatively identical to the old one. (Perhaps an essential property of my soul is that it can only animate *this* body – where 'this body' means in part a body consisting of *these* particles. So if *per impossible* my soul were to animate a different body the result would not be me. Or perhaps every configuration of particles that can possibly constitute a human body has it as one of its essential properties that it can be animated by one and only one soul.) But while logically consistent, this view seems to me exceed-ingly difficult to defend; it is hard to see how the suggested theses could be argued for.

Thus so far as the problem of personal identity is concerned, it is not easy to see why a defender of temporary disembodiment cannot dispense with all talk of God one day re-collecting the atoms, quarks, or whatever of our bodies. Perhaps human beings in this regard are unlike computers. Why not say God can award us brand new bodies materially quite unrelated to (although qualitatively similar to) the old ones? If the existence of the soul is sufficient for personal identity, and if the human soul never at any moment subsequent to its creation fails to exist, it will be us who exist after the resurrection in the kingdom of God whether or not our old bodies are reconstituted.

Furthermore, it needs to be noted here that identity of particles of bodily matter does not seem necessary to preserve the identity of an ordinary human person even during the course of a lifetime. As Frank Dilley says:

> We constantly replace our atoms over time and there is no reason to think that any eighty year old person has even a single atom in common with the newborn babe. If a person maintains personal identity over a process of total atom-by-atom replacement, it is difficult to see why such identity would not be preserved through a sudden replacement of all the atoms at once.[19]

Dilley's argument seems plausible, but we should notice that it does not necessarily follow. Perhaps gradual replacement of all the individual atoms of a human body is consistent with personal identity while all-at-once replacement of them is not. Perhaps some strong sort of material continuity is needed. One of the difficulties encoun-tered by philosophers who discuss personal identity is that different persons' intuitions run in different directions. For example, in a slightly different connection, Peter Van Inwagen argues that same-ness of person requires both (1) sameness of atoms and (2) regular and natural causal relationships between those atoms. So if God were now to try to raise Napoleon Bonaparte from the dead by omni-sciently locating the atoms of which his body once consisted and miraculously reassembling them, the result would not be Napoleon.[20] Now I do not agree with Van Inwagen here; I see no reason for his second stipulation. I raise his argument merely to show that his intuitions run in a different direction than do Dilley's. Since Dilley's

case of sudden-replacement-of-all-the-atoms-at-once seems to constitute something *un*natural and *ir*regular, Van Inwagen would doubtless deny that in such cases personal identity would be preserved.

What if there were, so to speak, some natural way of reassembling
persons out of totally new matter?' Derek Parfit considers in detail a
series of test cases involving an imagined Teletransporter.[21] This is a
machine that is designed to send a person to distant places like Mars
by (1) recording the exact state of all the body's cells (including those
of the brain); (2) destroying the body and brain; (3) transmitting the
information at the speed of light to Mars; where (4) a Replicator
creates out of new matter a body and brain exactly like the old one.
Suppose Parfit enters the machine and is 'teletransported to Mars'.
Would the resulting Parfit-like person on Mars *be* Parfit? Here again
our intuitions might differ, even in this relatively simple case (that is,
apart from complications like the original Parfit somehow surviving
on earth or 15 Parfit-like persons appearing on Mars). Those (like the
church fathers and Aquinas) who hold to some strong requirement
about bodily continuity will deny it is Parfit. Those who stress the
memory criterion are free to affirm that Parfit is now on Mars. So are
those, (for example, John Hick) who believe that identity is exact
similarity plus uniqueness. Those who think that identity is exact
similarity plus the right kind of causal origin or causal ancestry might
go either way, depending on whether they think the operation of a
Teletransporter constitutes an appropriate sort of causal origin for
the Parfit-like person on Mars.

The moral of the story thus far, I think, is that the fathers and
Aquinas may be right in what they say about resurrection, but it is not
clear that they are right. Their position may be consistent, but it does
seem implausible to hold both (1) that it will be me in the interim
period without any body at all (that is, the presence of my soul is
sufficient for personal identity), and (2) that it will not be me in the
eschaton, despite the presence of my soul, if the body which my soul
then animates consists of new matter. There may be other (perhaps
theological) reasons why we should hold that it is the very matter of
our old bodies that is raised, but so far as the problem of personal
identity is concerned, a strong case can be made that it will not
matter.

Recent and contemporary Christian theologians who discuss resurrection seem for the most part to have departed from the Patristic
theory. The more common thesis is that our glorified bodies will be
wholly different bodies, not necessarily consisting of any of the old

matter at all. As John Hick, an articulate spokesperson for this new point of view, says:

> What has become a widely accepted view in modern times holds that the resurrection body is a new and different body given by God, but expressing the personality within its new environment as the physical body expressed it in the earthly environment. The physical frame decays or is burned, disintegrating and being dispersed into the ground or the air, but God re-embodies the personality elsewhere.[22]

Frequently connected with this view is an exegetical claim, namely, that by the term 'the body', St Paul meant not the physical organism but rather something akin to 'the whole personality'. What will be raised from the dead, then, is not the old body but rather the *person*, and in being raised the person will be given a brand new body by God.

It is not hard to see why such a view has come to be widely adopted. (1) As noted above, personal identity does not seem to require the resurrection of the old body. (2) The Patristic theory seems to many contemporary Christians to be scientifically outmoded and difficult to believe; the idea that in order to raise me God must one day cast about, locate, and collect the atoms of which my earthly body once consisted seems to many people absurd. (3) Many such theologians want to hold in any case that the kingdom of God is not spatially related to our present world. It exists in a space all its own, and so can contain no material from this spatio-temporal manifold.

I am unable to locate any philosophical or logical difficulties in the 'modern' theory. It seems to me a possible Christian view of resurrection, and can fit smoothly with the other aspects of the traditional notion I am calling temporary disembodiment. Are there any theological reasons, then, for a Christian to retain the old theory, that is, to believe that our old bodies will be raised? Two points should be made here. The first is that the most natural reading of Paul in I Corinthian 15 is along the lines of the Patristic theory. That is, Paul seems to be suggesting there that the old body *becomes* or *changes into* the new body, just as a seed becomes or changes into a plant. Thus, just as there is material continuity between the seed and the plant, so there will be material continuity between the old body and the new; the plant is *a new form of* the seed. Note also Paul's use in verses 42 and 43 of the expression: '*It* is sown . . . *it* is raised . . . ', as if the one thing (a human body) is at one time in a certain state and at a later time in another state (see also vs 53 and 53).[23] Furthermore, as noted already, Paul's use of the term *soma* reveals that what he had in mind was a body; it is simply a lexical mistake to say that he merely meant 'the whole personality', or some such thing.[24]

The second point has to do with the difficulty of God one day collecting the atoms, quarks, or whatever fundamental particles human bodies consist of. This may well be the oldest philosophical objection ever raised against the Christian notion of resurrection. Virtually every one of the fathers who discussed resurrection tried to answer it, as did Aquinas. Such scenarios as this were suggested: What if a Christian dies at sea and his body is eaten by various fishes who then scatter to the seven seas? How can God later resurrect that body? Or what if another Christian is eaten by cannibals, so that the material of her body becomes the material of their bodies? And suppose God later wants to raise all of them from the dead, cannibals and Christians alike. Who gets what particles? How does God decide?

The move made by virtually all of the fathers in response to this objection is to appeal to omnipotence. You and I might not be able to locate and reconstitute the relevant atoms of someone's body, not surely after many years or even centuries have passed, but God can do this very thing. And as long as (1) the basic constituents of matter (for example, atoms) endure through time (as contemporary physical theory says they normally do); and (2) it is merely a matter of God locating and collecting the relevant constituents, I believe the fathers were right. An omnipotent being could do that.

But with the cannibalism case and other imaginable cases where God must decide which constituent parts shared at different times by two (or even two thousand) separate persons go where, the matter is more serious. The problem does not seem insoluble, but much more needs to be said. Perhaps some constituent parts of human bodies are essential to those bodies and some are not. That is, perhaps God will only need to collect the essential parts of our bodies and use them, so to speak, as building blocks around which to reconstruct our new bodies. And perhaps omnipotence must accordingly guarantee that no essential part of one person's earthly body is ever a constituent part, or an essential constituent part, of someone else's body. If these stipulations or ones like them are followed (for example, Augustine's idea that atoms will be raised in that human body in which they first appeared),[25] it still seems that the fathers were correct – an omnipotent being will be able to raise us from the ground.

Reacting against these and similar patristic appeals to omnipotence in order to rationalise resurrection, Paul Badham argues as follows:[26]

> Given belief in a once-for-all act of creation on the pattern of Genesis 1, then the act of resurrection cannot be difficult for an all-powerful God. Given that God made the first man by direct action, the restoration of a decomposed man becomes an easy task. Given that man consists of particles, it is easy to believe that omnipotence could reassemble these particles. But today each of these premises has lost its validity, and hence the conclusions drawn from them cannot stand. That man as a species is part of a slowly evolving process of life and in every respect continuous with the processes of nature from which he has emerged does not provide a congenial background for the idea of resurrection. Further, our increasing knowledge of the incredible complexity and constant changing of our physical components makes it difficult to see the resurrection as simply involving the re-collection of our physical particles. We are not composed of building bricks but of constantly changing living matter.

It is not easy to see exactly what the arguments here are meant to be. For one thing, Badham is right that nature is incredibly complex, as are human bodies; our bodies surely do consist of constantly changing living matter. But does any of this deny – or indeed does contemporary physics deny – the idea that our bodies consist of particles? I think not. Furthermore, it is hard to see how a commitment to evolutionary theory (a commitment I make) undercuts the ability of an omnipotent being to raise us from the dead. Perhaps it does undercut a simplistic argument which we occasionally find in the fathers, an argument which says, 'Since God already did the difficult job of creating me *de novo* by assembling the particles of my body, God can also do the far easier job of reassembling them in the eschaton.'[27] But surely claims about what is easy and what is hard for an omnipotent being to do are suspect anyway. The point the fathers were making is that whatever difficulties resurrection presents are difficulties that can be overcome by an omnipotent being. That point – still stands, and is not rendered improbable or implausible by evolution.

VII

Several philosophers have argued in recent years that the concept of disembodied existence is incoherent or at least that no disembodied thing can be identified with some previously existing human person. Antony Flew,[28] Bernard Williams,[29] D. Z. Phillips,[30] Terence Penelhum,[31] and John Perry,[32] among others, have jointly presented what might be called the standard arguments against survival of death in disembodied form. P. T. Geach,[33] has similarly argued against the notion of *permanent* disembodied existence, though he supports something like the theory I am calling temporary disembodiment. Now I am inclined to hold that the standard arguments have been successfully answered by defenders of disembodied existence;[34] that is, I believe the notion of survival of death (and even permanent survival of death) in disembodied form is intelligible and logically possible. Furthermore, one result of recent discussion of the puzzle cases in the area of personal identity is that many philosophers are now prepared to defend the notion that we can imagine cases where the memory criterion will suffice by itself. But since the arguments of Flew, Williams, and Phillips, and Penelhum have been discussed thoroughly in the journals, let me instead focus on the case John Perry makes in his excellent little book, *A Dialogue on Personal Identity and Immortality*.

Perry seems, in this dialogue, to speak primarily through the character of Gretchen Weirob, a mortally injured but still lucid philosopher who does not believe in life after death. And Weirob seems to present three main arguments against the conceivability or possibility of survival of death. All are versions of arguments we find elsewhere in the literature, but the virtue of Perry's work is that they are presented with great clarity and forcefulness. Perry's first argument has to do with the soul and personal identity; the second concerns memory and personality identity; and the third is an argument about the possibility of duplication of persons.

The first argument says that immaterial and thus unobservable souls can have nothing to do with establishing personal identity. Personal identity does not consist in sameness of soul, for if it did, we would never know who we are or who others are. Since souls are not observable, no thesis having to do with souls is testable (not even the thesis, 'My soul is me'). So I cannot know whether other human beings have souls, or even whether I have a soul; I have no idea whether I have one soul or several, or whether I have one soul for a time and then later a different soul. Thus there are no criteria for, and hence no way to make informed judgements about, 'the same soul'. It is possible simply on faith to assume criteria like, 'Same body, same soul', or 'Same mental traits, same soul', but since we never independently observe souls, there is no way to test these principles, and thus no reason to think they hold. But since we evidently are able to make correct personal identity judgements about persons, it follows that personal identity has nothing to do with souls. Personal identity must instead be based upon bodily criteria. Thus, concludes Perry, no thesis about my survival of death via the survival of my soul is coherent.

Perry's second argument is that the memory criterion of personal identity, which those who believe in immortality must rely on, is never sufficient to establish personal identity. This is because of the obvious fact that memory is fallible. Without some further criterion, we will never be able to distinguish between apparent memories and genuine memories. In fact, believers in immortality are committed to a kind of circularity – they claim that genuine memory explains personal identity (that is, a purported Jones in the afterlife really is Jones just in case the purported Jones genuinely remembers from Jones's point of view events in Jones's past), and they claim that identity marks the difference between apparent and genuine memories (the purported Jones can have genuine memories of events in Jones's past just in case the purported Jones *is* Jones – otherwise the memories are merely apparent memories). Thus again, the thesis that our souls survive death, which must rely on the memory criterion of personal identity, is incoherent.

Finally, Perry argues that the thesis of survival of death through immortality is rendered incoherent by the possibility of multiple qualitatively identical persons in the afterlife. Weirob says:[35]

So either God, by creating a Heavenly person with a brain modeled after mine, does not really create someone identical with me but merely someone similar to me, or God is somehow limited to making only one such being. I can see no reason why, if there were a God, He should be so limited. So I take the first option. He would create someone similar to me, but not someone who would *be* me. Either your analysis of memory is wrong, and such a being does not, after all, remember what I am doing or saying, or memory is not sufficient for personal identity. Your theory has gone wrong somewhere, for it leads to absurdity.

When told by one of the discussants that God may well refrain from creating multiple qualitatively identical persons in the afterlife and that if God does so refrain the immortality thesis is coherent, Weirob replies that a new criterion has now been added. What suffices for personal identity (that is, what makes it such that the purported Jones in the afterlife *is* Jones) is not just memory but rather memory plus lack of competition. An odd way for someone to be killed in the afterlife, she remarks – all God has to do is create, so to speak, an identical twin to Jones, and then *neither* is Jones; Jones has not survived death. Identity is now made oddly to depend on something entirely extrinsic to the person involved. Thus if memory does not secure personal identity where there are two or more Jones's in the afterlife, it does not secure personal identity at all. Weirob concludes it is best simply to abandon any thought of survival of death – when my body dies, I die.

Perry's first argument in favour of the notion that survival of death is incoherent is based on an element of truth, but is used by him in an erroneous way. Throughout his book he seems illicitly to jump back and forth between talk about criteria of personal identity and talk about evidence for personal identity. It is surely true that the soul is not observable, and that the presence or absence of a soul or of a certain soul is not something for which we can successfully test. What this shows, as I suppose, is that the soul is not *evidence for* personal identity. We cannot, for example, prove that a given person really is our long-lost friend by proving that this person really has our long-lost friend's soul. But it still might be true that the soul is *a criterion of* personal identity. That is, it still might be the case that the person really is our long-lost friend just in case this person and our long-lost friend have the same soul. It might even be true to say that a purported Jones in the afterlife is the same person as the Jones who once lived on earth just in case the purported Jones has Jones's soul. How we might test for or come to know this is another matter. Maybe only God knows for sure who has what soul. Maybe the rest of us will never know – not apart from divine revelation anyway – whether the purported Jones has Jones's soul. But it can still be true that if they have the same soul, they are two different temporal episodes of the same one person.

And the claim that personal identity consists in or amounts to the presence of the soul does not rule out the possibility of our making reliable personal identity judgements on other grounds, as Weirob seems to claim it does. Those who believe in the possibility of disembodied existence need not deny that there are other criteria of personal identity (for example, if the person before me has the same body as my long-lost friend, this person *is* my long-lost friend) and other ways of producing evidence in favour of or against personal identity claims.

Perry's second argument is also based on an element of truth – memory certainly is fallible; we do have to distinguish between apparent memories and genuine memories. So unless I have access to some infallible way of making this distinction, the mere fact that the purported Jones seems to remember events in Jones's life from Jones's point of view will not establish beyond conceivable doubt that the purported Jones is Jones (though it might count as evidence for it). As above, however, this does not rule out the possibility that memory is a criterion of personal identity – if the purported Jones does indeed remember events in Jones's life from Jones's point of view, then the purported Jones is Jones.

It is sometimes claimed that the memory criterion is parasitic on the bodily criterion and that use of the memory criterion never suffices by itself to establish identity. But such claims are surely false. We sometimes do make secure identity claims based on the memory criterion alone – for example, when we receive a typed letter from a friend. We hold that it is our friend who wrote the letter solely on the basis of memories and personality traits apparently had by the letter's author that seem to be memories and personality traits our friend has or ought to have. Of course if doubts were to arise we would try to verify or falsify the claim that our friend wrote the letter by the use of any evidence or criterion that might seem promising. We might check the letter for finger prints; we might try to see if it was written on our friend's typewriter; we might even telephone our friend. What this shows is not that we must always rely on the bodily criterion; there are equally cases where we might try to verify an identity claim originally based on the bodily criterion by means of memories. What it shows is that in cases of doubt we will look at both criteria.

But in the cases where the bodily criterion cannot be used – for example, during the interim period postulated in temporary disembodiment – can identity claims rationally be made? Can we ever be sure that a disembodied putative Stephen Davis *is* Stephen Davis? The problem is especially acute since memory is notoriously fallible; without recourse to the bodily criterion, how can we distinguish between actual memories and purported memories? I would argue that secure identity claims can be made without use of the bodily criterion, and that this can be achieved in cases where there are very many memories from very many different people that cohere together well. The context would make all the difference. If there are, say, 100 disembodied souls all wondering whether everyone in fact is who he or she claims to be, it would be irrational to deny that their memories are genuine if they all fit together, confirm each other, and form a coherent picture. Doubt would still be conceivable, but not rational. And something like this is precisely what defenders of temporary disembodiment claim will occur during the interim period.[36]

The third or duplication argument is one that critics of disembodied existence frequently appeal to, but is is one of the advantages of Perry's *Dialogue* that he grasps the defender's proper reply to it, and then moves to deepen the objection. After the comment from Weirob quoted above, Perry has Dave Cohen, a former student of hers, say: 'But wait. Why can't Sam simply say that if God makes one such creature, she is you, while if he makes more, none of them is you? It's possible that he makes only one. So it's possible that you survive'. This seems to me the correct response. Of course immortality or resurrection would be difficult to believe in if there were, say, 14 qualitatively identical Weirobs in the afterlife, each with equal apparent sincerity claiming to be Gretchen Weirob. But surely you can't refute a thesis, or the possible truth of a thesis, by imagining possible worlds where the thesis would be exceedingly hard to believe. Survival of death theses might well make good sense if in the afterlife there is never more than one person who claims to be some pre-mortem person. And since it is possible there will be but one Gretchen Weirob in the afterlife, survival of death is possible.

In response to this point Perry deepens the objection with Weirob's points about there now being two criteria of personal identity (memory and lack of competition) and about the oddness of God's ability to prevent someone's surviving death by creating a second qualitatively identical person. Both points seem to me correct, but do not render the survival thesis incoherent or even, as Weirob claims, absurd. What exactly is wrong with saying (in the light of God's evident ability to create multiple qualitatively identical persons) that memory plus lack of competition are criteria of personal identity? Lack of competition is a criterion that technically applies in this life as well as the next – we never bother to mention it because it rarely occurs to us that God has the ability to create multiple qualitatively identical persons here as well. And I suppose it *is* odd that God can prevent someone's survival in the way envisioned, and that personal identity is here made in part to depend on something entirely extrinsic to the person. These facts are odd, but they do not seem to me to impugn the possibility of the survival thesis.

Christians strongly deny that there will be multiple qualitatively identical persons in the eschaton. They would hold, however, that God has the ability to create such persons, so it is perfectly fair for critics to ask: How would it affect your advocacy of resurrection if God were to exercise this power? Now I prefer to hold that the existence of multiple qualitatively identical Joneses in the eschaton would place far too great a strain on our concept of a human person for us to affirm that Jones has survived death. Our concept of a person, I believe, includes a notion of uniqueness – there is and can be only one instance of each 'person'. Uniqueness or 'lack of competition' (as Weirob puts it) is a criterion of personal identity. So I would argue at the very least that we would not know what to say if there were more than one Jones in the afterlife (perhaps our concept of a human person would have to be radically revised to include amoeba-like divisions, or something of the sort). More strongly, I would argue that Jones (the unique person we knew on earth) has not survived death.

Accordingly, I see no serious difficulty for the survival thesis here. Although the view I am defending – temporary disembodiment – does not require the coherence of any notion of permanent disembodiment (like, for example, the doctrine known as immortality of the soul), I nevertheless would hold both to be coherent. As noted above, however, Geach argues strongly that only temporary disembodiment is coherent; what alone makes the problem of personal identity manageable as regards a disembodied person is its capacity or potential eventually to be reunited with a given body. Otherwise, he says, disembodied minds cannot be differentiated.[37] If Geach is right, only temporary disembodiment is coherent – immortality of the soul is not. Or at least, those who believe in the latter doctrine must add an item to their theory – perhaps something about a permanently disembodied soul permanently retaining the (forever unrealised) *capacity* to be reunited with a given body.

VIII

As can be seen from the preceding discussion, I do not consider that what I have been calling the Patristic theory is normative for Christians today. The 'modern' theory seems to me an acceptable interpretation of resurrection. God's ability to raise us from the dead in the eschaton does not seem to depend on God's ability to locate and reunite the very particles of which our bodies once consisted. Nevertheless, the Patristic theory also constitutes an acceptable understanding of resurrection for Christians. The standard objections to it are answerable, and the most natural exegesis of I Corinthians 15:35–50 supports it. Furthermore, respect for Christian tradition must (or so I would argue) grant great weight to views held by virtually all the fathers of the church unless there is serious reason to depart from what they say. It seems to me quite possible that God will one day raise us from the dead in the very way that the fathers and Aquinas suggest.

My overall conclusion is that the theory of resurrection I have been considering (which can be interpreted in either the Patristic or the 'modern' way) is a viable notion for Christians. Temporary disembodiment seems eminently defensible, both philosophically and theologically. I do not claim it is the only viable option for Christian belief about life after death; I do claim it is an acceptable way for Christians to understand those words from the Apostles' Creed that say, 'I believe in . . . the resurrection of the body'.

Much contemporary philosophy tends, in its understanding of human nature, in a behaviourist or even materialist direction. No believer in temporary disembodiment can embrace philosophical materialism, but such believers can have great sympathy with any view which says that a disembodied person would hardly be a human person, not surely in the full sense of the word. They too embrace the notion that a disembodied person is only a minimal person, a mere shadow of a true human person – not completely unlike a person who is horribly disabled from birth or from some accident but who continues to live.

Such Christians will accordingly embrace the notion that full and true and complete human life is bodily life. That is why they look forward to 'the resurrection of the body'. As Pseudo-Justin says:[38] 'In the resurrection the flesh shall rise entire. For if on earth He healed the sickness of the flesh, and made the body whole, much more will He do this in the resurrection, so that the flesh shall rise perfect and entire'.[39]

Notes

1. See Stephen T. Davis, 'Is Personal Identity Retained in The Resurrection?' *Modern Theology*, 2(4)(1986).
2. Cyril Richardson (ed.) *Early Christian Fathers* (Philadelphia: The Westminster Press, 1953) p. 389.
3. See Harry A. Wolfson, 'Immortality and Resurrection in the Philosophy of the Church Fathers', in Krister Stendahl (ed.) *Immortality and Resurrection* (New York: Macmillan, 1965) pp. 64–72. See also Lynn Boliek, *The Resurrection of the Flesh* (Grand Rapids, Michigan: Wm B. Eerdmans, 1962).
4. Alexander Roberts and James Donaldson (eds) *The Ante-Nicene Fathers* (New York: Charles Scribner's Sons, 1899) pp. 297–8.
5. Robert H. Gundry, *Soma in Biblical Theology: With Emphasis on Pauline Anthropology* (Cambridge: Cambridge University Press, 1976) p. 159.
6. Wolfson, op. cit., pp. 56–60, 63–4.
7. It does not seem to make sense to speak of some disembodied thing *x* being 'in the presence of' some other thing *y*, where 'in the presence of' means 'in the spatial vicinity of'. The notion may be coherently understood, however, as something like 'being acutely aware of and sensitive to'. This is why I am unable to provide a sensible construal of the notion of a disembodied and unconscious person being in the presence of God.
8. H. H. Price, 'Survival and the Idea of "Another World",' in John Donnelly (ed.) *Language, Metaphysics, and Death* (New York: Fordham University Press, 1978) pp. 176–95. I do not wish to commit myself entirely to Price's theory; among others, John Hick has detected difficulties in it. See *Death and Eternal Life* (New York: Harper & Row 1976) pp. 265–77. But Price's main point – that disembodied survival of death is possible – seems to me correct.
9. Thomas Aquinas, *Summa Contra Gentiles*, trans. by Charles J. O'Neil; Book IV (Notre Dame, Indiana: The University of Notre Dame Press, 1975) IV, 79.
10. Athenagoras, *Embassy for Christians and the Resurrection of the Dead*, trans. Joseph H. Crehan, S. J. (London: Longmans, Green, 1956) pp. 115–16.
11. Aquinas, op. cit., IV, 84.
12. Augustine, *The Enchiridion on Faith, Hope, and Love* (Chicago: Henry Regnery, 1961) LXXXVII.
13. Athenagoras, op. cit., p. 115.
14. Cited in P. T. Geach, *God and the Soul* (London: Routledge & Kegan Paul, 1969) pp. 22, 40.
15. Aquinas, op. cit., IV 81.
16. See Gundry, op. cit., pp. 164ff. For this and other points made in this paragraph, see C. F. D. Moule, 'St Paul and Dualism: The Pauline Concept of Resurrection', *New Testament Studies*, 12 (2) (1966), and Ronald J. Sider, 'The Pauline Conception of the Resurrection Body in I Corinthians XV. 35–54', *New Testament Studies*, 21, (3) (1975).

17. Augustine, op. cit., LXXXVIII.
18. See Irenaeus, in Richardson, op. cit., p. 388; Augustine, op. cit., XCI; Aquinas, op. cit., IV 83–7.
19. Frank Dilley, 'Resurrection and the "Replica Objection"', *Religious Studies*, 19, (4) (1983) p. 462.
20. Peter Van Inwagen, 'The Possibility of Resurrection', *International Journal for Philosophy of Religion*, IX, (2) (1978) p. 119.
21. Derek Parfit, *Reasons and Persons* (Oxford: Oxford University Press, 1986) p. 199f. I mention here only the most simple of the test cases involving teletransportation that Parfit discusses. Nor will I consider in this paper what I take to be the central theses of Part III of his book.
22. Hick, op. cit., p. 186.
23. Commenting on Paul's argument in I Corinthians 15:53, Tertullian says: 'When he says *this* corruptible and *this* mortal, he utters the words while touching the surface of his own body' (Tertullian, *'On the Resurrection of the Flesh*, in *the Ante-Nicene Fathers*, III (New York: Charles Scribner's Sons, 1899) L1).
24. Gundry makes this point convincingly (see op. cit., p. 186). See also Sider, op. cit., pp. 429–38, and Bruce Reichenbach, 'On Disembodied Resurrection Persons: A Reply', *Religious Studies* 18 (2) (1982) p. 227.
25. Augustine, op. cit., LXXXVIII. See also Augustine, *The City of God* (Grand Rapids Michigan: Wm. B. Eerdmans, 1956) V, XXII, p. 20.
26. Paul Badham, *Christian Beliefs About Life After Death* (London: MacMillian Press, 1976) p. 50. Despite my disagreement with him on this point, it must be admitted that in his book Badham does successfully rebut several unconvincing patristic arguments about bodily resurrection.
27. See, for example, Irenaeus, *'Against Heresies'*, in *The Ante-Nicene Fathers*, I (Grand Rapids, Michigan: Wm. B. Eerdmans, n.d.) V, III, 2. See also Tertullian. op. cit., XI.
28. See Flew's article on 'Immortality' in Paul Edwards (ed.) *The Encyclopedia of Philosophy*, (New York: MacMillan, 1967), and the articles collected in Part III of Flew's *The Presumption of Atheism and other Essays* (London: Elek/Pemberton, 1976).
29. See the articles collected in Bernard Williams, *Problems of the Self* (Cambridge: Cambridge University Press, 1973).
30. D. Z. Phillips, *Death and Immortality* (New York: St. Martin's Press, 1970).
31. Terence Penelhum, *Survival and Disembodied Existence* (New York: Humanities Press, 1970).
32. John Perry, *A Dialogue on Personal Identity and Immortality* (Indianapolis, Indiana: Hackett, 1978).
33. Geach, op. cit., pp. 17–29.
34. Among others, see Richard L. Purtill, 'The Intelligibility of Disembodied Survival', *Christian Scholar's Review*, V (1) (1975) and Paul Helm, 'A Theory of Disembodied Survival and Re-embodied Existence', *Religious Studies*, 14 (1) (1978). See Also Bruce Reichenbach, *Is Man the Phoenix?: A Study of Immortality* (Washington, DC: University Press of America, 1983).

35. Perry, op. cit., p. 3.
36. I will not try to answer Perry's circularity charge noted above because I believe Parfit has decisively done so via the notion that he calls quasi-memories. See op. cit., pp. 220ff.
37. Geach, op. cit., pp. 23–8.
38. Roberts and Donaldson, op. cit., p. 295.
39. I would like to thank professors John Hick, Jim Hanink, Jerry Irish, Kai Nielsen, and Linda Zagzebski for their very helpful and incisive comments on earlier drafts of this paper.

From Here to Eternity:
A Response to Davis
Jerry A. Irish

Stephen Davis has written a provocative and instructive paper in explanation and defence of Christian belief in the resurrection of the body. At the heart of his position is a theory of temporary disembodiment that accounts for preservation of personal identity from death to resurrection.

> I call the theory temporary disembodiment because it envisions the following scenario: We human beings are born, live for a time as psycho-physical beings, and then die; after death we exist in an incomplete state as immaterial souls; and some time later in the eschaton God miraculously raises our bodies from the ground, transforms them into 'glorified bodies', and reunites them with our souls, thus making us complete and whole again. (Davis, p. 120)

Professor Davis makes several points that I find unassailable and worth repeating briefly here.

Christian anthropology, true to its Hebraic lineage, assumes an indivisible person. Terms such as 'body' and 'soul' are, at best, distinctions within a unity. We depart from the earliest Christian tradition and, interestingly, from current secular or humanistic anthropology when we posit a dualism of body and soul: 'human beings seem rather to be understood in scripture as psycho-physical entities, that is, as unities of body and soul' (Davis, p. 119).

Resurrection of the body is, according to the Hebrew Bible and the New Testament, due to the miraculous intervention of God. It is part of an eschatological upheaval in which the world as we know it is utterly transformed by its creator. Immortality, understood as a natural survival capacity that comes with our humanity, is fundamentally incompatible with the biblical notion of death and resurrection. Professor Davis is consistent with Christian scripture in saying 'apart from God's intervention death would mean annihilation for us' (Davis, p. 119).

Post-death existence prior to the resurrection of the body, when such a state is described at all in the Bible, is highly attenuated existence. Sheol is uniformly gray, and its occupants are unable even to praise God. The apostle Paul's slumber imagery is only attractive because it is less negative.

Davis is on firm biblical ground in making these points. He is also quite correct in implying throughout his paper that the problem facing Christian belief in the resurrection of the body is personal identity in the meantime. The Kingdom of God as an eschatological image has its merit in providing cosmic solutions to intolerable problems now or in the very near future. In such a context resurrection of the body is logistically feasible and psychologically satisfying. It is only with the passage of time that we begin to get anxious about the continuity of personal uniqueness over decades, then centuries, now millenia. Davis, committed like his New Testament predecessors to an eschatological framework, tries to fill in the gap from here to eternity. He does so with a disembodied soul. 'There is no moment subsequent to our births in which you and I simply do not exist – we exist either as soul-bodies or as mere souls at every moment 'till eternity' (Davis, p. 121).

In defending the idea of a disembodied soul Davis winds up ignoring or confusing the very points he himself makes so clearly. He adopts an anthropology as dualistic as the theories of immortality he rejects; he shies away from the biblical meaning of death; in an unusual combination of faith and reason he offers quasi-philosophical support for the activities of an omnipotent miracle-working deity. In short, his solution to a dilemma posed by an ancient eschatological scenario undercuts the point of the scenario itself. Let me elaborate.

Davis rejects the concept of an immortal soul because it is so often linked with a 'classical dualism' in which 'the soul is the essence of the person and is only temporarily housed or even imprisoned in a body' (Davis, p. 119). For this immortal soul Davis substitutes a disembodied soul that turns out to have many of the same attributes. It is conscious and carries with it our mental abilities and properties. Human beings in the interim state between here and eternity have experiences, beliefs, wishes, knowledge, memory, inner feelings, thoughts and languages – 'just about everything that makes up what we call personality' (Davis, p. 123).

Despite Davis's repeated reminders that we are talking here about a diminished state of existence, an attenuated person, it is hard to keep in mind any significant difference between the disembodied soul and the immortal soul. The former carries with it personal identity and continuity. Though it cannot play catch, the disembodied soul can relate to God. Though it is only a temporary state, the apostle Paul has been at it now for close to 2000 years.

If the body is as important as Davis claims it is in affirming a holistic Christian anthropology, then to what degree and for how long can a human being be thought of as a person without his or her body? And even if one can imagine memory without brain cells and inner feelings without a central nervous system, can we so easily disassociate an individual's personality from the peculiarities of their body? Davis illustrates his confusion on this point when he likens someone who is horribly disabled from birth or accident to 'a mere shadow of a true human person' (Davis, p. 140). How can we envision the unique development of personal character in a Helen Keller or an Elephant Man apart from their bodies?

In stating his case for the disembodied soul as an explanation and defence of Christian belief in the resurrection of the body, Davis concentrates on God's miraculous intervention rather than death itself. Whereas the New Testament maintains a tension between the anticipated resurrection and the annihilation that is death, each giving meaning to the other, Davis dissolves the tension by avoiding loss of selfhood altogether.

Presently living persons (or only Christians – Davis does not say which) need not anticipate the agony Jesus experienced in Gethsemane or on the cross, nor the desolation of Jesus's followers after his death. Apparently God miraculously sustains the soul at what would otherwise be death. Then at the eschaton God either miraculously gathers the essential atoms of the old body, however far flung they might be at that point, and then miraculously transforms those atoms into a glorified body, or simply creates a new and different glorified body altogether. God's final miracle is performed in uniting the glorified body with the appropriate soul.

Whether God transforms the original matter of the body into a glorified body (the view held by the fathers) or simply starts from scratch in creating a glorified body (the 'modern' theory) seems to make little difference to Davis. That should not surprise us given the implicit body-soul dualism of his position. What is more disconcerting here is the mixture of appeals Davis makes in stating his case. On the one hand he sees no 'philosophical or logical' difficulties in the "modern" theory' (Davis, p. 131); on the other hand he could as easily adopt the view of the fathers by virtue of their appeal to God's omnipotence (Davis, pp. 132ff). I will not further confuse these matters by asking whether there is any consistent hermeneutical principle in Davis's numerous references to scripture. My point is simply that, in what is ostensibly a philosophical explanation and defence of Christian belief in the resurrection of the body, Davis actually increases the frequency of appeals to divine intervention. This is turn makes 'arguments' from 'puzzle cases' seem like so much window dressing (Davis, pp. 127ff).

Why does Davis go to such quasi-philosophical lengths, especially when working with an eschatological model that requires no such mental gymnastics? The answer to that question is what makes me sympathetic to the enterprise even where it fails. Few of us want to die. And so we talk, as Davis does, about 'surviving death'. What a wonderful conjunction of two incompatible concepts! No one survives death. Theories of immortality, however debatable, have the good sense to claim we do not die in the first place. And that is finally Davis's position in the paper before us. His theory that there is no temporal gap in the existence of persons from birth to eternity is in effect a theory of immortality or, as he might begrudgingly admit, attenuated immortality. The problem here is not so much the position itself, though I find it philosophically unconvincing, but Davis's attempt to link his views to a biblical anthropology and theology that is, on the whole, unsympathetic.

Davis states the biblical case for holistic personhood. But he is apparently unwilling to accept the consequences of that view for the meaning of death. Instead he dwells on Paul's philosophical and theological reflections in I Corinthians 15. I wonder sometimes what Paul would have said had he known those who had fallen asleep would not wake up for at least 1900 years. Obviously Christian philosophers and theologians since Paul's time have grappled creatively and often insightfully with the ever-widening gap between Jesus's death and our resurrection. Professor Davis joins a respectable tradition of Christian speculation. For my own part, as a student of such speculation and as a practicing Christian, Paul was at his best when he simply interpreted the cross and resurrection of Jesus Christ to mean that nothing, not even death, could separate us from the love of God.

God, the Soul, and Coherence: A Response to Davis and Hick

Kai Nielsen

I

I argue that belief in bodily resurrection is groundless and belief in disembodied existence is probably incoherent.[1] If we can come to believe in God, as 'God' is construed in orthodox Christianity, we can hope for bodily resurrection as a straightforward matter of faith, but viewed as an empirical hypothesis about how things are likely to be, such an eventuality is thoroughly unlikely. Disembodied existence, by contrast, is so problematic as to make it beyond reasonable belief given our resources for understanding. By contrast, the reasonableness of belief in bodily resurrection depends entirely on the reasonableness of belief in the God of Christian orthodoxy. Without that belief as a reasonable human option such a belief is irrational.

Against the analytical current, Stephen Davis has powerfully, and in an incisively analytical manner, argued that the very idea of disembodied existence is not incoherent.[2] There are, he claims, logically possible circumstances where the memory criterion by itself will suffice for establishing personal identity. We must, of course, be able to distinguish between apparent memories and genuine memories for the memory criterion actually to be a criterion. But it is Davis's belief that this can be done with disembodied agents.

Suppose Hans dies and suppose we say that Hans in a disembodied form goes to heaven. Hans, Davis argues, can be identified just in case the purported Hans can remember correctly the details of his former earthly life. If there is a coherent pattern of memories here, to which, in an ordinary way, only Hans would have had ready access, then it is reasonable to say, Davis would have it, that the purported Hans, bodiless though he is, is indeed the real Hans. We have genuine memories as distinct from only apparent memories, if we have such patterns of coherence in memories. In heaven the various people could be identified just in case we have, for each of the purported disembodied persons, such patterns of coherence. Suppose this came to pass, and it could, it is claimed, for it is, or so the story goes, consistently thinkable. We have described, that is, what would have to obtain for it to obtain, and then these purported disembodied persons are identifiable. The purported Hans does not just *seem* to remember, he *really* does remember if such a coherent pattern of memories obtain. The same holds for any other putative disembodied compatriots in heaven. If the purported disembodied Hans remembers such things happening to him, then, if these memories really fit in a pattern, it is reasonable to believe there really is such a Hans – a disembodied Hans.

The soul, what either temporarily or permanently is said to exist in a disembodied way, gives Hans, in those circumstances, his personal identity. But with such a conception we have nothing which is *testable*, for neither here nor in heaven do we have a way of observing such souls, and thus we have no way of knowing who Hans or anyone else is in such an alleged state and thus we cannot identify him. Since no thesis having to do with souls can be tested, the purported Hans cannot know whether he has a soul and nor can we.

Davis believes that to talk in this verificationist way confuses talk about *criteria* for personal identity with talk about *evidence* for personal identity. He argues 'that the presence or absence of a soul or of a certain soul is not something for which we can successfully test'.[3] Neither my Sarah example in 'The Faces of Immortality', nor the Hans example here, could count, if such things were to obtain, as evidence for disembodied existence. Such claims for disembodied existence, Davis avers, are not testable.[4] But while soul-claims could not count as evidence for personal identity, such things with the memory-claims they involve could reveal, Davis claims, a criterion for personal identity. However, having a criterion that we could never use because we would not know how to use it to make testable claims for the possible application of a concept (for example, disembodied existence), *particularly where the concept in question is already problematic*, is like having a fifth wheel. It is at best a decorative appendage doing no work. If this is verificationism and anti-realism make the most of it for, whatever we say in general about such doctrines, it is plain they have a point in certain contexts, for example, anti-realism about modalities or values. If no one can know whether there are disembodied beings, or what it would be like to identify them, then it is pointless to try to use such a concept to establish personal identity claims. Pointless, someone might say, but not incoherent. Well, to return to my wooden jetliner example in 'The Faces of Immortality', while not being a self-contradictory conception, still, when we think of what it would be like for such a thing to be, it is plain that it is an incoherent conception. Similar things obtain for the purported disembodied Hans, Sarah, Sven and Alice, somehow supposedly comparing their patterned memories in heaven. We have no idea of how we could go about establishing their identities. This being so we cannot sort out which memory patterns belong to which of these putative persons.

II

John Hick has no more room in his belief-system for bodily resurrection than I do. He remarks that 'from the standpoint of a modern biblically and theologically critical Christian faith the raising of physical bodies is one of the elements of the tradition that has been filtered out in the evolution of Christian thought'.[5] He is also not a defender of the soul as a disembodied reality but understands resurrection in terms of a replica theory. There are, however, at least two decisive objections to that:

1. Persons are such that they are unique. There can be only *one* instance of each person. A *replica* of Hans could not be Hans. (If this is a conventionalist's sulk so be it.)
2. If the replica was not a complete replica, but had a substance in common with what it was a replica of, namely a disembodied existent which, even in a second or two passed from the original to the replica, this still would not be a coherent conception unless disembodied existence makes sense.

Being temporary, even momentary, makes no difference at all. It is the very idea of disembodied existence that causes the trouble. Moreover, if in turn it is said, and said correctly, that a conception of the afterlife is entirely beyond our understanding, then it is beyond our understanding, and we cannot think it, or form beliefs about it, or take it as an article of faith. We can only have faith in what we in some sense understand; we cannot take Irglig on faith for we do not understand what it is to take it on faith.[6]

Hick thinks that between us there is essentially a clash of fundamental worldviews. From my atheistic worldview or standpoint, belief in God and the afterlife is implausible; for him, by contrast, from his theistic worldview or standpoint it is highly plausible. Hick rightly sees that I am not content just to accept a perspectival-relativism where we all just have our respective clashing viewpoints and there is nothing more to be said. It is just, given such an acceptance, a matter of which faith-perspective you take up or which grips you.

While not at all wanting to say we can leap over history and just come to know what is the case ahistorically, I am claiming that for someone living in our time in the west, and with a good scientific and philosophical training, it is not reasonable for such persons to believe in God or the afterlife. This is not to say that there are no good philosophers or good scientists who are Christians. There plainly are and it is not to claim atheists are generally more reasonable than theists. That is absurdly false. There are plenty of reasonable people on either side here as well as unreasonable people. But reasonable people can have, and frequently do have, some beliefs which are not reasonable. My claim is that for scientifically well-educated and philosophically sophisticated believers belief in God and in the afterlife is unreasonable. My basis for that claim is (1) my arguments for either the incoherence or falsity of these beliefs, their being one or the other depending on how they are construed, and (2) my claim that my arguments are not so arcane or so different from other arguments with widespread currency in our intellectual life that they are not widely available in intellectual circles. My claim is the hypothetical one that *if* my arguments are sound and non-arcane, then, for anyone who is in a position to be aware of them and with the capacity critically to appraise them, then, for that person, belief in God is irrational.[7] (He may be a generally reasonable person with an irrational belief here. That is common enough among both believers and non-believers.) I am further, and not unsurprisingly, claiming my arguments are sound and non-arcane. But I am not just trading faith-perspectives with John Hick, for I am fully *cognisant* that I may be mistaken. But I am also cognisant of the fact that whether I am mistaken or not is something that is in the public sphere for us – that is, we contemporaries – to reason out whether we are Christians, Jews, atheists or what not. It is not a matter of 'Here I stand, I can believe no other'. There are facts of the matter about what arguments are sound and what are not, and what is arcane and what is not, that are just there to be established.

Notes

1. Kai Nielsen, 'The Faces of Immortality', in this volume.
2. Stephen Davis, 'The Resurrection of the Dead', in this volume.
3. Ibid., p. 136.
4. Here his account makes a sharp contrast with that of Paul Badham's. See Paul Badham's 'God, the Soul, and the Future Life', pp. 36–52, in this volume.
5. John Hick, 'Response to Nielsen', p. 32, in this volume.
6. Kai Nielsen, 'Can Faith Validate God-talk?' in my *God, Skepticism and Modernity* (Ottawa, Ont.: University of Ottawa Press, 1988).
7. See the last chapter of *God, Skepticism and Modernity*.

6 *Memento Mori*: The Buddhist Thinks about Death
Francis H. Cook

Recently I had an interesting chat with a gentleman from a local mortuary establishment who wanted me to buy a prepaid burial plan, so that my family would be spared all the trouble when the time came. Better yet, there was a guarantee that the cost would never increase beyond what I had prepaid. This is surely a prudent way to prepare for the end. I did not buy the plan, but I did become fascinated with the salesman's talk. I listened for well over half an hour and not once did the words 'die' or 'death' pass his lips. I could not resist calling this to the man's attention and he confessed that such language depressed people. I suspect that the corollary was that it would be bad for sales. But here was a man who tried hard for almost an hour to get me to buy a plan that involved embalming expenses, caskets, and burial services, and never did he refer to a corpse, embalming, death, or burial. Rather, when I 'passed on', the 'remains' would be 'prepared' and 'interred'. The lucky remains would, however, never get caught in an inflationary spiralling of costs, and survivors would not even have to decide what suit the remains would wear throughout eternity.

The salesman reflected beautifully a widespread conspiracy of silence and evasion where death is concerned. A colourful array of euphemisms, from 'passing on' to the 'buying the farm' made popular in the Vietnam War, attempt to soften the blow of death. They allow us to talk circumspectfully and delicately about what is in effect a taboo subject. Even religion, sex, and politics are sometimes permissible in polite conversation but not 'It'. We in effect deny it exists by not permitting ourselves to think of it, as Heidegger showed so cogently. We in turn justify our evasions by relegating any frank discussion to the inadmissable category of the morbid. And morbid people are no fun to be with. Yet it is, as Heidegger points out, the most possible of all our possibilities.

The taboo nature of the discussion of death reflects, I believe, what is without question the case, which is that death is the gravest of problems for human beings. I believe that this is so obviously so that I shall not try to defend what shall remain a rather flat assertion. Though it is sometimes said in flights of rhetorical fervour that there are worse things than death, I would seriously doubt that anyone really believes this. Perhaps prolonged and irremedial pain may be an exception, but aside from this, the individual can *in fact* not think of anything worse than one's own death, which must be the greatest of evils. In fact, it shall be the overriding theme of this paper that human beings are primarily motivated in their everyday conduct to escape death and that they go to great lengths to deny its reality and finality.

I have come, in fact, to think that religion is the universal human response to the problem of death. Every religion I know anything at all about, from the animistic and tribal religions of the Native Americans or Japanese Shinto, to the so-called 'salvational' religions of Christianity, Hinduism, and Islam, has much to say concerning death. However, while the former religions respond in some way to the problem as part of a broader concern for such things as a plentiful food supply, mating, ritual purity, tribal unity, and harmony with natural forces, the salvational religions, by virtue of their special concern for salvation itself, seem to me to be fundamentally and primarily responses to the fact of death. I would go so far as to say that were it not for their attempt to provide a satisfactory way of dealing with the problem of death, they would have little attraction for most people. In saying this I am adopting an understanding of the sources and function of religion which operates within anthropology, which is to see any culture as a response to the environment. Religion as an important element of culture – sometimes pervasively so – must also be seen as a problem-solving strategy, whether the strategy consists of sympathetic magic or the belief in the immortality of the soul. Such an interpretation of religion has been suggested by E. O. James and others,[1] and in agreeing with their assessment, I am, at the same time, rejecting the possibility that a religion is divinely revealed, and hence that its pronouncements *vis-à-vis* immortality and the like are rooted in something other than the needs of people. In other words, to state it rather bluntly, people invent religion as a way of coping with life, and some religions seem to be mainly coping strategies addressing the urgent problem of death.

Now, this understanding of the origins and function of religion will not be acceptable to the Abrahamic religions, given their self-understanding as being religions revealed by a divine being. However, the situation is different with the Indic religions, which are not revealed religions and which tend to think of themselves as being primarily functional or instrumental. This is undoubtedly true as far as Buddhism is concerned, which acknowledges that it is merely a means to the end of liberation and has no absolute claim. This is very clear in the well-known parable of the raft, in which the Buddha has likened his teaching to a raft, which is contructed to accomplish the task of transporting one across the river (the 'world', perhaps in the Pauline sense) but which is no longer needed once the other shore (nirvāna, liberation) is reached. However, what I shall argue in this paper is that the task for which the *Dharma* has been constructed is that of overcoming the fear of death, although this is not the way Buddhism ordinarily articulates the existential problem, which is said to be that of craving, hatred, and ignorance, and the unsatisfactory mode of being generated by them.

Thus, Buddhism is certainly not unique or even unusual in addressing the problem of death. I think that what is unusual about it is, if I am not completely off base in interpreting it as a response to death, its self-admission of being primarily a coping response to death. What is unique about it is the *way* it solves the problem. But my main purpose in this paper is to respond to the highly challenging and novel demand of showing that Buddhism has *religious* reasons for rejecting the notions of a self, the immortality of this self in an afterlife, and, incidentally, a divine being who is the creator and lover of this self. In other words, although other philosophies reject these for some of the same reasons Buddhism does, Buddhism as a religion of salvation or liberation differs from them in seeing such a rejection as being crucial to salvation.

We can do no better than to begin with the well-known rubric of the 'Four Noble Truths' (*catur-āryasatyāni*) as a good way of getting at traditional Buddhist ways of analysing the human problem and offering a solution. In brief, the first truth is the truth of suffering or turmoil (*duḥkha*), and it asserts categorically the university of *duḥkha* among sentient beings. This is the human and religious problem, formally analogous to the problem of sin among Christians. The second truth is the truth of the cause or origin (*samudaya*) of *duḥkha*. The cause is located in craving (*tṛṣṇāḥ*), and expanded discussions amplify this by also asserting that hatred (*dveṣā*) and ignorance (*avidyā*) complete the list of the three 'fundamental poisons' which cause *duḥkha*. The third truth, the truth of cessation (*nirodha*), defines the religious goal as the cessation or stopping of craving, hatred, and ignorance, hence, *duḥkha*. The fourth truth is the truth of the path, or method (*marga*), which lists eight factors which bring about liberation, and these are often subsumed under the three broader categories of moral re-education, meditation, and wisdom or insight. All of Buddhism can be discussed in terms of the four truths. While traditional literature takes them in order, I shall begin with the second truth as a better place to begin for my own purpose.

The second truth finds the source of *duḥkha* in craving. Sometimes translated as 'desire', *tṛṣṇā* is a technical term with a very specific and limited meaning. *Tṛṣṇā* is a very powerful, persistent, mostly unconscious drive to perpetuate the self, to make it comfortable and happy, and to preserve its needed sense of self-importance and meaningfulness. Consequently, however the term is translated, it should be reserved to refer to this fundamental erotic drive for self-importance and self-preservation, and not to those actions we loosely categorise as desire, such as my desire to write this paper or when I want to eat because I am hungry. To Buddhistically quench desire or craving therefore does not entail ceasing to want lunch or write papers but does mean that the individual is no longer motivated primarily to preserve the self. *Karma*, then, is an intensified form of craving taking the form of vocal or physical acts designed to satisfy the craving. A lie, for instance, is seen as an attempt to avoid discomfort or worse for the self. A racial slur is an attempt to maintain a sense of self-importance through the demeaning of another. Any vocal act of this sort is always self-referential and self-generated in the sense that it is basically an attempt to maintain a sense of self-importance, self-integrity, and self-preservation. The same is true of physical acts motivated and preceded by intention or will of the same kind.

According to the Buddhist anthropology, craving and karmic action are expressions of an extremely deep-seated erotic urge towards self-preservation, which is clearly indicated by the stereotyped formula of the second truth, which speaks of craving for sensual delights and for being and becoming. However, the existential problem of *duḥkha* is created out of the self's inability to be satisfied that it is definitively secure. It never achieves a sure sense of invulnerability and significance in the face of real or imagined threats. It is frequently prevented from acquiring those things which it imagines will grant power and security, such as material things or immaterial things such as power, reputation, or philosophical certitude. Even if some things are actually required, they provide no definitive security, because it is the nature of the self to be fundamentally and irremediably insecure, suspicious, doubtful, and fearful. The Buddhist picture of human life, then, is not a pretty one. Our lives are portrayed as an unremittant cycle, in which a craving for security generates acts designed to ensure security, the act fails to achieve the security, and the frustration of this fundamental urge perpetuates and indeed intensifies the self's feeling of fragility and insecurity. Now, what I have been calling 'insecurity' is what Buddhism calls *duḥkha*, often translated as 'suffering' (somewhat misleadingly) but perhaps better translated as 'turmoil'. T. R. V. Murti has defined *duḥkha* as 'impeded willing, the inconsonance of our desires with objective circumstances'.[2] 'Turmoil' seems to capture the sense of the term inasmuch as it portrays the restless pursuit of the self for security which it cannot find anywhere. Thus, we have the cycle I spoke of:

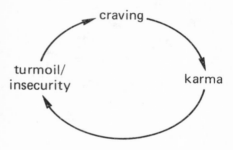

The object of Buddhism, as stated in the third of the Noble Truths, is to bring an end to the turmoil or insecurity by bringing an end to the craving, hatred (a negative form of craving), and delusion, the so-called 'three fundamental poisons'. The individual who has accomplished this is obviously a rather remarkable person, inasmuch as all craving of the sort I have spoken of has been eradicated and consequently his actions are no longer of the karmic sort. The transformed individual thus continues to live and function effectively in the world (the Buddha is said to have actively taught his discovery for 45 years after his own liberation and enlightenment), but unlike ordinary people, such a person is no longer driven compulsively by deep-seated urges to perpetuate the self. The Buddha, as a model of such an individual, is in fact appreciated as the ideal human being in being a perfect union of clarity of understanding (*prajñā*) and compassion (*karuṇā*).

As I have thought about this scheme of liberation and its anthropology for almost three decades, I have come to appreciate several insights which are muted in traditional literature or which are articulated in different language than that which I wish to use here. The first insight is that human beings in their unreconstructed state are severely and seriously neurotic in a way not recognised by western therapies. While most people would protest that they are healthy or 'normal', and indeed are, according to the canons of western psychology, Buddhism would on the contrary say that by its criterion, their so-called normal behaviour is conditioned by a universal and fundamental insecurity and that such behaviour is not really healthy. People are consequently victimised by a universal drive which lies beneath the threshold of self-awareness for the most part, and their normal behaviour is in fact destructive to others and to themselves. In this way, just about all of us are sick.

The second insight I find in Buddhism is related to the first and directly bears on the subject of this paper. Buddhism has, it seems to me, determined that it is a deep fear of death that is responsible for the insecurity that characterises the lives of ordinary people, and, consequently, it is the fear of death that must be overcome. In such biographies of the Buddha as Aśvaghoṣa's *Buddhacarita* (The Deeds of the Buddha), the young prince and Buddha-to-be is portrayed as being motivated to leave the palace and its pleasures after seeing successively an old man, a sick man, a corpse, and a mendicant monk. Aśvaghoṣa tells us that the prince was then in his mid-twenties and had been completely insulated from the knowledge of such things by a protective father. Encountering old age, sickness, and death was thus a revelation, and these sights filled his heart with overwhelming grief and turmoil. His decision to abandon the palace, with its power and unimaginable wealth, along with his lovely wife and newborn son, was prompted by the need to find a solution to the problems of old age, sickness, and death. But as is abundantly clear from the teachings that came out of his quest, the solution was not to deny the reality of such things as death, nor was the solution to be one of a literal escape from them. In fact, the Buddha himself died at the age of eighty of old age and illness, so his fate was to be that of all beings. He, and his successors, never taught that death is an illusion or that one's essential self, with its memories, its uniqueness, and its subjective enjoyment of experience, would survive biological death.

Death was not to be denied as really complete and final but seen realistically and honestly. The solution to the problem of death had to be found within the context of an absolutely realistic acceptance of death. Thus, if the fear of death spoils life, and death cannot in any sense be denied or escaped, then the only solution is to remove the fear.

Now, when I say that the strategy was to overcome the *fear* of death rather than overcome death itself, I mean that Buddhism, alone among the salvational religions, refused to adopt the strategy of other religions of denying that the self really dies. Hinduism taught, and teaches, that one's true self, the *ātman*, is immortal and either incarnates in new, different bodies or, freed from the cycle of rebirths, is absorbed into the divine in eternal life. In Christianity and Islam, the soul, once created, is also immortal. Even though the body dies, it lives on. The effect in these religions is *in effect* to deny the finality and completeness of death. Physical death then is seen as an unavoidable but brief interlude between one life and a better subsequent one. *In the end*, all will be all right, and as the scriptures say, death will not triumph, death loses its sting. As a gospel song says, 'there'll be no more cryin, there'll be no more dyin'.

Buddhism in all its forms has rejected this approach to the problem of death. The individual who achieves enlightenment and liberation does not achieve subjective immortality or even manage to avoid the headaches, indigestion, and constipation that ordinary beings are subject to. What he does achieve, on the other hand, is an unshakeable serenity in the face of complete death. It is, on the other hand, impossible for him to rationalise the experience away by assuming that he will somehow survive death, because, as is well known, the very cornerstone of Buddhism is the total rejection of any notion of some substance-like entity which can survive death, whether it be the more metaphysical *ātman* of Hinduism or the more intuitively-derived *ātman* found in introspection. As far as Buddhism is concerned, it doesn't matter whether one calls it a self (*ātman*), a person (*pudgala*), being (*sattva*), or life principle (*jīva*), it is a mere illusion and certainly not immortal. Even though Buddhism incorporates within its system the more widely-spread Hindu notion of rebirth, rebirth or reincarnation *must* be interpreted in some way that avoids the implication that it is a 'me' or 'self' which is reborn.[3]

The Buddhist approach was to achieve serenity in the face of death by attacking the problem at its source, which is the self which craves above all else to perdure and be happy. Now, when I speak of a self which craves, I mean a mind or a consciousness which is able by virtue of its structure to objectify itself in self-consciousness, to develop an overriding concern for its own preservation and contentment, and which can imagine its possible non-being and long for its continuation. I am not referring simply to what is often called the 'instinct for survival', which is common to all sentient beings, but to a capacity probably unique among human beings to be self-aware and to care about the assumed self found in that awareness. So, when I speak of the self's craving for perpetuation and happiness, I mean human minds which objectify themselves as something independent, substantial, and enduring and which can become self-concerned in a way non-humans cannot. Thus, if it is a matter of human minds construing themselves to be selves and craving the perpetuation of these imputed selves, the proper strategy must be to see clearly that the self is a fiction and in this way to eradicate the roots of craving.

Buddhism has consistently dealt with the problem of the self and its insecurity and craving through the use of techniques which in the west are called 'meditation'. In many forms, these techniques involve a temporary 'bracketing' of various intellectual and emotional obstacles that stand in the way of a clear, objective glimpse of the psycho-physical being. By temporarily anaesthetising fear, anger, sense-desire, and so on, the individual is enabled to experience himself objectively as being what is given in an empirical analysis, rather than as being what he is told to *believe*, what he *hopes* is there, what he *supposes* will be found, or what any so-called authorities have *claimed* is there. These techniques are basically analytical in nature, designed to decompose wholes into their components. The self or person is experienced as a locus of physical and psychological factors (*skandha*), each of which is experienced as a discontinuous stream of atomic events, each atomic unit coming into an extremely brief being on the basis of antecedent conditions, and then ceasing to exist, to be followed by a successor, and so on. Such an analysis divulges nothing of a substance-like entity in which these materials and psychic factors are imbedded, nor do these factors themselves satisfy the criteria for a substance or self, being conditioned, interdependent, discontinuous, impermanent. The deeply ingrained notion of self must, consequently, be abandoned in the face of objective, empirical evidence to the contrary. The enduring, substance-like self turns out to be nothing but the mind's mistaken self-image, a delusion, and a delusion which has an enormous impact on the quality of life and the nature of motivation. In this way, through these techniques, Buddhism arrives at the conclusion recently made by Derek Parfit, in *Reasons and Persons*, via different methods: it matters how we perceive ourselves, and our perceptions are surely mistaken.

According to all accounts, ancient and modern, the effects of insight meditation are remarkable. The individual *experiences* himself as a mere locus of incessant and extremely rapid change, a torrent of impermanent psychic and physical states ungrounded in any enduring and unchanging substance. The individual thus arrives at an experiential understanding of what he is and, more importantly, what he is not. He is led to conclude, on the basis of an objective self-analysis, that he is not the kind of self he had hitherto assumed. He is, that is, led to such a new self-understanding, not on the basis of reason, logic, or metaphysical speculation, but because a self is not given empirically in the experience of insight. Hence, the absence of a self is not a theory but a conclusion rooted in the experiential self-perception and self-understanding of a radically transformed consciousness.

The results of meditation are momentous for the individual. First, it is realised that there is nothing in the psycho-physical being of such a nature that it can or will survive the dissolution of the individual, and hence any hope for immortality must be realised as being groundless. Secondly and related to the first result, the experience of oneself as a mere configuration of conditioned and impermanent physical and mental factors must mean that one's own fate is no different from that of any other being, whether a tree, a stone, or a mosquito. There is not one shred of evidence that human life is exceptional or privileged. Such an insight must be not only extremely sobering but must be highly conducive to the eradication of the self-pride and anthropocentric arrogance synonymous with the belief in a self.

The insight I have spoken of must also have a crucial bearing on the problems of death. If, as Buddhism claims, a deep, unconscious (usually) anxiety about death has its origin in a mind-self which is by nature insecure and self-protective, then the dissolution of the idea of self-hood will remove the fear of death and its actional consequences. What is involved, which is to say the same thing, is that the individual in his new self-understanding as non-self comes to acknowledge himself, and unconditionally accept himself as essentially impermanent and mortal. What seems important here is that the individual *really* confront and acquiesce to the undeniable fact that there is no possible way to escape death. Also, of course, since he is no longer a self which is primarily concerned with self-preservation, the knowledge of his own eventual fate will have no emotional impact. 'Easy come, easy go', so to speak.

It might be said, then, that the Buddhist approach to death is to get it over with while still living, so that the business of life is no longer dominated and conditioned by the fear of death. In fact, there is a Zen expression which says, 'Die and become thoroughly dead while living and all will be well thereafter'. In Zen this is called the 'Great Death' (*daishi*) and it is the culmination of an often long and arduous religious training which is aimed at the dropping off of the self and its concerns. However, it is understood that the ultimate object is to enjoy the 'Great Life' which emerges phoenix-like from the ashes of the extinct self. One may presumably live joyously and creatively having effectively conquered death while still knowing without doubt that one will die absolutely. In Tibetan Buddhist iconography there is another reflection of this understanding that true self-understanding kills both the fear of death and its consequences. It is the image of Yamāntaka, who is the 'wrathful' or 'angry' manifestation of the Bodhisattva Mañjuśrī, who is turn represents understanding or insight (*prajñā*). *Yama* is in Hindu religious symbolism the lord of the underworld; he is death personified. *Anta* means 'end', and an *antaka* is an 'ender', so Yama-antaka is literally the 'death-ender' or 'he who puts an end to death'. The meaning is that the *prajñā*-insight of self-understanding as being non-self puts an end to death, even though we all end up in that underworld.

Buddhism is thus unique among the salvational religions in finding a solution to the problem of death that not only does not rely on the notions of a self, immortality, or a deity who creates the self and confers immortality, but sees the solution to the problem as necessarily requiring that such notions are rejected. The tendency to adopt a rather realistic and naturalistic view of death also stands in contrast to salvational religions which consider death to be the 'wages of sin', an unwelcome and alien intruder which will, in the final days, be banished forever. For Buddhism, death is simply the fate of all things which are conditioned and compounded, and there is no exception to this law. This tendency towards realism in Buddhism therefore leaves it no alternative but to insist that liberation and the subsequent cessation of existential problems must be accomplished within the framework of what appears to be the case empirically rather than within the framework of *beliefs* which may offer some comfort but which do not definitively solve the problem of the self and its overwhelming concerns. Thus, the invitation of the Buddha was not 'come and believe' but rather 'come and see' (*ehi passika*), an invitation to validate or invalidate any idea in the crucible of experimental self-understanding. He thus never rested his claims on the unseen and unseeable, although the unseen and unknowable might be pleasant to believe, but on the knowable and experiencable, although these might not be comforting. His solution to the human problem was not a religion of comfort but it promised to make a definitive end to the fear that plagues us.

Now, the above characterisation of the Buddhist approach to death must make it sound very much like recent trends in western philosophy in so far as there is a heavy emphasis on realism, a rejection of metaphysics, and an overwhelming trust in the empirical basis for knowledge. Buddhism also shares some conclusions with psychology, in so far as it assumes that such concepts as the self as an immortal entity and a protective, loving divinity who treasures the self are projections of deep-seated psychological needs. A contemporary monk-scholar from Sri Lanka, Walpola Rahula, says, in words that most Buddhists would probably endorse,

> Two ideas are psychologically deeprooted in man: self-protection and self-preservation. For self-protection man has created God, on whom he depends for his own protection, safety, and security, just as a child depends on its parents. For self-preservation man has conceived the idea of an immortal Soul or *Ātman*, which will live eternally. In his ignorance, weakness, fear, and desire, man needs these two things to console himself. Hence he clings to them deeply and fanatically.[4]

Following this rather blunt language, Rahula uses the clearly Freudian language of 'projection' and says, as I have, that the aim of Buddhism is to strike at the root of fear, desire, and weakness, which is the self.[5]

However, the Buddhist rejection of the concepts mentioned is not simply made out of a need for empirical consistency, a childish desire to thumb the nose at mass superstition, or even just because the notions are projections of need. After all, what is wrong with having a need for security? What is wrong with telling ourselves stories to make ourselves feel better? Is not a metaphysical whistling in the dark ultimately quite harmless?

What distinguishes Buddhism from western psychology and philosophy, despite some of their shared procedures and interpretations of
human experience, is the fact that Buddhism believes that a superior
life is possible if such notions are rejected. Actually, the distinction is
not that sharp, for Freud clearly sees a personal and cultural
advantage in the ultimate maturity of individuals who have been
healed of their childhood neurosis, in his *The Future of an Illusion*. I
am sure, too, that many western thinkers are also convinced that
humanity can only improve once childish, unfounded notions are
abandoned. However, I do not believe that the most sanguine
Wittgensteinian believes that the abandonment of such notions brings
about the profound kind of self-transformation envisioned by Buddhism. As Buddhism sees these notions, they are not merely projections, as Rahula says, but they are positively harmful, indeed
insidious in that they *aggravate* the self's fear and insecurity and
perpetuate the most fundamental of all problems. Consequently,
while on the one hand such ideas cannot definitively solve the
existential problem, on the other hand they are serious impediments
to an important self-transformation. It is this 'ultimate concern' for
self-transformation which makes the Buddhist critique of these
notions religious in a way the western philosophical and psychological
critiques are not.

My point is that the rejection of the assumptions I have been
discussing must finally be considered within the context of a programme which is ultimately aimed at the creation of a more perfect human
being, which I will call, in Zen fashion, the 'true man' (正人 ,
including, of course, both male and female). The 'true man' is true in
the sense that the individual has seen through and abandoned the
illusion of self-hood, and, along with it, the unrelenting craving and
hatred that express the self's insecurity. The whole Buddhist tradition
has been consistent in characterising this individual as an ideal union
of clarity of insight and compassion, as I remarked earlier. I, myself,
like to see such an ideal as a kind of ultimate maturity or full
adulthood, on the assumption that unfounded fear and insecurity,
conduct that for the most part reflects this insecurity, and fantasies
(Freud again) that serve mainly to comfort, are infantile, while an
objective and realistic view of life, and a compassionate caring which
refuses to interpret all decision-making and action in terms of
self-need and self-protection, is the mature flowering of a seed
potential contained within each embryonic human being. Such an

ideal may also be seen as the attainment of true health, assuming that a neurotic concern for self-preservation, with its compulsive and driven actional consequences, has been cured. In the most general sense, the ideal could be seen as the attainment of completeness and fulfilment.

Buddhism has also been completely consistent over the millennia in its conviction that the completeness and fulfilment of the 'true man' can only be attained through the complete transcendence or forgetting of the notion of self-hood. If the relationship between the self and human completeness is a necessary one, which I believe to be the case,[6] then not only is a naïve and uncritical assertion of self-hood inimicable to the achievement of completeness and fulfilment, but so likewise is the unfounded belief in the immortality of the self and in a divine being who creates and treasures it, in so far as these beliefs not only reinforce the need to believe in the reality of the self but, what is equally pernicious, they reinforce the sense of self-importance and anxiety for the fate of the self. This is what is religiously at stake in the affirmation or denial of these notions as far as Buddhism is concerned. The Buddhist must, that is, ask the question, in the total absence of any evidence that such things are objective realities, and in the face of the counter-evidence of meditational insight practices, that the self is not to be found in a careful empirical investigation, then what can such ideas be but, as Rahula says so forcibly, human inventions calculated to provide a sense of importance and security? But to cling tenaciously to the empirically and philosophically untenable in fact impedes and stalls the maturity, sanity, and completeness which are synonymous with selflessness. Selflessness by definition is totally antithetical to notions which are self-aggrandising, self-serving, and self-reinforcing, and so the notions *must* be abandoned as bad for the health.

However, the other side of the coin must be that the truly complete adult is one who accepts himself as a being who really, completely dies, and that there is no tragedy here, no cause for an incapacitating sorrow. To be a selfless self must mean that one has overcome the pathetic belief that oneself as a human being is special or privileged in escaping the end of all conditioned and compounded things. I must, in such a self-knowledge, indeed 'die like a dog', but this should not be thought of as demeaning or degrading. In fact, there can be positive benefits for sanity and health in modestly, humbly, affirming our strict continuity with the rest of living beings.

Such an appraisal of the ontological status of human beings and their fate is, from the perspective of human beings, dominated by fear and insecurity and who need individually and as a species to believe that they are 'really somebody', hard to take, to say the least. The Buddha was well aware that people by their very nature really wanted a teaching that affirmed their significance and comforted them, and he acknowledged that his teachings ran contrary to the deepest yearnings of the human heart. He said of his teachings:

> I have realized this Truth [*Dharma*] which is deep, difficult to see, difficult to understand . . . comprehensible only by the wise . . . Men who are overpowered by passions and surrounded by a mass of darkness cannot see this Truth, which is against the current, which is lofty, deep, subtle, and hard to comprehend.[7]

'Against the current' (*paṭisotagāmi*) is a clear recognition that what he had to say about the cherished self and its hoped-for immortality were not what people wanted to hear but which had to be said because it is Truth, *Dharma*. Consequently, as I have written elsewhere, such an approach to the self and its fate is part of a teaching which is rather chilly in its lack of warmth and comfort, and it is equally uncompromising in its insistence that a complete, perfected humanity is only possible with the utter abandonment of our most cherished notions.

This cool and uncompromising view of the self and its fate is characteristic of just about all forms of Buddhism, but it is particularly evident in Zen annals, where many stories are told of the nonchalant, matter-of-fact way the great Zen masters went to their deaths. I recount just one here, which is typical in many ways and has the proper Zen flavour about it. When Eshun, a Zen nun, was past 60 and about to leave this world, she had some monks pile up some wood in the monastery courtyard. Seating herself firmly in the middle of the pile of wood, she had it set fire around the edges. 'O nun!' shouted a monk, 'is it hot in there?' 'Such a matter would concern only a stupid person like yourself', answered Eshun. The flames arose, and she died.[8]

But along with edifying stories of this sort, what is particularly evident in Zen history and literature is that many of its great thinkers and practitioners saw their Buddhist practice as a response to the pressing problem of death, the overcoming of which would, as I have said above, release them to the 'Great Life'. Thus, in the thirteenth century the Japanese Zen master, Dōgen, tells us how as a young child he attended his mother's funeral and watched the smoke of the incense rise in the air and dissipate and disappear. His heart was stricken with grief and agitation at the thought that all things are impermanent and eventually disappear, like the smoke, and he became a monk at a very early age, determined, like the Buddha, to find a solution to this urgent problem. His search led him to take the perilous trip to China where he hoped he would discover the answer. Under the tutelage of the master, Ju-ching, he achieved what he called the 'dropping off of mind and body' (*shinjin datsuraku*), and liberated, returned to Japan where he founded the Sōtō line of Zen and became one of Japan's great literary, religious, and philosophical luminaries. What was the answer he found? Hee-jin Kim says:

> Dōgen did not indulge in aesthetic diletantism and sentimentalism as a way to escape from the fleeting fates of life [as many of his contemporaries did] but, instead, examined the nature of impermanence and its ultimate companion, death, unflinchingly, and attempted to realize liberation in and through this inexorable scheme of things.[9]

What Kim means by realising liberation 'in and through' impermanence and death is that Dōgen's response to them was to confront them seriously as the primary, fundamental, universal fact of one's own being and the fact of all being, and to accept and affirm them without reservation. The 'dropping off of mind and body', which is enlightenment, is the abandonment of all false and self-serving notions, and the dropping off of the body is the freedom from any attachment to the fate of the body.

Several centuries later a Zen master in Dōgen's line, Suzuki Shōsan, echoed this same concern for decisively disposing of the problem of death. 'I teach', he said, 'Buddhism for cowards',[10] 'I practice [Buddhism] because I hate death'.[11] 'No matter how long he lives, Shōsan has nothing special to talk about but death'.[12] Thus, Suzuki, like Dōgen and generations of Buddhists before him, displays the understanding that the belief in a self and the fear for its survival result in a tragic distortion of life that need not be. The abandonment of the illusion of self-hood, consequently, had the dual effect of eliminating the source of the fear and permitting the individual to understand himself and, most importantly, to radically accept himself without qualm or qualification as an ordinary conditioned, impermanent, brief coalescence of psychic and material factors. To die, then is nothing special.

It must be evident from my discussion that this rather realistic, naturalistic, no-nonsense view of the human animal, along with the basically empirical reason for doing so, is not in itself so very different from procedures and conclusions found in much recent western writing. The Buddha sounds very modern, or, I should say, modern philosophers and many theologians have become quite Buddhist in their anthropologies. I have mentioned Derek Parfit's book, *Reasons and Persons* earlier; he concludes his book with a chapter with the title, 'Buddha's View'. The British theologian, Don Cupitt, has written a book entitled *Taking Leave of God*, in which he argues that the Christian must do exactly that. Process theologians, following Whitehead, admit nothing more comforting than the possibility of 'objective immortality', the eternal remembering of our life experiences by God, but no subjective immortality is possible in the Whiteheadian metaphysics. The attitude of linguistic philosophers towards the soul, God, and immortality needs no comment. All such ideas seem to be being jettisoned as bad ideas under the probe of linguistic criticism, the dominance of empirical methods, the appeals of logic and other forms of reasoning.

The question, then, is this: is it really necessary to undergo years of strenuous meditation in order to decisively reject the self and its immortality and consequently accept death realistically and with equanimity? I think that it is certainly possible to reject the idea of a substantial self on the basis of reason, as Whitehead did, for instance, and there seems to be no empirical basis for believing that there is a kind of survival of physical death. However, the Buddhist position has always been that reason alone is inadequate in dealing with such problems as the self and its fate. To simply arrive at conclusions on the basis of mere reason is to very seriously underestimate the tenacity with which the mind clings to its belief in its self-hood and the power that the fear of death holds over the emotions, will, and conduct. In fact, it could be argued that a purely philosophically-based rejection of such notions as substantial self-hood are often little more than one more attempt on the part of the self to assert itself in some way. The self is understood by Buddhism to be capable of a thousand different ways of maintaining its sense of value, and often what appear to be objective and rational reasons for acting in a certain way are just the movements of an exceedingly cunning and resourceful self. But it is not that good old hard-headed reason will not go at least part way in disabusing oneself of untenable and pernicious notions. Buddhism has always known that reasoning can clear up a lot of bad thinking, but finally one must resort to techniques such as meditation which have in fact been devised with the specific objective of completely restructuring the personality in a way reason can not. Without that deep restructuring, one may loudly proclaim that there is no self or immortality but the fear remains, along with the destructive and distorting consequences.

Whatever reasons contemporary philosophers and humanists may have for rationally rejecting the notions of self-hood, immortality, and God – and there are several reasons – they are not *religious* reasons, and Buddhism, in all its atheism, and with all its rejection of the very essentials of the other salvational religions, is indubitably a religion. It is a religion because its reason for being is to make possible the ultimate transformation of the 'true man' in all his selflessness. But, because there is an unbridgeable contradiction between the 'true man' and the individual who believes he is a self and that that self is somehow special and privileged in a way no other being is, then the attainment of what Buddhism considers to be perfectly human can only be achieved through the forgetting of the self and a rejection of any form of immortality. To do so means that death itself must be grasped realistically, honestly, and unemotionally. In this way, the possibility of being perfectly human and the problem of death are intimately connected in Buddhism.

Buddhism is a tough religion. It offers not a shred of comfort or assurance regarding what is without doubt our greatest concern. It will not pat one on the back with a 'There, there, it will be all right', but, in its own way, will snatch away the last rag of hope, remind one that life is a flash of lightning in the darkness, a bead of dew on the morning grass, and suggest that one use one's time to settle this one great matter once and for all. A monk once asked Zen master Ta-sui, 'When the great conflagration flares up at the end of the world and the great cosmos is completely destroyed, I wonder, will "It" perish also?' Ta-sui said, 'It will perish'. The monk persisted, 'Then, will "It" be gone with the other?' Ta-sui said, 'It will be gone with the other'. What a sweet, kindly reply.

Notes

1. Besides James, E. R. Goodenough, in *The Psychology of Religious Experience* (New York: Basic Books, 1965) takes a similar approach.
2. T. R. V. Murti, *The Central Philosophy of Religion* (London: Allen & Unwin, 1965) p. 221.
3. There are several ways to interpret rebirth. The first, which is the literal reading, is clearly not a possibility for Buddhism, since Buddhism rejects the possibility of anything about the individual surviving physical death. This must be mythical and requires demythologisation. A second interpretation widely accepted by Buddhists is that it is the craving which continues on after death to become re-embodied. Craving is thus seen as the builder of this world. The relationship between individual *A* who dies and individual *B* who is born is said to be one of neither identity nor complete difference. They are *not* the same person, but they are causally related. A third interpretation is that of 'instantaneous' rebirth, which sees the individual as dying and being reborn incessantly, somewhat analogously with the process of actual entities in Whitehead's thought.
4. Walpola Rahula, *What the Buddha Taught* (New York: Grove Press, 1959) p. 51.
5. Ibid., p. 52.
6. I have written extensively on this in 'Dōgen's View of Authentic Selfhood and its Socio-ethical Implications', in Wm LaFleur (ed.) *Dōgen Studies* (University of Hawaii Press, 1985) pp. 131–49.
7. Rahula, op. cit., p. 52.
8. Recounted in Paul Reps, *Zen Flesh, Zen Bones* (Garden City, New York: Doubleday, 1961) p. 27.
9. Hee-jin Kim, *Dōgen Kigen: Mystical Realist* (Tuscon: University of Arizona Press, 1975) p. 183.
10. Royall Tyler (transl.) *Selected Writings of Suzuki Shōsan* (Ithaca: Cornell University East Asian Papers, no. 13, 1977) I:72.
11. Ibid., III:12.
12. Ibid., III:29.

Zen and Death: A Response to Cook

Paul Badham

I would like to thank Professor Cook for his thought-provoking interpretation of Buddhist teaching and for the striking parallels to which he draws attention between aspects of the Buddha's 'no-self' doctrine and some contemporary philosophical writing on the self. Let me start my comments first on the substantive issue of what follows from a thorough-going acceptance of a post-Wittgensteinian, or as Cook argues, a post-Buddha understanding of personhood as a constantly changing succession of impermanent psychic and physical states with no enduring self or centre. It does seem to me correct to argue that when this understanding of personhood is adopted all notions of a personal life after death do lose their coherence and death can, or at any rate should, cease to be perceived as of any great significance. If there is no satisfactory way of defining our identity now, how much more must that be the case in the hypothesis of a life after death! It is indeed not at all surprising that contemporary philosophers of mind who are increasingly attracted to such views see the notion of life after death as a total non-starter.

Moreover, I would also take Cook's point that if this view of personhood is true, then psychological balance and maturity require us to accept it as such. For I would agree that not to live in accord with perceived reality is the mark of a neurotic, or of a person suffering psychological disorientation. But whether this view of the self is in accordance with reality is what needs to be discussed. Rahula cites Asanga's remark, 'There is the fact of no-selfness',[1] but whether this is a fact, and what is meant by the claim, need first to be weighed. For I do not for one minute accept Professor Cook's belief that all the empirical evidence is on one side. What I would most dispute in his paper is the view that 'there is not one shred of evidence that human life is privileged'.[2] On the contrary, what is really daunting about teaching a graduate course on the empirical evidence for survival, as I do, is the sheer amount of solid and apparently well-documented empirical evidence now available. I don't mean that the evidence is necessarily compelling for it obviously isn't, but the reason for this is not any shortage of data, but the difficulty of reconciling this data with the well-founded picture of reality built up over the centuries by the natural sciences. As C. D. Broad points out, when weighing evidence 'we always have to take into account the probability or improbability of an alleged event, relative to the rest of our knowledge and well-founded belief other than the special evidence adduced in its favor'.[3]

Turning from the issue as to whether or not these notions of the self are true, I wish to raise the further issue of whether or not they can be characterised as Buddhist. At one level, of course, the picture Francis Cook paints is Buddhist in that it is put forward as an interpretation of some key Buddhist scriptures. It is a perspective which has been presented by other western scholars and has some precedent in elements in the Zen Buddhist tradition. And yet I am uneasy about it because I find it hard to square this view with some of the most deeply established elements in the Buddhist tradition. I was very struck at a previous conference on Life after Death held in Korea by the reaction of other Buddhist scholars to a paper by a Zen priest from Japan who gave a comparable picture to that presented here by Francis Cook. For their reaction was not simply disagreement, but utter bewilderment that any Buddhist could say such things!

It does seem to be the case that with the possible exception of some elements in the Zen tradition, Buddhism as a living religion has never equated death with extinction, but has had a deep and abiding conviction of the reality of a future life. As Edward Conze puts it in his preface to the section of his edition of Buddhist Scriptures which deals with other worlds: 'The horizon of Buddhism is not bounded by the limits of the sensory world, their true interests lie beyond it . . . many Buddhists believe they possess definite knowledge of life after death'.[4] This is also true of popular Buddhism. The popularity of the tales of Buddha's former lives, the institution of Lamaism in Tibetan Buddhism, and the fascination of Buddhist monks and laity in reported claims to remember former lives only make sense in a context of widespread belief in a fairly concrete understanding of rebirth. Then think too of the vast literature of the pure-land tradition with its pictures of heavenly existence, and think also of the vivid descriptions of purgatorial hells, or look at the detailed descriptions in the *Tibetan Book of the Dead* of the experience the mind is to encounter in the Bardo world. And in the realm of culture, the ethos of funerals in Thailand displays an attitude of mind where life after death is not simply *believed in* but is treated as an unquestioned *fact of life*, a kind of conviction far deeper than anything we know today in so-called Christian countries. Moreover, I believe that the basic reason for the American defeats in Vietnam and Cambodia was the failure of American strategies to take into account the total fearlessness of death that a still living tradition of belief in reincarnation had given to their opponents.

The problem we have to face is that the doctrine of rebirth is at least as deeply rooted in Buddhism as is the no-self doctrine, and any exposition of Buddhism which is to do justice to the complexity of the theme requires that both doctrines be given full weight. I do not believe that Mrs Rhys Davids was right to say that in the light of the rebirth doctrine we must interpret away the no-self belief,[5] and by parity of reasoning I think Cook ought not to say that in the light of the no-self doctrine we *must* demythologise the doctrine of rebirth.[6]

Any valid presentation of Buddhism must take the two beliefs into account. So let us look again at the no-self doctrine. Cook is of course right to say that the Buddha denied the immortality of the self, but he should have gone on to mention that in the next verse the Buddha went on to deny the extinction of the soul of death.[7] In this, as in other doctrines, Buddha sought a 'middle path'. We may wonder how a middle path is possible in such a context, yet I suggest that it does make considerable sense. In one sense death clearly marks the end of life, but if one assumes the reality of rebirth, as the Buddha did,[8] then in another sense death is not the end.

Every denial has to be understood against its opposing affirmation. Buddha's denial of the self is a denial of one very specific understanding of the self, the concept of *ātman*. Buddha denied that there is a permanent *unchanging* spirit which can be considered self or soul or ego as *opposed* to matter. He believed that the idea of an *abiding immortal substance* called *ātman* was a mental projection. In particular he objected to an identification of this *ātman* with a supposed world soul. As he taught, 'the speculative view that the universe is *ātman* and that I shall be that after death – permanent, abiding, everlasting, unchanging, and that I shall exist as such for eternity, is not that wholly and completely foolish'.[9]

I can only say that I think Buddha was absolutely right in what he denied. The concept of *ātman* is just not a valid understanding of what it means to be human. To be human is to be developing, changing, moving on. Only a dynamic concept of self-hood does justice to experience or empirical reality. But none of this excludes

Buddha's belief in rebirth, or indeed other possible ideas of a future life.

However, keeping with the Buddha let us note that he did believe that something went on. Cook rightly says that Buddhism rejects the idea that the *ātman*, or the person (*pudgala*), or the being (*sattva*), or the life principle (*jiva*), goes on.[10] But he does not mention what Buddhism affirms, namely that what goes on is 'linking-psyche' (*patsandhi viññāna*) – a mental unit which leaves the body at death and is subsequently reborn.[11] This linking-psyche, while clearly very different from the Hindu *ātman*, is not necessarily very different from what western scholars think of as the subject of the claimed out-of-the-body experiences. Certainly Saeng Chandra-Ngarm, Professor of Religion in Chiang Mai University in Thailand, has claimed near-death experiences as proof of the reality of the linking-psyche leaving the body at death, and hence as evidential support for the Buddhist understanding of life after death.[12]

I accept that this may go too far for some western interpreters of Buddhism, yet even Walpola Rahula, whose concept of the self Cook cites with approval, insists on real continuity through death. As Rahula says, 'what we call death is the total non-functioning of the physical body'. Yet he claims this does not imply that our physical and mental forces or energies also stop:

> Buddhism says 'no'. Will, volition, desire, thirst to exist, to continue, to become more and more, is a tremendous force . . . This force does not stop with the functioning of the body, which is death; but it continues manifesting itself in another form, producing re-existence which is called rebirth.[13]

I suggest that will, volition, desire and the thirst to exist is quite a lot to survive, and certainly very different from total extinction.

Buddha himself explicitly denied that death meant extinction. Indeed he described the notion as a 'wicked heresy',[14] even when put forward as an interpretation of the final state of parinirvana! How much more when describing the simple passing on from one life to the next. The fact that it is difficult to identify our self-hood in the here and now was never perceived by the Buddha as any kind of ground for doubting the truth of the doctrine or rebirth. A child grows to be a man of 60. Certainly the man of 60 is not the same as the child of 60 years previous. But nor is he another person. Similarly, when a person dies here and is reborn elsewhere. He is neither the same person, nor is he another person.[15] The popularity of this analogy in Buddhist sources indicates that Buddhism sees no *more* difficulty in establishing identity between lives as *within* life. The problem of the self remains, but it never in Buddha's view constituted any objection to his firm belief that the human destiny is to move through many lives in many worlds in the long journey to our true fulfilment.

Notes

1. Walpola Rahula, *What the Buddha Taught* (New York: Grove Press, 1959) p. 56.
2. Francis Cook '*Memento Mori*: The Buddhist Thinks about Death' p. 161.
3. C. D. Broad, *Lectures of Psychical Research* (London: Routledge & Kegan Paul, 1962) p. 14.
4. Edward Conze, *Buddhist Scriptures* (Harmondsworth: Penguin Classics, 1959) p. 221.
5. Rahula, op. cit., p. 55, note 4.
6. Cook, op. cit., p. 159–60, and also p. 170 note 3.
7. *Visuddhimagga* XVIII, cited in H. C. Warren, *Buddhism in Translations* (New York: Athenaeum, 1973) pp. 132–5.
8. Buddha refers to the doctrine of rebirth in his First Sermon, in his Fire Sermon, and in the Dhammapada. As such it is present in the most ancient documents of earliest Buddhism.
9. Rahula, op. cit., p. 59.
10. Cook, op. cit., p. 159.
11. Saeng Chandra-Ngarm, 'Life, Death and the Deathless', in Paul and Linda Badham (eds) *Death and Immortality in the Religions of the World* (New York: Paragon House, 1987).
12. Ibid.
13. Rahula, op. cit., p. 33.
14. *SamyuttaNikaya*, XXII 85, in Warren, op. cit., p. 138.
15. Rahula, op. cit., p. 34, 'Questions of King Milinda', in Conze, op. cit., p. 150.

Response to Cook
John Hick

Frank Cook's paper is enormously interesting, and is as challenging as it is impressive. He says many wise and (I believe) true things about our attitude to death and the way this colours the whole of life, and about the ideal of a selfless stance in which death is no longer a source of anxiety. But he also, I want to suggest, makes two dubious philosophical moves, to correct which would not affect his more practical and existential thoughts but which would change some of his more theoretical positions. I also want to raise the question whether these theoretical positions agree with the teachings of the Buddha as we have them in the Pali scriptures.

First, then, much depends, in this kind of enquiry, upon how one poses the issues and upon what is presupposed in so posing them. And I want to suggest that at two rather crucial points Cook has operated within assumptions that have to be questioned. The first comes early on when he characterises religion as a human problem-solving strategy responding to basic problems, including death as the most basic of all problems. He then says that in agreeing with this assessment of a number of anthropologists 'I am, at the same time, rejecting the possibility that a religion is divinely revealed, and hence that its pronouncements *vis-à-vis* immortality and the like are rooted in something other than the needs of people' (p. 176). But the choice between divinely revealed pronouncements and human projections is much too restricted. The basic issue is not whether religious beliefs are the supernaturally revealed pronouncements of a deity (rather than, say, valid human religious insights), but whether they are true. The truth or falsity of the belief in a transcendent reality in relation to which the human spiritual project continues after bodily death, does not depend upon whether or not this is a divinely revealed proposition. And when we see that the central issue does not concern propositional revelation but truth we see that to conclude from the fact that religion meets basic human needs to its being false is a regrettable logical *faux pas*. The suppressed premise that if religion meets human needs its affirmations must therefore be false obviously needs to be stated and defended. Without an explicit and convincing defence it cannot function as the logical plank over which anyone can step from religious beliefs as problem-solving to religious beliefs as false. At this point Cook has, I suspect, simply taken over the modern western naturalistic worldview, with all its assumptions.

A second over-simple either/or comes, I want to suggest, in his treatment of the self. He identifies a self, such as might conceivably continue to exist after bodily death, with a substance, which he defines as something that is unconditioned, independent, continuous and permanent – this is on p. 160. A few lines later he further equates the idea of the self with that of an 'enduring and unchanging substance'. Thus he is assuming the alternative: either a continuous, permanent, unchanging, unconditioned, completely independent self, or no self at all. Cook's definition of a self does indeed fit the Hindu conception of the *ātman*, and it was presumably this that the Buddha was rejecting in his *anātman*, no-*ātman*, teaching. But it would be arbitrarily, and I suggest unjustifiably, restrictive to assume that there can be no notion of a self other than this. For western conceptions of the self have typically held that the human self is radically dependent upon God for its existence; that it is temporal, having been created at a certain time; that it is alive and therefore changing all the time; and the modern personalist movement of thought, going back to the early years of this century, stresses that personality is essentially interpersonal, the self existing in interaction with other selves. I suggest therefore that it is not realistic to argue: no immutable, eternal, independent self, therefore no self.

Finally, may I return to the Buddha's teachings and ask where in them we can find the rather bleak view of the human situation that is implied in Cook's paper. By this 'bleakness' I mean the idea that the goal of human existence, called *nirvāṇa*, is one that can in practice only be attained by a fortunate few, and that for the large majority our human experience consists in a short and chancy life pervaded by *duḥkha* and terminated definitively by death. For if, as Cook asserts, the spiritual project which is taking place in each individual life ends at death and becomes as though it had never been, then only those few who attain to *nirvāṇa* in this life ever attain to it at all. This means – does it not – that only a very small proportion of human beings have ever attained or (in all likelihood) will ever attain this fulfilment. And that, I suggest, constitutes bad news for the human race as a whole.

Now in contrast to this the Buddha's teaching, as reflected in the Pali canon, affirms the idea of repeated rebirths, so that each individual spiritual project will continue through life after life until *nirvāṇa* is attained. What is thus continually reborn is indeed not the Hindu *ātman*, as an eternal, immutable, self- existent psychic entity. It is, on the contrary, a continuant that is ever changing as it moves towards the realisation of the eternal Buddha nature. This continuant includes unique threads of spiritual development and of memory. I reap directly my own *karma*, not yours; and it is in principle possible for me, in certain circumstances, to remember having lived bits of my own past lives but not having lived bits of yours. Thus the Buddha, during the hours of his enlightenment experience, is said to have remembered his own past lives and traced his own approach to final enlightenment. This enormous enlargement of the field of spiritual change makes possible the eventual universal salvation which became a prominent theme of Mahayana Buddhism. Again, another part of the Buddha's teaching, reiterated several times in the Pali canon, concerns the *avyākata* or unanswered questions. One of these is the question about the state of the Tathagata or Buddha beyond death. The person in process of becoming perfect is reborn to continue the process; but what of the person who has become perfect and who is now a Buddha or Tathagata? The Buddha rejected the four propositions that such a one exists, does not exist, both exists and does not exist, and neither exists nor does not exist, after death. He was, I believe, thereby saying that none of the options that our unenlightened categories of thought can offer is applicable. And he added, 'Freed from denotation by consciousness is the Tathagata, he is deep, immeasurable, unfathomable as is the great ocean' (*Majjhima Nikaya*, II, 487, E.T. p. 166). This coheres with the familiar picture of the individual spiritual project continuing through life after life and then finally attaining to an eternal state which is beyond the present scope of our minds and imaginations.

But this whole dimension of Buddhism is omitted from Cook's version. He has taken from the tradition only what fits the presuppositions of contemporary western naturalism. But in doing so he has transformed the Buddha's teachings from good to bad news, and from a universal to an élitist gospel

These are, I know, strong words. But if they are justified they would leave Cook's practical wisdom intact, though not his philosophical superstructures. But justified or not, they are uttered in the spirit of co-operation in the difficult search for truth.

Response to Paul Badham's Response

Francis H. Cook

Paul Badham's response to my paper reflects a long-standing difficulty for westerners in confronting Buddhist teachings concerning the self and the allied question of post-mortem existence. He mentions several Buddhist teachings which make the answers to these questions either more ambiguous than I have made them out to be or which cast some doubt on my own answers. I would like to briefly respond to his thoughtful reflections on my paper.

First, does Buddhism deny the existence of any kind of personal entity that might persist after death? If fact, there are many scriptural passages and systematic texts in which the rejection of such an entity is made quite categorically. To mention just two well-known sources, the eighth chapter of the encyclopedic *Abhidharmakośa* and the *Questions of King Milinda* are both authoritative texts and both categorically deny the existence of any real self, person, soul, or substance. The *Kośa* marshalls a number of logical arguments which sound very much like those used by many contemporary western philosophers. The *Questions of King Milinda* reduces the assumed self to the status of a mere convenient, conventional label for a certain configuration of impersonal psychic and material factors. The monk Nagasena tells King Milinda that although he is called Nagasena by his fellow monks, there is *in reality* no such a thing as 'Nagasena', only a concatenation of mental and physical factors (*skandha*). Such texts are common, and many others could be cited.

Now, Paul Badham is quite correct in pointing out that in Buddhism the really correct answer to the question of the existence of the self is neither a categorical 'yes' nor a categorical 'no', because the Buddhist 'Middle Way' (*madhyama-pratipad*) tries to avoid either flat affirmation or flat denial when dealing with questions. Here, with regard to the self, a flat affirmation would be an affirmation of what in fact is not given in a careful, objective analysis of the psychophysical being, where, instead, only momentary (*kṣanika*) flashes of mental and material energy are found. On the other hand, a

180

categorical denial would be a denial of an unquestionably real, numerically distinct individual. Such a flat denial could be misleading. The truth is more complex than simple affirmation or denial; when certain mental and physical factors combine in mutual dependence, there exists an individual which we may conventionally label a 'person' (and the Buddha himself used language in this non-realistic manner). However, the label is merely a convention and a convenience; the label does not indicate an objective reality. Thus, in Buddhism, 'person' and 'self' are nothing but nominal realities, like 'army' or 'city'.

But if this is the correct approach, as Badham notes, why do texts such as the *Kośa* categorically deny the existence of self and person? They do so because the human, existential problem of *duḥkha* – the unceasing turmoil of insatiable but unfulfilled and unfulfillable craving – is rooted in the belief that one is a self. The solution to the problem lies in the clear realisation that the self is a fiction. Thus, the ultimate objective of every form of Buddhism that ever existed has been to force the individual to understand experientially via meditation that the assumed real self, which is the origin of almost all decision-making and action, and consequently the source of all frustration, grief, fear, longing, and anxiety, is a mere delusion, a serious misinterpretation of the true facts of psycho-physical being.

If there are in reality only impersonal mental and physical aggregates which are impermanent and which disperse and decay upon death, then what could possibly survive death? Badham seems to see the doctrines of *karma* and rebirth as some support for a Buddhist belief in a post-mortem existence. Many students of Buddhism these days, myself included, tend to see this doctrine as a 'convenient fiction'. The term 'fiction' is self-explanatory. Rebirth interpreted literally is a problem in Buddhism because it does not mesh easily with the central teaching of no self and, moreover, is a violation of the fundamentally empirical approach of Buddhism. However, it is 'convenient' because it serves as a powerful inducement to live the kind of moral life that is a prerequisite to liberation. Interpreted literally, it serves to promote the kind of social climate that is important for both the larger society and the community of monks and nuns dedicated to liberation and which requires the support of the larger community. I find no empirical support for the notion of literal rebirth; good Bultmannian that I am, I have no recourse but to understand it in a radically demythologised and existentially more relevant manner.

As Paul Badham is obviously aware, the Buddhist teaching concerning rebirth is that the relationship between the person who dies and the person who is subsequently born is 'neither identical nor different'. Now, 'not identical' must be understood most literally. The man who dies and the dog who is born are not the same 'person'. The dog has none of those markers of personhood that characterised the dead man: memory, objectives, attitudes, tastes, emotions, and so on. The man and the dog are two different beings. They are not the same self.

However, Buddhism also says that the two are 'not different'. Now, the relevant texts show clearly that 'not different' means that there is a necessary *causal link* between the two. This means that the life of the dead man – meaning his unresolved craving, primarily – serves as a cause for the arising of the new being, the dog. However, the craving which survives the man's death is just craving; it is not personal in the form of memories, attitudes, tastes, and so on. Consequently the two beings are 'not identical'. The idea that craving is perpetuated through many lives is simply a recognition of what seems like a fact, which is that will or volition does outlive us to create later consequences. Karmic consequences seems to be empirically evident in the fact that we are aware of being touched and moved by even the long dead. But the long dead and ourselves are not just two forms of the same person or self transmigrating through the ages on a quest for moral perfection. That is not the Buddhist vision.

I therefore must reaffirm the point made in my paper; I find nothing in Buddhism to support the idea of personal post-mortem existence. A person may 'exist' in some very impersonal manner, such as in the memories of others, in one's writings, as a causal factor for the lives of later beings, and so on, but this is not any kind of *personal* survival in which I can find comfort or meaning. However, aside from the philosophical arguments concerning selves and post-mortem existence, what is of greatest importance to the Buddhist is the fact that the belief in self-hood, and the self-interest and self-attachment reflected in the longing for self-preservation even beyond death are, to the Buddhist, inimicable to spiritual health. Therefore, even if I am a self, I had better proceed through life as if not one.

7 A Possible Conception of Life After Death

John Hick

It has often been assumed that the notion of human survival of bodily death poses a straightforward question, 'Do we live on after bodily death?', which rightly expects a straightforward 'Yes' or 'No' answer. Few have indeed thought that the true answer is easy to come by; but many have thought that the question itself is easy enough to ask. Much of the empirical evidence, in the form of 'spirit communications' through mediums, seems at first to support that assumption. A deeper analysis however has opened up more complex possibilities. To a great extent this deeper analysis was achieved in the classic period of parapsychological research towards the end of the nineteenth and early in the present century. The observations, analyses and theorising of some of the workers of that period were of the highest order and have indeed seldom been equalled since. Modern parapsychologists have, of course, at their command greatly superior technology, more sophisticated mathematical techniques, and a more impressive line of jargon; but not often a better, or even an equal, theoretical power and intellectual penetration. In praising those classic contributions I am not referring to work on physical phenomena – spirit materialisation, direct voice mediumship, poltergeists and so on – which does often seem to have fallen far short of the rigorous standards of control, aided by such devices as infra-red photography, that we rightly require today. I am referring rather to work in the field of *trance mediumship*, including *automatic writing*, and in particular to the investigations of the small group of outstanding mediums, such as Mrs Piper, Mrs Verrall, Mrs Leonard, and Mrs Willett (whom we now know to have been Mrs Coombe-Tennant). It is true that such researchers as Richard Hodgson, Mrs Sidgwick, William James, and others would have been aided by tape-recorders if these had then been invented; but not, I think, to an extent that would have made any significant difference to their conclusions. Their reports are now buried in the back numbers of the *Proceedings of the Society for Psychical Research* (*P.S.P.R.*) and a subsidiary reason for my referring to them here is to draw attention to a very rich store of what is today largely neglected material.

When we read the transcripts of the trance communications, and the texts of the automatic writings of Piper and Leonard, our first impression is one of the presence of still-living personalities who have passed through bodily death. We find the 'spirits' (I shall use invisible quotation marks around the word in the rest of the paper) talking very much as though they were living people communicating from a distance by telephone or letter. Sometimes, of course, the person on the phone (speaking, that is, through the entranced medium) or writing the letters (that is, producing automatic scripts through the medium's hand), is a 'control' (again, invisible quotation marks henceforth) who is relaying messages from some other deceased individual who is thus communicating indirectly through both control and medium. But whether operating through a control or directly through the medium, these spirits, and also the spirit controls, seem essentially like living people who have moved to a distant part of the world, or better, if we may anticipate the likely technology of the future, who have emigrated by rocket to live on the surface – or perhaps beneath the surface – of another planet. They seem to be the same conscious individuals, with memories connecting them continuously with the time when they were here on earth. They speak the same language, and apparently operate in terms of the same system of concepts and framework of presupposition. They are, so to speak, still on the same mental wavelength as we are and still very much interested in our goings-on in this world

There is, however, one puzzling feature of most of the well-known published trance material. This is that the spirits say very little about their own world and their own lives in it. We gain no impression of their activities apart from the brief periods when they are communicating with us on earth. I know that there are exceptions to this; but the prevailing general impression is that expressed, back in the classic period of trance communications, by Professor J. H. Hyslop when he said, in his long discussion of the Piper mediumship, that 'there is not one sentence in my record from which I could even pretend to deduce a conception of what the life beyond the grave is'.[1] It is almost as though the spirits' whole life took place in the seances, with only blank periods in between! And this is precisely what some very experienced and thoughtful early students of the phenomena concluded might well be the case. William James, for example, in his study of the Piper material, favoured the idea of the communicators 'all being dream creations of Mrs Piper, probably having no existence except when she is in a trance, but consolidated by repetition into personalities consistent enough to play their several roles'.[2] For example, Mrs Piper's spirit control Phinuit claimed to be a French doctor, Jean Phinuit Scliville, who had practiced in London as well as in France and Belgium in the first half of the nineteenth century. However, that he was not what he claimed to be was established by Richard Hodgson by ordinary detective methods. Phinuit could not speak French; he displayed no special medical knowledge; and there was no record of his having attended the medical schools at which he claimed to have studied. In order to understand what he was Mrs Sidgwick drew upon the phenomenon of hypnosis. Mrs Sidgwick, who was Principal of Newnham College, Cambridge, was one of the most powerful intellects of her generation, and what looks in the bibliographies like a modest article in the *Proceedings of the S. P. R.* called 'A Contribution to the Study of the Psychology of Mrs Piper's Trance Phenomena',[3] is in fact a book-length study (of 657 pages) which constitutes one of the most important contributions that we have to parapsychological literature.

Under hypnosis – as many have today witnessed in the performance of stage hypnotists – people may exhibit considerable powers of impersonation. If the hypnotist suggests to them that they are, say, visitors from outer space, they will play out this role, mobilising their relevant knowledge and a latent dramatic ability and inventiveness to sustain it, and will, at least on one level of their consciousness, actually believe that they are the persons being impersonated. Sometimes another level of consciousness monitors all that is going on without, however, being able to intervene, whilst at other times the whole person is completely immersed in the hypnotic role and on return to normal life has no memory of what took place under hypnosis. Mrs Sidgwick suggested that Phinuit, as also Mrs Piper's other controls, were Mrs Piper herself in an auto-hypnotic state, impersonating spirits who had been suggested to her jointly by the spiritualist sub-culture of her time and by her circle of sitters. Phinuit accordingly existed only in this intermittent context; but in it he elaborated and solidified his own character, developing his identity from seance to seance.

Thus far, then, we have the hypothesis that the medium goes into a self-induced hypnotic state in a context which suggests to her the role of a spirit control relaying messages between the spirit world and earth. If we add the further feature, for which there is independent evidence, that genuine (that is, not-fraudulent) mediums tend to be excellent ESP subjects, we have a possible explanation of how it is that, to a much greater extent than could be accounted for purely by chance, the spirit messages are appropriate to the deceased individuals from whom they purport to come. For it could be that information in the sitters' minds about a deceased person, including fairly complete character impressions, affects the medium's mind in its highly suggestible hypnotic state, and is built into the drama of spirits presenting themselves to the control, who then relays their messages to the sitters.

However both Mrs Sidgwick and Richard Hodgson, who spent so much time investigating the Piper mediumship, thought that her controls may well sometimes have displayed information going beyond what might have been derived telepathically from her sitters. And they point out that if human personality survives bodily death there may be ESP between living persons and disembodied survivors, as well as between the living. And so one possibility is that deceased persons sometimes try to use a medium's personation of them by impressing her mind with the information which they want to have conveyed, in this indirect and hard-to-control way, to the sitters on earth. This might account for the very uneven quality of the material. However, yet another possibility to be considered is that the medium receives telepathic impressions of the deceased Mr X, without Mr X himself being consciously involved. For telepathy does not normally require the conscious intent of the sender. In this scenario it would not be correct to say that Mr X is, from his own point of view, communicating through the medium with relatives and friends on earth. The situation would be more like someone else writing letters in his name and without his knowledge. Yet a further possibility to be noted is that Mr X no longer exists as a conscious person, but that when we die there remains something like what C. D. Broad called a psychic factor,[4] consisting in a more or less coherent nexus of ideas, character traits and memories which persist for a longer or shorter period until it gradually disintegrates, and that it is this that a medium is able to tap for impressions that feed her hypnotic impersonations. This latter hypothesis could perhaps even be stretched to cover those cases – such as the famous Chaffin will case – in which information which was not at the time known to any living person is presented through a medium.

This range of possibilities – reflecting our ignorance rather than our knowledge – shows how difficult it is, with our present evidence, to establish the straightforward survival hypothesis. That hypothesis is fully compatible with the facts, but represents by no means the only possible way of accounting for them. Many who have personally conversed through a medium with what professes to be a deceased relative or friend have been unable to doubt that this was indeed the person whom they had known on earth, still intellectually alive and with the same distinctive character, emotional pattern and personal mannerisms. But those who have not had that experience may well feel that it is possible in such a situation to be mistaken, misled by a natural desire for contact with loved ones who have died and for assurance that they have not finally perished.

Where then does the empirical research leave us? It leaves us at present in uncertainty. One of the most recent attempts to weigh up the parapsychological evidence is that of the veteran psychologist, and former President of the Society for Psychical Research, who died in 1988, Dr Robert H. Thouless, in a lengthy discussion in the Society's 1984 *Proceedings* of the question 'Do we survive bodily death'?[5] He concluded:

> There seem to be many converging lines of evidence which suggest that [death] is the passage to another life, but we cannot yet be certain that this is the case. It is a future task of parapsychology to reduce to a minimum this uncertainty and to find out all we can about the nature of this future life. This task is very far from being yet completed. (p. 50)

This could seem to be a fair, if not very startling or newsworthy, conclusion at this point in time.

But, needless to say, the fact that we cannot as of now establish life after death by empirical evidence does not mean that there is no life after death. We must not mistake absence of knowledge for knowledge of absence! We should therefore keep in mind the other possible ground for expecting such a continuation, namely that offered by the world's religious traditions. I am not going to attempt here to justify religious belief – though I have tried to do that elsewhere – for the subject is much too large to be treated within the limits of the present paper. Accordingly what now follows is addressed primarily to those who are convinced that the religious experience of humanity does not consist purely of human projection – although it does undoubtedly involve a considerable human element, varying from culture to culture – but is at the same time a cognitive response to a divine reality transcending physical nature and human consciousness. Each of the great historical ways of experiencing and conceiving that reality has found that it must include within its understanding of the universe a belief in a larger human existence that transcends our present life. But this belief takes a number of very different forms. I propose to treat these different religious conceptions of life after death as providing our range of options, and then try to see if there are any considerations that can reasonably guide us in an attempt to choose among them.

One major difference between the traditions concerns the time scale of the formation of perfected or fully developed human creatures. Each of the great religions holds that the ultimate human state – whether it is to be attained by all or only by some – is one of union or communion with the divine reality. From our present earthly standpoint the difference between union and communion seems considerable, but in that final state it may perhaps be transcended – somewhat as in the Christian conception of the Trinity as three in one and one in three. At any rate the traditions all point in their different ways to an eschaton which lies beyond our present conceptuality. But when we turn from that ultimate state to possible penultimate states, and thus from eschatology to pareschatology, we meet more clearly defined options. The big distinction is between the western doctrine of a single temporal life, and the eastern doctrine of many such lives. The dominant Christian (and also Jewish and Muslim) view is that our temporal existence, during which moral and spiritual change and growth are possible, is limited to this present life; and after this comes a divine judgement followed by eternal heaven or hell, or heaven via a purgatorial phase which is not, however, thought of as a further period of active living and growing. Our existence, according to this view, consists of two very unequal phases – an eternal state, preceded by this brief earthly life in which we exercise a fateful freedom and responsibility. Thus it is assumed that the function of our present life is to be the arena in which we become, through our own free responses and choices, persons to whom either eternal heaven or eternal hell is appropriate. But is this picture morally realistic? Consider the facts that (a) a large proportion of the human babies who have been born during the last hundred thousand years or so, a proportion probably approaching, and quite possibly exceeding, 50 per cent, have died at birth or in infancy, so that for them it would seem that the purpose of life has remained unfulfilled; (b) the circumstances into which people are born and in which they have to live vary so greatly in their propitiousness for moral and spiritual growth that it is hard to see how we could be fairly assessed on our performance in this one brief and chancy life; and (c) very few people can be said to to be morally fitted, by the time of their death, for either eternal bliss or eternal torment. To some extent this last point is met by the fact that, in traditional Christian theology, the diverse judgement is not so much ethical as theological – the saved are those who believe in Jesus Christ as their Lord and Saviour and who put their trust in the efficacy of his atoning death. However, in our pluralistically conscious age this seems arbitrary and implausible; and much Christian thought has moved decisively away from it. Such a move may well lead Christians to consider again the alternative view of the Hindu, Buddhist, Jain and Sikh traditions, or some further variation of its central theme. The basic thought here is that one life-span is not enough for the transformation of human beings from the self-centredness of our natural state to the unity or community with the divine reality which the ultimate aim of human existence. And I think we must admit that this is a morally realistic view. But another important insight accompanies it. This is implicit rather than explicit in most Hindu and Buddhist discussions, but can be made explicit as follows. It is the very finitude of our earthly life, its haunting brevity, that gives it shape and value by making time precious and choice urgent. If we had before us an endless temporal vista, devoid of the pressure of an approaching end, our life would lose its present character as offering a continuum of choices, small and large, through which we participate in our own gradual creating. There is thus much to be said for the view that the formation of persons through their own freedom requires the boundaries of birth and death. But if one such natural span is not sufficient for our growth to a total unitive or communitive centredness in the divine reality, then our present life would seem likely to be followed by further such finite phases, rather than by a single limitless existence continuing without end. And so perhaps we should consider seriously the basic eastern option of a series of finite lives, the series ending only when we have attained to a final self-transcendence, when the discipline of temporal life is no longer needed.

Eastern thought has always assumed that any such further lives will be lived on this earth. The Hindu and Buddhist traditions do indeed speak of a great range of other spheres of existence, heavens and hells, in addition to this earth. But they also hold that it is only as human beings in this world that we can make substantive progress towards final liberation from the self-centred ego. I see in this belief an implicit recognition of the need for the boundary pressures of birth and death to make possible any profound development of the self. Hindus and Buddhists accordingly see it as a rare privilege to have been born into this world; for here and here alone do we have the opportunity of spiritual growth.

However, when we turn to the empirical evidence for reincarnation or rebirth we find, in my opinion, the same kind of ambiguity and uncertainty that we discovered in the empirical evidence for survival. There are innumerable claimed memories of former lives, including spontaneous memories of children, and sometimes of adults, and also memories systematically induced under hypnosis. A large collection of spontaneous memories has been made by Professor Ian Stevenson of the University of Virginia in his four volumes of *Cases of the Reincarnation Type*[6] from India, Sri Lanka, Lebanon and Turkey, and Thailand and Burma; and many further instances of apparent memories of previous lives have been garnered through hypnotic regression, some of the best known being the Bridey Murphy case[7] and the cases reported by Alexander Cannon.[8] But although the best examples in both categories are impressive, and satisfy some people, they are not objectively convincing in the sense of convincing any and every rational person who studies them. I think it must be admitted that the majority of people who dismiss this range of evidence as insufficient have never in fact made a serious detailed study of it, and are therefore expressing a prejudice rather than a responsible judgement. But, nevertheless, there are some who have looked rather carefully at the detailed reports – I would include myself among them – who still do not consider that they constitute conclusive or even nearly conclusive evidence. Almost invariably the reported spontaneous childhood memories of a previous life come from societies in which reincarnation is a matter of general belief. The believer in reincarnation will say that it is in these societies that children with such memories are allowed to express them rather than being treated as over-imaginative or untruthful. The skeptic on the other hand will say that in those societies the idea is suggested to children by their surrounding culture, and sallies of the imagination can be too readily accepted as previous-life memories and encouraged by the family. Further, the interest of investigators, particularly visiting foreign investigators, may enhance the family's local importance and may in general be something for the village to encourage rather than discourage. Again it was inevitable that Stevenson's well-recorded cases were not investigated as soon as the child had begun to speak of a previous life but after a longer or shorter lapse of time during· which the story had time to develop, to become consolidated, and to attract supporting testimony that was later hard to test in any rigorous way. It is also regrettable, from an ideal point of view, that in almost all cases the investigation had to be conducted through an interpreter, with the consequent difficulty of totally discounting all possibility of bias or misunderstanding. Yet another difficulty, of a different kind, is suggested by the range of options which we noted concerning human survival. Could it be that those who have 'memories' of previous life are good ESP subjects, receiving genuine impressions of persons who have died derived either from those persons, still existing in a spirit world, or from a 'psychic factor' or set of mental traces left behind by them? Once again, it is impossible to banish the spectre of ambiguity. And there is also ambiguity in the hypnotic regression cases, witnessed to by the controversy which has always surrounded them.

However, these ambiguities and uncertainties are only ambiguities and uncertainties. They do not authorise us to dismiss the idea of reincarnation. Nor should we necessarily treat it as a simple all-or-nothing issue. Conceivably some people reincarnate and others not. And there is a yet further possibility which deserves to be identified and considered. This is that we do indeed go through a series of lives, each having its own beginning and end and being a sphere for the exercise of freedom and responsibility, but that these are not all in the same world, but on the contrary in different worlds. Perhaps Hindu and Buddhist teaching is right in holding that there are many spheres of existence but wrong in holding that none of them, other than this earth, is such as to provide opportunity for further moral and spiritual growth. If we are seriously going to consider the idea of other worlds why should we exclude the possibility that they may be at least as appropriate to a person-making process as is this world?

If there should be such other worlds in which continued person-making can take place, where are they? Contemporary physics and scientific cosmology are in such a state of flux that they intensify the general ambiguity. But, nevertheless, they do seem to speak today of the possibility of plural spaces within a single superspace. Thus Paul Davies, Professor of Theoretical Physics at the University of Newcastle, England, says that 'what is usually regarded as "the universe" might in fact be only a disconnected fragment of space-time. There could be many, even an infinite number of other universes, but all physically inaccessible to the others.[9] A plurality of spaces might include a plurality of worlds, some of them sustaining intelligent life, each such world having its own unique history, its own proper concerns and excitements, achievements and dangers, and each constituting a possible environment for moral and spiritual growth through practical challenge and response.

Let us, then, tentatively entertain the thought that having died in this world we are, either immediately or after an interval, born in another physical world in another space. This thought also, of course, carries with it the possibility that we have already lived before in another such world.

Major questions now arise. One concerns the nature of the 'we' who are to be thus re-embodied. What precisely is it that reincarnates?

We have noted the effect of temporal boundaries in giving shape, character and meaning to our present life. This insight has a further implication which can be expressed by saying that we human creatures, living between birth and death, are essentially historical beings, constituents of a certain particular segment of the human story. And as historical beings we are largely formed by the culture into which we were born. There are no such things as human beings in general, but only beings who are human in this or that particular cultural pattern and as part of this or that stage of history. Thus you and I are not incidentally but essentially twentieth century western persons. We cannot be abstracted from our cultural and historical setting. This, at least, is true of what we may call the empirical self, created by heredity and environment within a particular historical and cultural setting.

But this is not a complete account of us. In addition to this empirical or public self, formed in interaction with others within a common historico-cultural matrix, there is a basic moral and spiritual nature, or dispositional structure, for which I propose to use the traditional name 'soul'. I said that this exists in addition to our empirical self. But that may be a misleading way of putting it. For our empirical self and our basic nature are not two distinct entities. The terms refer rather to two continuously interacting levels on which the stream of self-consciousness which I call 'me' operates. One is the level of moral and spiritual response and choice. Here our fundamental nature is expressing itself. Such basic dispositional attitudes as a tendency to be compassionate, generous and forgiving, or to be unloving, grasping and resentful, and again, to be open or closed to the divine mystery, can express themselves through a variety of different empirical selves enmeshed in different historico-cultural contexts. They could be lived out, or incarnated, in the lives of, let us say, a male Tibetan peasant of the fifth century BCE and a female American lawyer of the twentieth century CE. In these extremely different circumstances the same basic dispositional structure would result in very different empirical lives. Further, we must not think of the soul, as our more basic nature, as fixed and unchanging. On the contrary, like the empirical self, it is changing in some degree all the time as we respond to life's tasks and experiences. The main distinction, for our present purpose, is that whereas our empirical self can only be described in terms of a particular historico-cultural context, our basic nature or soul can be described independently of the concrete ways in which its basic traits express themselves in particular circumstances.

You will appreciate that I am not here propounding a dogma but constructing a thought-model to stimulate reflection. This thought-model suggests that what is going on in human life is the growth of a multitude of souls – individual moral and spiritual natures – towards union or communion with the divine life. And it may be that in this long process souls are embodied a number of times as different empirical selves. What reincarnates on this view – which is fairly close to both Hindu and Buddhist teaching – is not the empirical self but the basic moral and spiritual dispositional structure, the soul. At bodily death the empirical self, with its culture-bound personality and time-bound memories, begins gradually to fade away, our consciousness becoming centred in the moral/spiritual attitudes which constitute the soul; and that soul, or dispositional structure, is then able to be embodied again to engage once more in the creative process.

A further question that arises for this hypothesis concerns its relation to time. Do all these supposed worlds exist within the same time-frame, so that our life in world two is subsequent in the same time-sequence to our life in world one? If we are relating the plurarity-of-worlds conception to the physicists' talk of a plurality of spaces, we must be prepared also to follow them in what they say about time. They seem to have abandoned the Newtonian notion of a single absolute time within which each event occurs either before or after or simultaneously with each other event. Time is conceived of as relative to the observer, and spaces that are not spatially related to one another will accordingly not be related within a single time-

frame. It would thus not be appropriate to say that life two comes
after life one; and neither would it be appropriate to say that it occurs
before it or simultaneously with it! On the other hand, the idea of
re-embodiment in many worlds does seem to require a causal
relationship between these worlds such that the basic character of my
empirical self in world two depends upon the basic character that I
had when I died in world one. The distinction that we have already
drawn between the basic moral/spiritual character, or soul, and the
psycho-physical self, is relevant at this point. For the causation
involved between worlds one and two will not be physical but more
like the kind of mental resonance that occurs in ESP. It will involve
the transmission of information, but information whose content is a
basic character, or system of moral/spiritual traits. This body of
information is called in some Hindu systems the *linga sharira*,
sometimes translated as 'spiritual body', and in some Buddhist
systems is called a karmic system, and is regarded in each as
constituting the continuant from life to life. However, whereas
Hinduism and Buddhism hold that the karmic system or *linga sharira*
influences the development of a new empirical self within the
evolution of life on this earth, I am suggesting the possibility that it
may influence the formation of a new individual within the process of
life in another world which is part of another space.

Understood from a religious point of view such a series of lives
constitutes a long creative process leading to unity with or community
within the divine life. The formation of new empirical selves will go
on as long as they are needed as vehicles for the development of the
deeper self or soul. Then, eventually, temporal life will be subsumed
into eternal life, *samsāra* into *nirvāṇa*, history into the Kingdom of
Heaven.

Let me return in conclusion to the parapsychological evidence for
survival. I suggested that this evidence remains inconclusive. But,
nevertheless, it may be of interest to relate it to a plurality-of-worlds
hypothesis such as I have very sketchily outlined.

If after death our basic nature is embodied again as another
empirical self, it is, of course, theoretically possible that this happens
immediately. The Theravada tradition within Buddhism teaches
precisely that. On the other hand the Hindu tradition, and much of
the Mahayana tradition, speak of an intermediate period between
embodied lives, and if we want to keep open the possibility of
incorporating the spiritualist evidence we shall opt for this possibility.

Let us entertain the hypothesis, then, that after bodily death consciousness continues, in a now disembodied state, as a centre both of moral and spiritual freedom and of memories and personality traits formed in relation to this world. In this next phase, as it is described in the classic Buddhist *Bardo Thödol*, there is no new sensory input, and the environment of which we are aware is a mind-dependent projection of our own memories, desires, fears and beliefs. Such a dream-like phase would seem to correspond with what in western Spiritualist literature has been called Illusion-land or Summer-land. The *Bardo Thödol* describes the experiences that a devout medieval Tibetan Buddhist may be expected to have in this state. But a modern western and largely secular mind might well project the kind of banal continuation of the present life that we find in, for example, the Raymond communications through Mrs Leonard, recorded by Lodge – this being one of the notable exceptions to the generalisation that the spirits tell us practically nothing about their own world.

But this *bardo* (meaning 'between two') phase only lasts for a certain time, during which the memories and characteristics of the empirical self gradually fade and the deeper nature, now at the centre of consciousness, moves on to a new phase which is evidently beyond the possibility of communication with persons in this world. In the Spiritualist scenario this next phase is roughly equivalent to the *deva* worlds of Buddhist and Hindu cosmology. I have, however, been suggesting the possibility that the phase after the *bardo* period may be (as the *Bardo Thödol* itself teaches) a new embodiment; and that this may be in another world which is part of another sub-space within this unimaginably vast and complex universe. In Christian terms, of course, such a re-embodiment is the resurrection of the dead, and the novelty, from the Christian point of view, of this idea is that it includes a series of resurrections instead of only one.

I need hardly say that this thought-model is highly speculative. It is offered as an attempt – a feeble attempt whose only merit might be to provoke others to make their own attempts – to discriminate among the options offered by the great religious traditions and by such ambiguous empirical evidence as we have.[10]

Notes

1. J. H. Hyslop, 'A Further Record of Observations of Certain Trance Phenomena', *Proc. S. P. R.*, 16 (41) (1901) p. 291.
2. William James, 'Report on Mrs Piper's Hodgson-Control', *Proc. S.P.R.*, 23 (58) (1909) p. 3.
3. *Proc. S.P.R.*, 28 (71) (1915).
4. C. D. Broad, *The Mind and Its Place in Nature* (New York: Harcourt, Brace, 1925).
5. *Proc. S.P.R.*, 57 (213) (1984).
6. University of Virginia Press, 1975–83.
7. M. Bernstein, *The Search for Bridey Murphy* (New York: Doubleday, 1956).
8. A. Cannon, *The Power Within* (New York: Dutton, 1953).
9. Paul Davies, *Other Worlds: Space, Superspace and the Quantum Universe* (London: J. M. Dent, 1980).
10. For a further development of these and related ideas see my *Death and Eternal Life* (London: Macmillan and New York: Harper & Row, 1976; revised 1987).

Conceivability and Immortality: A Response to John Hick
Kai Nielsen

I

I am perplexed as to where to start and indeed as to what issues to pursue in responding to Professor John Hick's rich and reflective thought-model. I am one of those who, rightly or wrongly, believe that the religious experience of humanity is purely a human projection, though, like Ludwig Feuerbach and George Eliot, I think it is often a morally complex and morally significant projection. But a human projection I believe it to be and not, as Hick takes it to be, 'a cognitive response to a divine reality transcending physical nature and human consciousness'.[1] But his 'A possible Conception of Life After Death' is addressed to those who would share with him that religious assumption and would accept some conception of life after the death of the present body. That is a fair enough limitation of his task. All deliberation and argument, including philosophical argument, is not between belief and unbelief but sometimes it is between belief and belief. And it is that task that Professor Hick sets himself in his present essay. Since I am skeptical about a common background assumption of many otherwise very different religious belief-systems, the very possibility (metaphor apart) of there being any life for us in any form after the death of our 'present' bodies seems very problematical to me. Given this skepticism, I find it very difficult to get exercised over the different alternatives of the western strands of the religious life and the eastern strands. Still, initially bracketing all questions about the plausibility and coherence of both conceptions, and, for a moment, looking only at their moral dimensions, I want to consider their comparative moral attractiveness.

They both have their matching virtues and defects, yet if either were a live option for me I would Pascalian wager on the eastern option. Both the eastern and western religious traditions, at least as Professor Hick reads them, hold 'that the ultimate human state . . . is

one of union or communion with the divine reality'.[2] Where they
most centrally part company is that the western doctrine is 'of a single
temporal life and the eastern doctrine of many such lives'.[3] The
Jewish-Christian-Islamic strands have a single temporal existence
followed by divine judgement, while the Hindu-Buddhist strand, with
its belief in incarnation, makes for a whole series of temporal lives in
which through those lives in a developmental sequence there can
finally be, through a series of moral and spiritual changes, the
attainment of a state of union with divine reality and with that eternal
life. The western conception – speaking purely morally now and
setting aside all consideration of comparative cosmological plausibility – gives, with its 'one shot hypothesis', an attractive stress on our
taking responsibility for our lives and on our actively struggling to be
a certain kind of person, while the indeterminately large number of
chances the eastern way affords could encourage passivity, resigna-
tion and a kind of fatalism. However, this is more than counterba-
lanced when we consider the extensive infant mortality in the world,
the incredibly blighted lives of many people (people – to take a key
example – experiencing very severe and very early malnutrition) with
nothing like a realistic chance for moral development. But that is in
fact the fate of millions of human beings. Here there certainly seems
to be something very unfair about the one shot deal. The eastern
option, in spite of its propensity for passivity, seems, on balance, if
we view the matter purely morally, the more attractive option. Such a
world will be fairer, more humane, giving far fewer hostages to the
arbitrariness of the wheel of fortune. We have, with the eastern
option, a connected series of finite lives in which the series ends only
when a final self-transcendence has been attained. Moreover, it is
something we, since we all are in such a series, will all attain in the
end. No one will be permanently damned. Whatever we might think
about its cognitive coherence (and it seems no worse than the western
way), taking it pictorially and looking at it from the moral point of
view, morally speaking it is more compelling than its western
counterpart. It would, that is, square better with our considered
judgements in *wide* reflective equilibrium.

II

Let me now turn to something in which both cosmological issues and
conceptual issues come to the fore. Hick argues that the empirical

evidence for both reincarnation and the survival of the death of our 'present' bodies in either a disembodied state or with a new resurrected body is ambiguous and uncertain. The phenomenon, taken as evidence for either, that religious believers of either tradition appeal to, can be, and reasonably is, variously interpreted. Sometimes the interpretations are religious and sometimes secular. We, Hick tells us, certainly have no conclusive evidence or even strong evidence that would require a reasonable, fair-minded person, faced with the phenomenon – phenomenon taken by some to be evidence – to believe in either reincarnation or survival.[4] Hick is surely right when he goes on to claim that the following facts are not in themselves sufficient to dismiss either religious belief (that is, either reincarnation or survival), namely (a) the fact that we do not have conclusive or even nearly conclusive evidence for either survival or reincarnation, and (b) the fact that the alleged evidence can plausibly be read either in a secular fashion or in a religious fashion. These things *by themselves* are not sufficient to dismiss either a belief in reincarnation or survival.[5]

Hick, after he has characterised and contrasted east and west, proffers, in an admittedly speculative way, a thought-model that might, as he views it, have something of the advantages of both while escaping their disadvantages. We should, he argues, consider seriously, and indeed from a religious point of view, the possibility 'that we do indeed go through a series of lives, each having its own beginning and end and being a sphere for the exercise of freedom and responsibility, but that these are not all in the same world, but on the contrary in different worlds'[6] Following some speculations of a theoretical physicist, Paul Davies, Hick seeks to give a non-metaphorical sense to 'different worlds'. It is possible, he tells us, that there are plural spaces within a single superspace. It might well be the case that 'what is usually regarded as "the universe" might in fact be only a disconnected fragment of space-time. There could be many, even an infinite number of other universes, but all physically inaccessible to the others'.[7] Something like this would have to obtain for it to be possible for each of us to go through a series of lives in different worlds. But this, taken just like that, will not yield anything like reincarnation, for these different universes, these different space-time fragments in one super-space, are less tendentiously described as disconnected (*contingently* disconnected) fragments of space-time in one big universe: 'little universe', if you will, in a super-universe. In saying these space-time fragments are physically inaccessible to each other we can only be saying that they are contingently inaccessible. Indeed how could it be otherwise if they are in single super-space (that is, the 'big universe')? All we need mean in saying that we are at different times in different worlds is that we are in those different space-time fragments in the big universe at different times. Indeed we could keep bodily continuity and all of that. Dying in this world might be like a battery going dead in this world only for it, after it was transported there, to be re-activated in another part of space-time. This does not take one to reincarnation and, unless we wish to multiply conceptions beyond need, we can be thoroughly materialistic here.[8]

Hick says that besides our particular cultural-historical selves there is a dispositional structure which he calls the soul which is not so cultural-historical. But dispositions and dispositional structures are not things (beings) that can have an independent existence. There must be some being which has the dispositions and the dispositional structures. Rather than speaking of a soul it is less complicated and conceptually problematic to speak, as Marx did, of human beings as beings who have needs, some of which are historically and culturally particular, and some of which, as the need for security, for meaningful work and a sense of self-identity, are pan-human. There is no need, and indeed no justification, for making what is distinctively historical and particular into the 'empirical self' and what is pan-human into a 'non-empirical self'. Rather they are just different, equally empirical, facets of an empirical self. There is no need to multiply selves or worlds beyond necessity.

The picture that Hick is trying to give us is of human life constituting the growth of a multitude of souls, that is, individual moral and spiritual natures, moving toward communion or union with divine life. But, on his reading, the soul is not an entity or person but, as a dispositional structure, a property a person has, just as being energisable is a property a battery has. For us to be able justifiably to say that the same battery was first energised, then went dead, then was energised again, we need to establish a physical continuity that this is indeed the same battery. Similarly, since a dispositional structure is not an entity, we need to establish or to have established some bodily continuity between *A* and *B* in different space-time fragments to know whether it was the same disposition reincarnated in *A* and *B* rather than its being the case that *A* and *B* have dispositional structures of the same type. The 'deeper self' or 'soul', *as a dispositional structure*, is not a being who could be an independent continuant between lives but is an attribute of a person: an embodied being. As such it could not be some mysterious independent continuant in some utterly problematic way existing between embodied lives. We have no more understanding of what it could even mean for dispositional structures to exist independently, when there was nothing for them to be dispositions of, then we understand what it would be for the energising capacity of batteries to exist independently when there were no batteries about to be energised. All we can coherently say is that as batteries are the sorts of things that, when they actually exist, can be so energised, so similarly human beings are the sorts of beings such that when they are alive – there in the flesh and blood – they have certain dispositional properties. No sense has been given to how the soul, as a purely dispositional structure, could exist unembodied so that it could persist between different empirical selves or when there was no longer an empirical self.

III

I have – to go back to the beginning of Hick's essay – a fundamental difficulty with Hick's whole project. The very idea that after death consciousness continues in a new, an utterly disembodied state, a state Buddhists call *Bardo Thödol*, seems to me incoherent. This suspicion of mine, a suspicion reasonably widely shared, leads me to agree with Hick that the question of human survival after bodily death is not a straightforward empirical question to be answered yes or no. Hick points to the existence of a wealth of exotic psychological phenomena such as trance mediumship, trance communications and automatic writings and the like. They seem to suggest, at least to many religious people, 'the presence of still-living personalities who have passed through bodily death'.[9] We have the impression of spirits talking, albeit by proxy, very much as if they were living people talking from afar. It is rather as if someone in Yellowknife were called up by their relatives from the Falkland Islands.

However, Hick points out that, while the survival hypothesis is compatible with all those strange psychological facts, it is 'by no means the only possible way of accounting for them'.[10] He makes similar remarks about the evidence for reincarnation. In both cases, Hick maintains, the evidence can be reasonably interpreted in either a religious or a naturalistic manner.

Plainly Hick is right in claiming that from the fact that we cannot now establish that there is life after death by empirical evidence, it does not follow that there is no life after death. My difficulty is a logically prior one about coherence. If some putative proposition *p* is literally incoherent then no question of evidence for or against its truth can possibly arise. But where talk of life after death involves some claim (putative claim) to a self existing in a disembodied manner, even if only for a short time, then it seems to me we have a notion which is incoherent. (I have argued this in my 'The Faces of Immortality'.)[11] *If* that is so, then there can no more be empirical evidence for such disembodied existence than there can be empirical evidence for the truth of 'Procrastination drinks melancholy'.

Two analogies may help. Suppose someone tells me his basil plant suffers from anxiety. (Someone actually did that in the village once.) I remain incredulous. He replies, 'Look, if I talk to it soothingly it grows rapidly. If, on the other hand, everything else remaining constant, I do not talk to it or I shout at it, it ceases to grow and begins to wilt'. Suppose the chap is not a liar and suppose, further, that in many people's houses the identical phenomena occurs. Even so, I would still argue that evidence could not show that plants suffer anxiety because the very idea is incoherent. (If that is fundamentalism, so be it.)

The second analogy is this. Suppose every time Carnap, Ayer, Flew, Nielsen and Company produced an argument for the incoherence of God-talk, the following night the stars re-arranged themselves so that everyone in the Northern Hemisphere could see patterned in the heavens what could quite unambiguously be read as 'God exists'. I would, of course, be stunned – indeed shattered – and I would certainly give up drinking aquavit. Still, if the very idea of God as a disembodied infinite individual transcendent to the universe (Hick's super-universe) is incoherent, such strange happenings would not constitute evidence for the truth of the incoherent proposition. What transpired would shake us up all right, but it still would not count as evidence for the truth of that theistic proposition or to help us understand any better what we did not understand before. If, that is, we do *not* understand what it means to speak of such an infinite individual such happenings, we will be no better off after such happenings. Indeed such occurrences will not in the slightest help us to understand such God-talk where we did not understand such talk before.

In both cases it is just the case that we have some weird causal connections that we cannot now explain. Somehow, soothing talk, we know not how, helps basil plants grow or at least so it seems.

My claim is that talk of persons having a disembodied existence is similarly incoherent. If the arguments for that claim are sound there can be no evidence for such a belief even *if* we at present have no plausible alternative explanations for the supposedly evidencing phenomena. Moreover, contrary to what some have thought, this is not *a priorism* and a denial of fallibilism, the alter-ego of Christian or Islamic fundamentalism, for I do not take it as an *a priori* truth that such talk is incoherent. Argument is always relevant here and there is no certainty here any more than there is anywhere else. But since Peirce's devastating assault on Cartesianism this should not be the least bit surprising or disturbing. It is just irrational to go on a quest for certainty.

Notes

1. John Hick, 'A Possible Conception of Life After Death', p. 183 in this volume.
2. Ibid., p. 188.
3. Ibid., p. 188.
4. Ibid., p. 190.
5. Ibid., p. 191.
6. Ibid., p. 191.
7. Ibid., p. 192.
8. It has been said that I am going back to Newton and ignoring Einstein here. But I see nothing at all incompatible in what I say with Einstein's account of relativity. I was, as I think is proper in such metaphysical contexts, sticking close to our common-sense way of describing things. That, I believe, is a matter of reasonable caution faced with such problematical metaphysical claims. The burden of proof here should be on those who would challenge such common-sense characterisations to show that they are incompatible with modern physics or that they distort the phenomena or ignore certain phenomena. It is my claim that they do not. I think we should take a leaf from Susan Stebbing here.
9. Ibid., p. 184.
10. Ibid., p. 187.
11. Kai Nielsen, 'The Faces of Immortality', p. 1 in this volume.

Index

The names given in brackets after headings are those of the contributors referring to the subject. In the case of titles of books, etc., two names appear, denoting, respectively, the author of the publication and the contributor quoting it. Apart from the above, contributors are indexed only where discussed by other contributors. See Contents, pages v–vi, for list of contributors' papers.